WITHDRAWN

REGULATING SOCIAL HOUSING

REGULATING SOCIAL HOUSING: GOVERNING DECLINE

David Cowan

and

Morag McDermont

Routledge·Cavendish
Taylor & Francis Group
a GlassHouse book

First published 2006 by Cavendish Publishing

Transferred to digital printing 2007
by Routledge-Cavendish
2 Park Square, Milton Park, Abingdon, Oxon, OX14 4RN

Simultaneously published in the USA and Canada
by Routledge-Cavendish
270 Madison Avenue, New York, NY 10016

A GlassHouse book
Routledge·Cavendish is an imprint of the Taylor & Francis Group, an informa business

Typeset in Sabon by Newgen Imaging Systems (P) Ltd., Chennai, India

British Library Cataloguing in Publication Data
Cowan, David (David S.)
Regulating social housing: governing decline
1. Low-income housing – Great Britain 2. Housing policy Great Britain
I. Title II. McDermont, Morag
363.5' 8'0941

Library of Congress Cataloging in Publication Data
A catalog record for this book has been requested

ISBN10: 1-904-38582-6 (hbk)   ISBN13: 978-1-904-38582-0 (hbk)
ISBN10: 1-904-38540-0 (pbk)   ISBN13: 978-1-904-38540-0 (pbk)

Publisher's Note
The publisher has gone to great lengths to ensure the quality of this
reprint but points out that some imperfections in the original
may be apparent

Contents

Acknowledgements |

Writing any book is a collective enterprise, more particularly so when one works in a field where there are close relationships between the 'experts'. We are fortunate enough to work in two such fields – housing and socio-legal studies – and have benefited greatly from our interactions with colleagues in both. Some people, however, must be singled out as they have been particularly influential on the final text.

First, Peter Malpass who supported Morag through her PhD and allowed us to open our book with an email correspondence between him and Dave. Peter also read a number of chapters of this book. Nobody has a more in-depth knowledge of housing history than Peter, and we have particularly received the benefit of this expertise throughout our association. Almost certainly, Peter will not buy into many (if any) of our arguments, but that just makes his assistance more generous. Second, Helen Carr who consistently offered inspiration when it was lacking, and who acted as a reader of the text offering considerable insight (as well as picking out our errors). Third, Sally Wheeler who read this book as a non-expert and has given us confidence in its ability to reach beyond a pure housing audience. Fourth, Caroline Hunter who also read this book and has supported us over more years than we care to remember, as well as being responsible (as part of the 'Sheffield Hallam School') for some of the most important socio-legal research in this area. We have particularly drawn on this research in Chapter 6. Fifth, we need to acknowledge Alex Marsh, without whom this book simply would not have been possible. Indeed, it would be impossible to underestimate Alex's contribution. Alex and Dave have worked together for nearly 10 years. This book, to a very large extent, grew out of their work on Choice-based Lettings (discussed in Chapter 3) and the Private Rented Sector (discussed in Chapter 7). Finally, Simon Halliday read and commented on Chapter 1 and contributed much stylistically.

We should also acknowledge the inspiration we have received from the housing group at SLSA, especially (although it is somewhat invidious to name names) Sarah Blandy and Martin Partington.

We should acknowledge that parts of this book have been carved out of work published elsewhere in articles, although we have updated and edited them as appropriate: Cowan D. and Marsh A. (2005a) 'From need to choice, welfarism to advanced liberalism? Some problematics of social housing allocation?' 25(1) *Legal Studies*; Cowan, D. (2003) ' "Rage at Westsinster": Socio-legal reflections on the power of sale', 12(2) *Social and Legal Studies*

177–198; McDermont, M. (2004) 'Housing associations, the creation of communities and power relations', 19(6) *Housing Studies* 855–74. We are grateful to the journals for publishing those articles in the first place and for our ability to draw on that work.

Others are influential just by being there and picking up the pieces. Dave wishes to dedicate this book to the 'barking boys', Jake and Finbar, and to Professor Gabi Ganz who was an inspirational teacher/colleague at Southampton. As usual, Dave's partner is probably happier than he is that this book is finished. Morag wishes to dedicate this book to her family, June, Rosie and Brendan, without whose support and tolerance this project would not have reached fruition; and to Tom, who provided inspiration and creativity, and much food for thought.

Some of you may think, when (if) you reach the end of this book, that it finishes rather precipitately. Well, the process of writing a book together has been fantastically creative for both of us; we like to think that the whole is more than the sum of the parts. However, when attempting to come up with a concluding paragraph we discovered that there were some things we just could not agree on – so, rather than bring our five-year working partnership to an abrupt end, we thought it less destructive that the book should be brought to an abrupt end.

Dave Cowan and Morag McDermont
Bristol, January 2006

List of Abbreviations |

ASB	Anti-social Behaviour
CBL	Choice-based Lettings
CCT	Compulsory Competitive Tendering
CHAC	Central Housing Advisory Committee
COS	Charity Organisation Society
DETR	Department of Environment, Transport and the Regions
DOE	Department of the Environment
DSS	Department of Social Security
DTLR	Department of Transport, Local Government and the Regions
DWP	Department of Work and Pensions
GLC	Greater London Council
HHSRS	Housing Health and Safety Rating System
HIP	Housing Investment Programme
LCC	London County Council
LSVT	Large-scale Voluntary Transfer
MHLG	Ministry of Housing and Local Government
MUD	Moral Underclass Discourse
NFHA	National Federation of Housing Associations
NHF	National Housing Federation
NPM	New Public Management
PRS	Private Rented Sector
ODPM	Office of the Deputy Prime Minister
RED	Redistributionist Discourse
RSL	Registered Social Landlords
RTB	Right to Buy
SID	Social Integrationist Discourse
TPC	Tenant Participation Compact
SORP	Statement of Recommended Practice

Prescott pledges action on sink estates

> Homes on some of Britain's worst sink estates are to be offered for sale and rent to higher income groups as part of a plan to tackle areas of concentrated poverty, the deputy prime minister, John Prescott, pledged today. The mixed communities initiative will aim to break up sink estates by creating a greater mix of housing types in areas that are dominated by social housing tenants. ... Ministers are concerned that these areas, and others like them, have become ghettos for people on benefits. They believe that the key to regenerating such places is to encourage working households to buy homes there.
>
> Matt Weaver, *The Guardian*, 31 January 2005

Such is the power in the present-day imagination of social housing that our publisher was able to construct a book jacket, which precisely reflected the issues and themes of this book, before they showed it to us. The concrete, prison-like block on the front cover tell a similar story to the one Matt Weaver is spinning – an image of social housing as 'ghettos', 'sink estates', providing accommodation for marginalized households. In Weaver's story this picture is made more stark by setting it alongside others tenures – home owners, 'higher income groups', 'working households'. Of course, *The Guardian* would lay claim to only reporting the news: the 'pledge' to take action by Deputy Prime Minister John Prescott, whose department has responsibility for housing, regeneration and much else (in the typical mish-mash of policy areas that emerge from governmental re-organizations).

But what this article also demonstrates is the central thesis of this book – that social housing is both constructed and contingent, and most critically, an arena for *regulation*. This book is an attempt by both of us to work through some of the conditions that made possible the present-day imaging of 'social' housing, and its supposed Other, the private sector. In making this statement we do not want to oversimplify by juxtaposing the private sector *against* social housing. Indeed, in this book we argue that one cannot draw such a neat line around social housing – perhaps somewhat controversially, we argue that 'ownership is social housing in the imagination'. Indeed, in understanding social housing we must look beyond the 'public housing' provision of municipal councils as well as the ambiguous 'social housing' provided by housing associations (now referred to as 'registered social landlords', hereafter RSLs). We argue that we must also consider the role played by the private rented sector and, at the very least, seek to understand social housing's relationship with owner occupation. They cannot be divided off from each other but work with, on, against and through each other. The relationship between them is complex – for example, the private sector often describes itself as 'social' and, though the development of municipal-owned housing was one of the major innovations of the twentieth century, it was always contingent.

In writing this book we acknowledge that there have been a great number of influences – we pick out two as being central to this work. First, our practical experience: for one of us, 13 years of empirical socio-legal research into housing 'systems'; for the other, 15 years experience as an officer working in local authority housing departments and housing association development. We come to this work as socio-legal scholars, our different backgrounds drawing us to the mundane and the everyday; our legal training frequently drawing us towards case reports as sources for our analysis. However, our interest in such reports is somewhat different from that of doctrinal lawyers. Our fascination is seldom with the actual pronouncements, the principle of law, created by the law lords and judges who preside over these cases, but is frequently with the way in which the courts approach their tasks, their description of the national interest or underlying assumptions about the housing systems. Thus, our attention focuses on variously, the evidence presented to the courts by the parties, and in the statements of 'fact' that the judges accept, and present, as 'truths'.

Our second influence has been our theoretical 'encounter' with the work of Michel Foucault and the 'governmentality' scholars – we would indeed like to say that our book is driven by this theoretical perspective. Michael Power wrote that a theoretical commitment is not so much 'a set of theoretical propositions ... as a style of addressing problems, of seeing and writing' (1997: xiii). For us too, the greatest impact of our theoretical encounter has been to change our way of seeing the world. So, while in Chapter 1 we set down the theoretical propositions that guide our thinking, in the rest of the book we attempt a rethinking and reworking of the plentiful literature and data about housing looking through the 'lens' of Foucauldian scholarship and governmentality.

In creating this analysis, our book has a number of interlocking 'themes' running through it. Although we expand on these themes in our conclusion, we raise them here as a guide for the reader, in seeing the kinds of questions we are asking in this book as well as the analytical tools deployed in their consideration. We begin with a question which has troubled us for some time – what is 'social' about 'social housing'? This question is principally addressed in Chapter 1 in that we consider it explicitly at that point. However, it also permeates the other chapters as we seek the characteristics and imaginings of the social.

Second, we are concerned with the relationship between regulation and government. We see two streams of overlapping thought here which have not yet been connected in a sustained way. Our particular interest in the regulation literature lies in that which seeks to develop a 'decentred' understanding as that fits with a Foucauldian instinct. One of our main purposes in this book has been to let these two sets of literatures collide and see what happens to the pieces. Again, we consider this literature explicitly in Chapter 1 and then implicitly thereafter.

Third, we argue that social housing has always provided a site of moral regulation. Although this can be seen negatively as further evidence of the expansion of the social control of the poor (for example, as a result of the focus on anti-social behaviour), it can also be productive. Productivity emerges not necessarily out of a preconceived design (although it might be, such as through reforms to housing selection and allocation) but out of an elision of different, sometimes unconnected tensions.

Fourth, and perhaps the linking theme in this book, is an understanding that obscurity forms a potent technique of governance. Social housing provides an arena which is pretty much governed through obscurity. Obscurity is also productive – of expertise to decipher it, of communications to uncover its principles and their individualizing effect, and of expanding the objects of government.

Our last theme is about the shifting boundaries of the social and its regulation. We see this quite clearly when we think about the different ways in which 'social housing' has been conceived over time, as well as how the key actors conceptualize their roles in the process. Private renting was thought of for some time as part of the social housing nexus; this then waned; but was reborn in the 1980s as fulfilling a social role. Key actors – from members of the government, civil servants, co-opted civil servants, and industry 'leaders' – have thought of the private sector in this way. These are just a few examples of the way social housing has been manipulated over time.

We now turn to explain the chapters of this book individually.

About this book

The rest of this book represents an attempt to grapple with this perhaps awkward combination of studies in regulation/governmentality, and to extrapolate them through a series of subject-specific chapters. The structure of the book is designed to enable readers to dip in and dip out if they want, or read the whole. The chapters can be read on their own to suit your interest although we hope that, having read one, you'll want to read more. In order to convince you of the value of each and the whole, we now outline the scope of our discussion in each chapter. We hope that this book will be read by a wide audience, not just those with an interest in housing, and so we have tried to keep out the acronyms that plague the housing literature, the academic and the practitioner.[1]

In Chapter 1 we set out our theoretical perspectives, arguing that the literature concerning regulation and Foucauldian approaches to government have much in common. Indeed, we argue that the former can be seen as a technique of the latter. We begin by addressing the question 'what is social housing?' and, perhaps more pertinently, 'what is social about social housing?'. As we argued earlier, underlying these questions are some of the most pressing issues that form part of the current problematization of housing, the new 'housing question'. Our understanding of the term is that social housing is expansive. What we seek to demonstrate is that all housing tenures – whether for a profit or not – form part of the understanding of social housing at the level of political rationality. Social housing is a contingent term that has become linked to ideas about regulation, government and control. It operates by dividing off households between two broad tenures, the 'social' and the private.

Following this discussion, we set out understandings from the developing literature on regulation which we believe to be most methodologically and theoretically useful in the context of social housing, particularly drawing from the 'decentred' thesis and the regulatory space literature. We then seek to demonstrate how these perspectives can be integrated into, and enhance, the academic literature which draws on Foucault's theoretical perspective of 'governmentality'. In particular, we draw on Rose's understanding of the 'social' to draw out the ways in which a sector termed 'social housing' has set the terms for the ways in which moral, political and intellectual authorities have thought about and acted upon those who inhabit this particular 'social' space. We seek to address those critics who might consider our project as either impossible or incommensurate (or both): as discussed above, we argue for a broad use of the term regulation; and in addressing those who consider Foucault's concept of governing as taking place 'beyond the state' to be at odds with the strong concept of the state and sovereignty in the regulation literature, we draw on the governmentality theorists who seek to bring law back into a concept of governance.

In Chapter 2, we set out a historical context for our exploration of the governing of social housing by looking at the various ways the 'social' has been imag(in)ed in housing. Our intention is not to provide a history as historians might view it, but in Foucauldian style we seek to develop a history of the present of social housing. In this chapter we examine the various discourses that have shaped and impacted upon social housing. Foucault's approach of developing 'histories of the present' focused on the importance of history in creating what is thinkable and practicable. Medical discourses brought about some of the earliest regulation of nineteenth-century housing conditions through a focus on sanitation and water supplies, and continued to have an impact on the development of municipal housing estates throughout the twentieth century. Equally, the approach of nineteenth-century philanthropists such as Octavia Hill, whose concern was on reforming the moral character of poor tenants, was adopted by housing officers in municipal and voluntary housing organizations. We explore the emergence of council housing; the emergence of the 'management' paradigm; the role and function of the charitable and not-for profit sector; as well as the developing debate about the public or private nature of social housing providers.

In Chapter 3, we follow that analysis with a search for the purpose of 'social' housing as it developed through the municipal housebuilding programme. We find that the purpose of social housing was ambiguous at the outset but that it germinated into a particular set of questions that coalesced around the potentially problematic character of certain future occupiers in the context of economic crisis in the early 1930s. The principle that social housing is about meeting housing need can be traced back to this time, which also provides a link with the development of housing management and the sometimes difficult relationship between municipal authorities and housing associations/RSLs. The welfarist principle of 'housing need' is one which has a strong discursive hold on the social housing community, but which, in fact, is often manipulated to suit various other ends. We argue that other concepts, such as risk and responsibility have begun to dominate. In particular, we focus in this chapter on the governance effects implied in the shift to 'choice-based lettings' and the requirement for recipients of social housing to exercise their capacities of self-government in order to access this sector.

In Chapter 4, we focus on the economy of social housing. Subsidy arrangements and controls over rent-setting have frequently been used by central and local government as mechanisms to regulate both access to housing and the providers of social housing. The concern of this chapter is not to explain the minutiae of housing finance, but is with the *mentalities* of governing as they have impacted upon the pragmatic practicalities of the housing finance system. Although this subject is usually thought of as an example of classic 'top-down' governance, we suggest that it is more messy than this, in that systems of economy and subsidy are continually in action working through both power and resistance.

Of course, in choosing to approach the subject from the perspective of governmentality we cannot avoid being also concerned with the day-to-day practical and mundane application of the rules and procedures of housing finance, for it is in this application, and resistance to such application, that new mentalities of rule appear. The chapter approaches the subject of finance through a series of problematizations. The *affordability* problematization has created the need for technologies of governing that enable the less well off to have access to housing that they can afford. But a further two problematizations have dominated mentalities of housing – the need to ensure *supply*, and the need to control *standards*. The last is now the driving force behind the transfer of housing from local government to RSLs, bringing with it new rationalities and technologies of private sector funders, who increasingly regulate housing providers.

In Chapter 5, we draw on the Foucauldian focus on the *techne* of governing, the mundane, pragmatic, everyday practices that act as regulatory mechanisms, and Hoggett's notion of 'centralised decentralisation', to develop an understanding of the diverse sites through which 'social' housing providers are regulated. Our starting point is that the 'meaning' that becomes attached to regulation, and the types of technologies employed, depends on who is asking the questions. Early attempts at 'regulation' were carried out from the perspective of those with detailed, scientific training – the medial officers, architects and surveyors whose gaze rested on the minute detail of scheme design. Later, concerns to marketize social housing required the overview technologies of the auditors and accountants, technologies that themselves shaped social housing. We consider the role of competition law, compulsory competitive tendering and performance management, as mechanisms for the self-regulation of the major social housing providers. In examining the role of housing associations/RSLs, we consider their relationships with the state regulator, the Housing Corporation, alongside other central government agencies, local government and private funders. We show how regulation is seldom linear or hierarchical, and that it is often difficult to distinguish the regulator from the regulatee.

In Chapter 6 we consider three ways in which occupiers of social housing are treated differently from those in the private sector through different uses of the medium of contract: tenant participation; anti-social behaviour and court proceedings on the basis of non-payment of rent. Although we are talking in part of this chapter about enforceable contracts, enforceability is not our primary concern. Despite its late appearance in this sector, contract is now used in a variety of ways as it offers a particularly potent incitement to self-government both through the self and by reference to the other. The contractual metaphor offers a way to responsibilize occupiers, to take part in their own management. In this conception, they are the experts, not their managers. Contract is also the method commonly used to control the behaviour of occupiers, although here the contract is also combined with potent powers of discipline and control implied into these contracts and related to them. Breach of the contract for non-payment of rent offers a way of seeking an identification of the 'social'. Here we draw on interviews with District Judges engaged in the apparently mundane eviction procedure to demonstrate their vision of the social contract. In each of these three different topics, we have an underlying research question – why treat social housing differently?

Chapter 7 shifts the focus of the book. Up to this point, we have been concerned mostly with housing provided by councils and housing associations/RSLs. In this chapter, we begin to focus on the Other with an examination of the private rented sector. It seems almost bizarre to think now that at the turn of the twentieth century, practically all households lived in this tenure. Yet it lost its dominance for a variety of reasons. This loss has been contested and resisted. In the opening section of this chapter, we consider the different frameworks of that contestation and resistance through a series of official reports the purpose of which was to analyse whether controls placed on the sector during the First World War should continue.

The general view was that the controls should be phased out to enable the sector to rejoin its historic mission of providing housing for the vast majority (a view particularly prominent at the height of financial crisis). We consider this dissonance through the apparent divide between regulation and freedom, a division which still dominates the discursive narrative of the sector. Indeed, the focus of the subsequent section is on the current division between 'good' and 'bad' landlords on which regulatory policy is premised. This simplistic division, however, underlays an important conjunction of regulation and freedom in the mechanisms of the Housing Act 2004. In the final section, we turn to consider the problematization of a particular body of tenants – those reliant on state subsidy (housing benefit) – and demonstrate how policy now seeks to work through the enterprising souls of this group, disciplining the market through their entrepreneurial ability.

In our final chapter, we focus on owner-occupation. We develop an argument which will, no doubt, be familiar with the housing audience concerning the ways in which policy has sought to activate our supposedly natural desires to become 'home' owners. Drawing on Rose's observation that this is used as part of a strategy of 'government through the calculated administration of shame' (Rose, 1999: 73) – that is, shame not to be a home owner, shame to be within the 'social' system – we argue that ownership operates as the essence of the dividing off of social housing. We demonstrate how the ownership experts – the building society movement – operated at the intersection of the social, constructing themselves as providing a social service and, indeed, constructing themselves into a powerful movement. We then go on to analyse a principal device in this shaming process, the right of council and certain housing association/RSL occupiers to buy their properties. In the final part of this chapter, we go on to 'map policy onto the local' through an analysis of the sales policy pursued by Westminster City Council in the late 1980s, about which much is now open after the intervention of audit and law in the so-called 'homes for votes' scandal. What all of this tells us is how ownership has been promoted as social housing, as meeting housing need, providing consumer choice and activating individual desires, even though ownership simply swaps one set of controls (through the landlord) for another (through the mortgage lender).

Chapter 1:
On Social Housing, Decline, Regulation and Government

Peter, you're probably the only person I know who can answer this question and, if you've got time I'd be grateful. When does the descriptor 'social' be linked to 'housing'. My understanding is that it occurred at some point during the 1980s and was used as a means of 'doing down' the sector – as part of the discursive narrative of housing at the time – and subsequently came to be adopted generally. Is that right? ...

best, as always
Dave

Dave

It is my understanding and recollection that [the term] social housing was not introduced with any pejorative implication, but it was reacted to in that way by (some) tenants on the basis that it sounded too much like social security and being 'on the social'. They thought it was a way of identifying them with dependency, but ... the term arose as an alternative to the government's preferred label [, 'the Independent Sector'].

I think the whole thing could have been avoided if we weren't so wedded to a 3 tenure model of housing in Britain. After all, there is no real need to bracket Local Authorities and Housing Associations together.

A final observation would be that the difficulty of using a term like social these days indicates the distance we have travelled from the collectivist days after 1945, and therefore the difficulty of overcoming social exclusion. It seems to be a measure of resistance to policies promoting cohesion and solidarity. Depressing isn't it?
Peter

[Email conversation between one of the authors and Professor Peter Malpass; reproduced with permission]

While the content of this book seemed fairly obvious to us, we spent a disproportionately long time considering its title. 'Regulating Social Housing: Governing Decline' was what we came up with, with some assistance from the then Glasshouse Press commissioning editor. We can't claim that this title is perfect (by any means); however, it does carry with it the key theoretical, empirical and conceptual messages that we aim to discuss in this and subsequent chapters. The purpose of this chapter is to provide an outline of those messages, and hint at some of the major shifts in thought which have accompanied the development of 'social' housing in England and Wales.

'Social housing'?

The conjunction of the words 'social' and 'housing' represents a relatively recent, and perhaps paradoxical, truth-claim in the history of state involvement in the provision of housing in the United Kingdom. In the early 1990s, at a time when we questioned the existence of the social, or talked of its crisis, the term began to be applied to rented housing provided by local councils and housing associations in a rapidly demunicipalizing not-for-profit rented sector. It was in an attempt to recover both a distinctiveness and commonality of purpose in the face of fragmentation that the term 'social housing' belatedly came into currency.

We like to think about the creation of the term 'social housing' as being a site of resistance to Conservative housing policy, as in Dave's original email to Peter Malpass cited above. However, Peter's response suggests a different type or set of resistances being deployed, a response from tenants attempting to resist being placed within a particular framework or category. We return to this issue later.

One way into the term is to see it in terms of what it was designed to replace. For much of the twentieth century, housing policy had drawn on the idea of the 'public' to describe the state's intervention in housing provision. However, by the 1980s that term just would not do; it simply did not describe the vision of this type of housing held by the Conservatives who became obsessed in housing, as in so many other areas, by the idea of the mixed economy of provision. In their 1987 housing White Paper, the Conservatives coined the phrase 'the independent rented sector' to cover housing provided by housing associations *and* private landlords. This was a fairly clear message in itself; yet, by 1995, it was clear that the term social housing had stuck and it seemed to describe the provision of 'not-for-profit' housing by councils and housing associations. In that year, for example, another White Paper talked about the 'social housing product' (incidentally also seeking to extend the term to profit-seeking providers).

Between those periods, the term came into currency in both academic and professional discourse. For example, Ball *et al* (1988) use the term without discussion, and Hughes and Lowe (1991) talked about a new century of social housing again without pinning it down. Housing professionals, rapidly losing the local authority/housing association distinction as the transfer of stock from the former to the latter altered the policy landscape, used the term to demarcate their own area of expertise. Indeed, until recently the term 'social housing' has been used by professionals and academics alike, almost without question – we instinctively think we know what it is, or alternatively, its meaning is so difficult to pin down that it is too difficult to question definitions. Nevertheless, we believe that the term *is* meaningful, and that it is worth spending time attempting to untangle and understand its meaning. Indeed, you can tell from Peter's email that the term is both controversial, critical and tells us/him some rather depressing things. But the most critical reason for attempting to pin it down is that current professional discourse at least appears to be attempting to remove the word 'social' – our concern is that in abandoning the term we are in danger of 'abandoning the social' altogether from housing.

Defining 'social housing'

Michael Harloe, in a discussion paper tellingly entitled *The Social Construction of Social Housing* (1993), attempts a definition in a footnote:

> The term 'social rented housing', let alone 'social housing', has a variety of meanings. But social rented housing can be broadly characterised as having three major characteristics. First, it is provided by landlords at a price which is not primarily determined by considerations of profit. Second, it is administratively allocated according to some conception of 'need'. Third, government control over social rented housing is extensive and has become more so over time. (ibid, 3)

Now, while Harloe here makes a distinction between 'social housing' and 'social *rented* housing', in the remainder of the pamphlet he, like most academics, uses the term 'social housing' without consideration of whether we are only talking about one tenure or not. Producers of 'social housing' have recognized elements of owner occupation as being part of their remit for some considerable time: for example, the 1950s promotion of self-build by the housing association sector; and leasehold schemes for the elderly, shared ownership and other low cost home ownership schemes developed by municipalities and associations from the 1970s. It is true that this provision has been seen to be at the margins, but from the beginning of the 1980s government housing policy promoted home ownership not simply through the right to buy, but also by increasingly providing subsidy for low cost home ownership schemes more generally (at the expense of rented housing). This is particularly evident since the publication of the Barker Report (2004), but the roots of this shift were evident much earlier (Murie *et al*, 1976). Government housing policy now talks in terms of 'affordable housing' (ODPM, 2005), and the Government obsession is with 'key worker housing'. Even a survey of affordable housing by *Roof*, an editorially independent magazine produced by Shelter (a campaigning organization for the homeless and housing), is concerned with affordable home ownership. It is therefore arguable that being tenure blind, or only being concerned with rented housing, misses the point, both in terms of historical meanings of social housing as well as the current environment.

Meeting 'need'

Arguably, it is Harloe's second category, of being 'administratively allocated according to some concept of "need" ', that is most commonly considered to be the defining characteristic of social housing. In fact, this statement has two parts: 'administratively allocated' signals that social housing is housing managed by some form of administrative, or bureaucratic organization – organizations provide social housing, not individuals. And these organizations employ administrative, not market mechanisms. The latter are not synonymous with social housing because they cannot be deployed to allocate according to need.

On the other hand, the current policy focus seeks first and foremost to promote 'choice' in the social rented sector, which thus challenges even these assumptions. As the housing Green Paper in 2000 (DETR/DSS, 2000: ch 9) conceptualized it, there is a need to move away from bureaucratic 'allocation' towards 'letting' property. In this new conceptualization, the role of the managers is to act as facilitators of choice.

The 'concept of "need" ' invoked by Harloe is also problematic. It is regularly employed by academics in their appreciation of the underpinnings of the sector:

> Social housing is conventionally conceived of as breaking the link between income and housing quality – a mission characterized as 'meeting housing need' – its existence justified in large part by merit good and equity arguments. (Marsh, 2004: 201)

> It has almost been a mantra in housing circles that social housing is allocated according to 'need'. (Cowan et al, 1999: 403)

'Need' is here being used as a unifying concept – in reality, we find unity neither over time, nor in space. There are clearly difficulties in using the term 'social housing' as an identifying term over time because it has only been in circulation for the last twenty or so years. But an even greater difficulty appears when one begins to attach attributes such as 'need' to the term, because it is difficult (perhaps impossible would be more accurate) to find a unifying concept of 'housing need' over time. The philanthropic housing trusts termed need as being connected with being 'in poverty', in part arising from seventeenth-century definitions of 'charitable'.

State housing policy from the end of the nineteenth century directed housing subsidy towards the 'working classes', but this was removed as an official definition by the Housing Act 1949. Post-Second World War, housing shortages were so widespread that housing 'need' was a concern for 'an extensive spectrum of income and socio-economic groups' (Harloe, 1993: 2). In the 1980s and 1990s, housing need came to be attached to an increasingly marginalized (Forrest and Murie, 1991) section of the population. This last definition of need – a concept of social housing being for the most vulnerable households – would probably equate to the present day assumptions of most academics and professionals about 'need'; except that government housing policy is now inverting the meaning of the term. *Need* has become an issue of the needs of society; the necessity to house for teachers, policemen and other 'key workers' in the overpriced and unaffordable south-east.

Social housing is non-profit-making

Harloe's first criteria, of price being set in accordance with principles that do not take profit as being the primary motive, is one that is echoed by other housing scholars, as a subsequent email from Peter Malpass demonstrates:

> My view is that if social housing is to mean anything it has to be based on the following principles: that decisions about provision are determined on the basis of some judgement of need rather than profit; that rents are set on a non-profit basis, and the distribution of

dwellings to individual households is on the basis of need rather than ability to pay and first come first served.

As Peter goes on to say, this definition would exclude any consideration of the private rented sector within a definition of social housing; indeed, it also excludes ownership. However, we argue that both the private rented sector and ownership play an important role in social housing *policy*. Historically, throughout the first six or so decades of the twentieth century, private renting played a critical role in providing for low income households. Octavia Hill's intervention in housing was not through removing properties from the private sector into a not-for-profit ownership, but was to take over the management of privately rented housing, improving the housing as well as the tenants. And even in the twentieth century, when council housing became a significant sector, we should recognize that some households have been forced to live in the private sector for a number of reasons – discrimination or ineligibility being two particularly prominent causes. Rex and Moore (1967), in their classic study of discrimination and inequality of access to accommodation in Sparkbrook, talked about certain types of housing as providing a 'twilight zone'. They were not talking about public housing as such, but the more transient private housing – rooms in a lodging-house; some owners who had to rent out rooms to pay off short-term loans; and private tenants. And finally, to add to our argument that private renting is important to social housing, we would point to the actions of local authorities in the 1980s and 1990s. Faced with increasing demands from households in acute housing need, they turned to the private rented sector (PRS) to house homeless households on a temporary basis, through a variety of schemes in which private sector homes were leased to local authorities or housing associations.

However, given the acceptance that private renting is now a *profit-making* sector, governments have been self-constraining in refusing to exercise regulation of rent levels. They have turned to the housing benefit system to provide subsidy to the households in order to make the housing affordable. We recognize that mixing subsidy and housing benefit risks accusations of mixing provision with consumption. It is argued (see, for example, Malpass, 2004) that housing benefit is simply another form of social security benefit that happens to be made available to pay for housing costs. Just because people in receipt of social security benefits choose to spend their benefit elsewhere does not in itself make those locations 'social'. Even so, we say that housing benefit supports the social housing sector even if defined in the narrow sense – systems for paying this benefit direct to the landlord have been in place for some time, and are critical for housing association cash flow, since over 70 per cent of their income is derived from this source. Second, and more critically, the availability of a welfare benefit to enable low income, vulnerable households to pay high rents, is precisely what has made it possible for local authorities to use the private sector to meet their statutory duties under homelessness legislation. Indeed, such is the interchangeability of these two sectors that *the system could not function without private landlords*.

Social housing is regulated housing

Harloe's final characteristic is potentially the most controversial and challenging – but at the same time links two themes of this book, social housing and regulation. Harloe argues that government exercises control through social housing, and that this level of control, or regulation as we prefer to term it, is more significant than ever before. This characteristic of social housing, we believe, is critical to present discourse and has been so for a very long time.

But it has not just been the state that has seen 'social housing' as a mechanism for control. The social reformers of the nineteenth and early twentieth century, such as Edwin Chadwick and Octavia Hill, also saw social housing as a means by which tenants could be 'improved', in their morals and their daily practices (Malpass, 1999b), what Hunt (1999) terms 'moral regulation'. However, it must be recognized that this desire to regulate is not only directed at the *occupiers* of social housing, but also at the *providers*. Social housing organizations have always been subject to high levels of control. But the desire to regulate extends beyond the boundaries of local government and housing association provision, to attempts to regulate private landlords who house 'vulnerable households'. Demands to regulate the PRS have arisen not from those high income households in rented housing, but from households (and those professionals supporting vulnerable households) who become housed in the sector because there is no other choice. One of the mechanisms for regulating the quality of social housing, the decent homes standard, has been extended to take in the most vulnerable private rented tenants after criticism of the ODPM from the Parliamentary Select Committee (2004). Furthermore, as we argue in Chapter 8, property ownership in itself has been regarded as a particularly important method of regulating, or controlling, the owners – indeed, it is this way in which individual ownership is constructed as being social.

What is social about social housing?

The above discussion then begs the question: 'what is social about social housing'? This poses a rather tricky question, particularly when one opens up the category to include certain parts of the profit-making private sector. Once you've asked the question, though, you just can't let it slip away (or you can't if you're us). It should be said in our defence, the question would be just as tricky if one regarded the sector as including simply local authorities and RSLs because recent shifts towards a focus on the 'social housing product' means that who provides it is less relevant – thus, there is now the possibility that private sector developers can bid for public money to build housing for low/no income households. In an era when rent collection officers are renamed income maximization officers, in which the public service ethic is being replaced or manipulated by faux private sector values, in which the size of your surplus determines your risk rating (and, therefore, your ability to obtain private money), notions of 'social' simply seem misplaced.

However, asking this question is central to the distinctiveness of our analysis of 'social housing'. As scholars influenced by the work of Michel Foucault, we would be bound to answer this question in a typically frustrating vein – that the social is a political rationality, a way of thinking about the world. As Rose (1996: 329) puts it, 'within a limited geographical and temporal field, it set the terms for the way in which human intellectual, political and moral authorities, in certain places and contexts, thought about and acted upon their collective experience'. One might say, then, that the discussion in the previous paragraphs and Peter's email says more about us, and about our construction/reception of the notion of the social.

There is also a more serious point to make here – if one follows the neo-Foucauldian line, there is at least an argument (and this probably understates it) that patterns of thought have shifted away from the 'social' to what Rose refers to as 'advanced liberalism' and others refer to as 'neo-liberalism'. This shift implies a new and different way of thinking about the world, which we will discuss further. Here, though, it explains why we described the recent conjunction of the social with housing as being of some interest. To talk of some housing as being 'social' also involves a division, a separation, a typology of housing, which makes value-laden assumptions about occupiers and tenures. Thus, these are more than just words put together – they are intended to mean something and take advantage of common sense understandings of social. They create a 'regime of truth', to use Foucault's words, and in so doing shape a set of questions and answers. The point is that the term 'social housing' tells us little about this type of housing, but much about the changing mentalities of its government. Thus, rather than posing a big question (i.e. what is social about social housing?), our analysis seeks to unfold this claim to truth.

Social housing as welfare housing?

An earlier version of our title used the term 'welfare housing' to encapsulate those varieties of housing providers which we think make up this sector. It had the benefit of breaking the link between 'the social', 'social' and housing, but we discarded that title as being too problematic in itself. In fact, throughout the twentieth century, the relationship between housing and the welfare state oscillated, sometimes strongly and sometimes attenuated, as successive governments pursued different visions for council – and latterly social – housing. Perhaps this also reflected different rationalities of the social.

Nevertheless, as Peter Malpass (2003) has gone to some lengths to demonstrate, the relationship of housing to the welfare state in the post Second Would War period was trammelled by a pre-war rationality of housing policy. Housing 'remained the least decommodified of the main social services' because of a fundamental assumption at the heart of the debate about reconstruction after the Second World War; and Labour's position in the immediate post-war period was for municipal housebuilding by the private sector. Decommodification of housing was a temporary solution, after which, it was assumed, the private sector would be able to build to demand. Longer term solutions were not considered. Thus:

> The lack of housing rights, the retention of user charges and the persistence of a predominant market sector all contributed to the distinctive position of housing in relation to the welfare state and subsequently made the public sector vulnerable to attack from governments less committed to public provision. (Malpass, 2003: 604)

Indeed, as Cole and Furbey (1994: 64) note, in the post-war period, public housing fell short of the twin objectives of welfarism: universalism and minimum subsistence levels. As they put it: '[public housing] was neither universal in coverage nor did it assist those in greatest need'.

By now, any housing academic will probably have had their heckles raised by this section. They will be thinking, why just write about social housing? You can't possibly understand social housing and its consumption without placing it within the wider housing system. We would not want to deny this. The consumption of housing has been determined – indeed, manipulated – by the diverse ways in which tenure has been used by different governments. There are two answers to this criticism. First, a focus on social housing enables us to square up to the quite different ways we think about it; and, it follows, the quite different problems and solutions offered, which would be obscured in a longer, less focused text. Thus, it allows us to ask some really important questions about the 'unity' of social housing, its regulation and differential treatment. For example, in the early to mid-1990s when politicians became so exercised about responding to the phenomenon of anti-social behaviour, why did they focus first on housing provided by local authorities, adding housing associations subsequently? And second, our construction of social housing as including *all* tenures – not-for-profit and profit-making – enables us to demonstrate the kind of values underpinning different understandings of the social in housing.

So what we might say is that the term 'social housing' both closes off, and opens up, a terrain of government – indeed, the conjunction of the words 'regulating' and 'social housing' in our title begin to appear somewhat tautologous. However, to use the term 'social housing' marks out an inside and outside. The very creation of the term implies a sense of shared ethical values, a way of thinking about this sector of housing – though we will demonstrate below that this is not one rationality but several, often running concurrently. For most, the term social housing is now relatively uncontested; it is part of the purpose of this book to contest that proposition.

'Decline'?

Our title is also slightly impish. The social housing sector has rarely looked more innovative, or more awash with professionals and experts. Social housing is said to be a key tool in the shed of the police, social work and other therapeutic practitioners. Compared with the private sector, the social sector offers (usually) relatively cheap and often good quality accommodation with the important asset of long-term security of tenure for a large proportion of its occupants. Although there is some unevenness, it is generally extremely well managed by a cadre of committed, well-qualified officers and managers. And, in terms of sheer numbers, the sector caters for just under 4.5 million households. Finally, government policy as outlined in the housing Green Paper is clearly to deliver quality social housing: 'We will *ensure the provision of a wide range of good quality, well managed, affordable social housing* to help meet their needs' (DETR/DSS, 2000: para 1.9; original emphasis).

Nevertheless, it would be difficult for any observer of the politics of social housing not to be aware that this is a sector which is in crisis; indeed, the professionals of the housing association sector are currently engaged in 'rebranding' the sector under the slogan 'iN Business'. Social housing agencies have been pilloried for building housing which nobody wants (or not enough to meet demand – Barker, 2004); which is badly managed, requiring intervention from a variety of different inspectorates, ombudsmen, auditors, quangos and other agencies; and which houses dangerous people in dangerous environments. As Cowan and Marsh (2005a) have put it:

> A diagnosis of failure might point to an uncertainty in the mission of social housing – what is its purpose and who is it for? – an uncertainty in its status within the economy – who should pay for it? – and its dangerousness – how can we manage it?

All of this has led to turmoil and rapid evolutionary change. You don't need a crystal ball to recognize that, whichever political party has power, *publicly provided* housing is likely to cease to exist within 20 years. It is already being diffused into different 'group structures' or organizations. Although there is no question that a sector providing low cost, quality housing with long-term security of tenure is regarded as an unquestionable truth in housing policy, the various problematizations of social housing have been translated into practical and policy action in a variety of different ways, not all of which have been consciously strategized or uniformly developed.

However, a central point of this book is that 'decline' is not a new phenomenon – there has always been an uneasy feeling about public provision, regulation and control of housing; even during the times of exponential growth, it was believed that such growth was a temporary phenomenon, a stop-gap, until the private sector could take over again. Perhaps the best example of this, which occurred at around the same time as notions of housing 'need' became linked with the sector, was a letter written by the London County Council to 300 of its tenants. The letter suggested that they vacate their properties in the interests of those persons whose need was greater – half of the recipients apparently did vacate (Ministry of Health, 1934: 160).

There is a further way in which decline is a central narrative of present-day social housing. Whereas earlier generations saw public housing as an aspiration, it is clear now that social housing is a tenure of last resort for those for whom 'home ownership' is impracticable at the time. Home ownership has become regarded as 'natural' – it is the norm – and now around 70 per cent of the population enjoy this natural state. As Craig Gurney (1999b) notes, this naturality is presumed down to the level of the aphorism. As Flint (2004a: 901; drawing on Bauman, 1998) points out, the social housing occupier becomes regarded within this discourse as a flawed consumer:

> Housing is one of the most explicit examples of this branding of goods, in which distinctions are drawn between 'normalised' consumption choices (in this case owner-occupation) and the reliance of marginalised 'flawed consumers' upon collective, state-allocated provision. In housing, tenure marks the fault line of this differentiation. UK housing policy is characterised by a strong promotion of owner-occupation as the natural and desirable form of housing consumption. Through this process, social housing is rationalised and portrayed as an inherently flawed and problematic housing product, framed within a language of dependency and residualisation. The dominant housing discourse inherently links owner-occupation with desirable self-conduct.

The word 'decline', then, is used particularly to refer to the exit or non-use of this tenure; but it is also used to denote that strategies have been designed, in recognition of this decline, to 'revive' the sector. Such strategies work through the occupier's freedoms – such as the exercise of choosing housing – and draw intimate connections between the social and the private housing domains (Marsh, 2004). These strategies tend to contain an apparent paradox: what makes social housing anti-social?

Regulation and Government

We searched our souls far less when it came to this part of the title – the conjunction of the words 'regulation' and 'governing' were always there. These terms define a particular methodology which, indeed, governs our approach in this book. Our primary field of reference is the work which amplifies Michel Foucault's suggestive line of enquiry, developed somewhat later in his life, around 'governmentality' (see in particular Dean, 1999; Foucault, 1991; Miller and Rose, 1990; Rose and Miller 1992). However, we also operate on a more pluralistic – or less methodologically pure – plane in that our approach is also seeking to capture some of the more thoughtful approaches of the regulation scholars. It has seemed to us for some time that, although these sets of literatures exist side-by-side, there is little overlap (with one or two exceptions). Yet, it would be difficult for a regulation scholar to say what is not regulatory about studies in governmentality, and vice versa. We argue that there is some considerable scope for them to be melded together, or at least engage in some form of dialogue. In the rest of this section we outline some of the key themes of each for the uninitiated, and discuss how they might work together. In the following section we discuss each of the chapters in this book in turn, and seek to demonstrate how each approach has a suggestive line of enquiry with which we engage.

'Regulation'

We discuss below the potential impossibility of our project, which adverts us to the fact that, when we talk about 'regulation', we need to be sensitive to the context in which it is used. Adopted definitions serve functional purposes. For example, Parker *et al* (2004) were able to define regulation narrowly because their project sought to combine regulatory theory with elements of the core curriculum of law. Others have needed more expansive definitions in order to delve more deeply into broader regulatory environments. So, for example, for Baldwin and Cave (1999: 2) the term can encompass 'all forms of social control or influence'.

Hierarchical regulation

Thinking about regulation has evolved considerably over the last two decades. The dominant approach to conceptualizing regulation has been in terms of independent, public agencies exercising vertical 'command and control' regulation in pursuit of some notion of the public interest. Such vertical approaches to regulation have lost currency as a plausible description of, or prescription for, the typical regulatory process (c.f. Baldwin, 1997). Indeed, the abbreviation – 'CAC' – perfectly summarizes the feelings of some current authors to its utility. As Black (2001: 105) puts it, 'the term is used to denote all that can be bad about regulation: poorly targeted rules, rigidity, ossification, under- or over-enforcement, unintended consequences' (see Baldwin, 1997: 66–8). When one talks about regulation as the vertical implementation of a set of legal rules, questions of enforceability frequently dominate, and the 'regulation-as-burden' argument comes to the fore.

Cowan and Marsh (2005b) draw attention to the dichotomous way in which regulation is viewed by policy-makers in relation to privately rented housing. On the one hand, there is the widely accepted argument that without some form of regulation the market will fail to deliver an acceptable standard of management and quality of accommodation across the board: the regulation-as-facilitator argument. On the other hand, the diagnosis of the decline of the tenure widely accepted particularly among politicians is that regulation, and the uncertainty generated by a history of successive de- and re-regulation, was the primary cause: the regulation-as-burden argument. These dichotomous positions have rarely surfaced when considering social housing that is funded by the state.

It has simply been a given that the state should exercise regulatory responsibility as a *quid pro quo* for its provision of funding. This argument can also be seen to operate in relation to private renting where the state supports that tenure by paying rent on behalf of the tenant. Having said that, though, the methods used by the state to regulate social housing have shifted in line with broader regulatory strategies so that much of the current regulation is of a reflexive variety, often related to measured and measurable performance. Indeed, changes in emphasis within social housing have led to the 'regulation-as-burden' argument becoming prominent in recent debates.

Until the 1980s, CAC was not a particularly dominant feature of the social housing regulatory landscape. There was a 'hands-off' approach, which originated in 'the traditional expectation that councils should *govern* their local areas, rather than simply administer centrally defined services on an agency basis' (Loveland, 1992: 344). When the state did seek to tighten its regulatory embrace – over council rents – in the 1970s, there was such an outcry combined with marches from Clay Cross that the law never came into effect. However, from the 1980s successive Thatcher governments prescribed ever-increasing regulatory instruments with ever-increasing specification over council housing. Examples considered later in this book include prescriptions over finance, tenant's rights, and the right of tenants to buy 'their' property. The 1980 Act demonstrated that the Thatcher government had learnt lessons from its experiences in the 1970s: councils retained powers to set their rents at the level they wanted, provided it was 'reasonable' (a word used since 1936 to define rent levels), but the increasing controls over their finance, as well as what counted in each accounting item, meant that the control they had was far less than it seemed.

Similarly, housing associations were largely left alone until central government began to see them in the 1960s as a means for breaking the municipal monopoly of rented housing. From that moment on, they have been the subjects of more intrusive regulation through the quangocratic arm of the state, the Housing Corporation, a body notable for its combined role of both funding and regulating the sector. Legislation now gives the Corporation considerable powers of intervention in the affairs of housing associations and their regulatory guidance and oversight goes into some degree of specification so that it may be considered to be of the command and control variety. Nevertheless, in both the municipal and housing association sector, explanations of regulation as hierarchical control offer only limited explanatory power.

'Decentred' regulation

It is the 'decentred' thesis that we believe is theoretically and methodogically more useful in the context of social housing. For some time socio-legal theory has proposed more horizontally oriented analyses based around the ideas of 'regulatory space' or 'decentred regulation'. Both ideas, on some versions, owe much to systems thinking and autopoietic theory in particular, which in socio-legal studies is strongly associated with the work of Teubner. Teubner (1987: 390) argues that processes of juridification are related to a new type of law – 'regulatory law ... in which law, in a peculiar fashion, seems to be both politicised and socialized'. This type of law has derived from the structural coupling of law with other systems, such as politics and economics. For Teubner, law has become 'instrumentalized for the purposes of the political system'.

Yet, Teubner sees limits to regulation in terms of the 'regulatory trilemma' produced by the problematic nature of the coupling of law to other social systems; that is, every regulation which goes beyond self-regulating processes 'is either irrelevant or produces disintegrating effects on the social area of life or else disintegrating effects on regulatory law itself' (ibid: 408). Teubner's thesis is not, however, a deregulatory one; rather, he advocates reflexive regulation, a shift towards indirect, procedural regulation – 'law confines itself to the regulation of organization, procedures and the redistribution of competences'. Julia Black's recent work has focused on the possibilities and problems of this proceduralization (2000) as well as reconsidering the different types of self-regulation available to policy-makers through a 'decentred' approach (2001; 2002a). As she puts it (2001: 104), following Teubner, '[r]egulation of self-regulation is the new challenge. But the prescription is for governments to regulate self-regulation in a "post-regulatory way" '.

The decentred approach to regulation emphasises 'the dynamics, complexity and diversity of economic and social life, and in the inherent ungovernability of social actors, systems, and networks' (ibid: 111). The fragmentation of knowledge and the exercise of power, autonomy, interactions and interdependencies mean that goals set for hierarchical, CAC approaches to regulation are inherently unobtainable. In this respect, the analysis shares much of its diagnosis with the *regulatory space* thesis (although Black is critical of it (2001: 109)). Regulatory space is a descriptive term which draws attention to the 'interdependence of powerful organizations' and their relations over time (Hancher and Moran, 1989). The thesis argues that the central role ascribed to 'public' sector agencies in shaping the regulatory process needs to be called into question. Rather, a range of organizations – public, private and voluntary – occupy the regulatory space, seeking to influence regulation and excercise power, what Colin Scott (2001: 335) refers to as negotiated interdependence.

In the 1990s, if not before, this regulatory mix has come to hold a particular purchase on the ways in which we think about social housing. There has been a shift towards a public/private mix, with a considerable amount of money raised in the form of loans from private lenders which has had impacts on the ways in which social housing providers see and present themselves. Thus, there has been talk since 1995 of a 'social housing product', of customers not tenants; RSL accounts increasingly reflect corporate modes (see, for example, Mullins, 1997), and credit ratings by non-public agencies have become increasingly prominent indicators of success. These are significant, if emblematic, of a broader restructuring of social housing provision which seeks to operate on housing management through a variety of different performance-related mechanisms.

Like many other areas of social life, housing too is being reshaped by the norms and values of audit and accreditation (see Power, 1997). Housing agencies are increasingly subject to audit and inspection – significant in this respect has been the restructuring of RSL inspection which now falls under the Audit Commission's Housing Inspectorate, along with local authority inspection. In this structural description of housing's regulatory space, one must also then take account of the role of meta-regulatory agencies – that is, those agencies responsible for the regulation of regulation. Plenty of examples now exist of this type of regulation in the United Kingdom – for example, the

Better Regulation Unit or the National Audit Office – and they operate 'at the intersection of an increasing legalization of politics and a growing reliance on nonjudicial mechanisms of accountability' (Morgan, B., 2003: 517). Such organizations play an important role in overseeing the regulation of housing. The National Audit Office's oversight of the Housing Corporation, combined with the DoE's (as then was) 'y2k review' of the role of the Corporation, speak volumes about the importance of what Bronwen Morgan (2003) refers to as the 'embedded reliance of economic rationality in such meta-regulatory systems'.

Enforcement

In parts of this book, we give considerable emphasis to discussion about the enforcement of regulation. Although there is some discussion in the housing literature of the imbalance between the great swathes of regulation and limited enforcement mechanisms, broader literature on regulation has developed quite sophisticated models. On the one hand, a casual observer of socio-legal works on enforcement would note that such studies demonstrate extreme variability, but the predominant focus is on compliance often through what Black describes as 'regulatory conversations' (2002b). The classic study is Hawkins' (2002) analysis of the work of the Health and Safety Executive which deftly examines the framing of such compliance-based behaviour.

On the other hand, various models have been developed which seek to integrate such compliance work with other regulatory enforcement strategies. Most prominent is the pyramid of regulatory interventions developed by Ayres and Braithwaite (1992) which models regulators as able to 'speak softly' when 'carrying big sticks'. It is the principle of escalation in regulatory oversight – moving up or down through the pyramid – that they see as especially important. They advocate delegation of regulatory tasks to firms themselves, public interest groups, and the firm's competitors as the best way of ensuring that action is responsive. Later chapters in this book consider the interaction between these types of enforcement approaches and the social housing sector. For now, we might say that, for example, the role of the Housing Corporation approximates to both – it operates at a compliance level often, precisely because it carries both big sticks and the carrot of funding. On the other hand, local authorities, which are responsible for enforcing the regulation of the private rented sector, operate within a pyramid that is at best bottom heavy.

Towards Foucault?

However, of equal importance in the decentred thesis must be the characteristics of those excluded from the space, and the range of issues which may be regarded as available for regulating, and those that are not. For example, how are the occupiers of social housing included in this regulatory space? – after all, public interest theories assume that the mass of regulation is for their benefit. They might be included on RSL boards of management but there is some antipathy towards their involvement and voice. In this sense, perhaps a better analogy would be that of Paul Hoggett and others who talk about forms of 'centralised decentralisation' (see Hoggett, 1996). For us, this is a highly suggestive term, a kind of 'swivel plate', in that the exercise of power appears to have been decentralized away from the state, but at the same time remains in the centre through the prescription of performance indicators and targets. Housing association boards may feel they are in control of their organization's future, but, Malpass (2000: 260) argues that, in reality control largely remains with the state:

> It is fanciful to think that [RSL board members] are in control of strategy in any real sense – it is the government and the Corporation that decide what housing associations will do, and therefore any strategic thinking at the level of individual organisations takes place within narrow and well-defined limits.

The same statement could be read for local authority housing managers and councillors for whom the decentring analogy works just as well. It is elegantly summarized in Peter Vincent-Jones' chapter title, 'from housing management to the management of housing' (2001). Here, he discusses the decentring techniques of the government's Best Value regime, with its emphasis on resident consultation, and other mechanisms designed to remove the provision and regulation of social housing from the local state, while at the same time 'steering' local authorities in particular directions through the 'responsibilization' agenda. However, as we will show throughout this book, while the state is an important centre through which power operates, the way in which interests are able to coalesce around the idea of the state means that it is not just 'the government and the Corporation' who are exercising power. For example, in the housing association sector a now dominant regulatory influence comes from private financial institutions (Mullins, 1997).

Black argues that decentring regulation involves a shift away from state-based regulation towards 'instrument mix' (2001: 113). In this mix, self-regulation has an important role because it is indirect and harnesses the self-governing capacities of organizations, 'but never directly telling and never directly trying to control' (126). In this, the analysis presented by writers proposing decentred regulation shares much with Foucauldian analysis (Braithwaite, 2000) and Black has sought to incorporate and modify some of the approaches within the Foucauldian literature (see, for example, 2002a: 258–9). This analysis offered by Black, Scott and others in the regulatory compliance literature (such as Parker, 1999) promises much in opening our horizons regarding the players and processes involved in regulation. Yet, reflexive regulation has attracted criticism as being as flawed as CAC (Baldwin, 1997; Ogus, 1994; Tombs, 2002). In particular, by offering arguments for the ultimate futility of vertical regulation by the state and an emphasis in its stead on industry-based self-regulation, critics characterize the move as a 'retreat' to reflexive regulation and compliance strategies. As Tombs (2002: 124) suggests:

> The range and nature of the neutralization techniques currently offered in a society such as Britain can only be understood in the context of the facts that the spirit of

entrepreneurialism, ideologies of free enterprise and the illegitimacy of external
regulation have become elevated to the status of almost unquestionable moral truths.

Nevertheless, by seeking to problematize vertical approaches to regulation, the
decentred regulation analysis advances both our understanding of the realities
of regulatory processes and thinking regarding the efficacy of policy
alternatives.

'Governmentality'

So far we have implied that there is some considerable degree of overlap
between understandings of regulation and the governmentality literatures. Yet,
the focus in the latter is rather different. Regulation studies tend to focus most
clearly on types of regulation, or regulatory strategies and their enforcement.
In this, they tend to hold a concept of the state as exercising a guiding hand or
some form of oversight (even in the decentred analysis). Governmentality
scholars, on the other hand, focus on the *mentalities of government* – their
interest in regulation lies in what it tells us about political rationality and the
ways in which we think about governing.

Equally, for governmentality scholars, the concept of the state itself is
highly problematic. Thus, governmentality understands power as localized,
operating through 'capillaries of power'. This is not to say that the state is
unimportant, but that relations of power 'necessarily extend beyond the limits
of the state' (Foucault, 1980: 122). However some, like Hunt, are clear that
the centralization of power, through state institutions and other mechanisms,
plays an important role – power is 'condensed in centralised sites' (1992: 11).
The interest lies in an atomistic approach – 'governing at a distance', and the
ways in which we are made the subjects/objects of regulation.

However, there is clearly an overlap between regulation and
governmentality – Gordon (1991: 2), for example, refers to governmentality as
'a form of activity aiming to shape, guide or affect the conduct of some person
or persons'; and we would position the different modes of regulation described
above as *technologies of government*.

Governmentality, or, to use Foucault's phrase 'the conduct of conduct',
refers to two particular complimentary mentalities of government: first, to the
techne, that is the practices of government which have sought to ' "make up"
subjects capable of exercising a regulated freedom and caring for themselves as
free subjects' (Rose, 1993: 288); second, governmentality 'is a way of
problematizing life and seeking to act upon it' (ibid). Problematizations – or
the calling into question of some aspect of the conduct of conduct (Dean,
1999: 27) – are a central starting point for the process of governing.
Government is an inherently problematizing activity in this conception (Rose
and Miller, 1992: 181–3).

Governmentality finds its early formulation in the ancient concept of
pastoral power – 'adapted and elaborated by Christianity, as the care of souls'
(Gordon, 1991: 8) – and reason of state. The latter is summed up by the then
current usage of the word 'police' – in which government was constructed as 'of

all and of each', a form of totalizing power based upon an understanding of the intimate relationship between population and state. The strength of the state, in this conception, lay in the 'strength and productivity' of all and each (ibid: 10).

Subsequent processes of liberalism led to government being problematized differently and paradoxically – the concern became how to rule without ruling. Broadly, governmentality allows us to explore this tension between the urge and reluctance to govern. Liberalism presupposed limits to political authority at the level of the individual – 'a natural realm of freedoms and activities outside the legitimate sphere of politics' (Rose and Miller, 1992: 179). This new problematic of government required a new technology of government, 'action at a distance', or government beyond the state. Direct control was substituted by a variety of different programmes of government beyond the state in which the individual was made *active* in their self-government. This was made possible by the development of experts and expertise as well as, for example, mass education. The role of the state in this process was as 'guarantor of both the freedom of the individual and the freedom of the capitalist enterprise' while developing a welfare state which 'socializ[ed] both individual citizenship and economic life in the name of collective security' (Rose, 1993: 293). Technologies of government became a 'complex assemblage of diverse forces ... such that aspects of the decisions and actions of individuals, groups, organisations and populations come to be understood and regulated in relation to authoritative criteria' (ibid: 183). It was the 'humble and mundane' mechanisms, such as examination and assessment, which became significant in this respect (Foucault, 1977a).

What is important here is a focus not on constraints as in some of the regulation literature, but on inherent freedom. Government operated through freedom, inciting the individual to self-control and self-responsibility. The individual becomes responsibilized to their own self-government. The individual is both the object of government, but also the subject. Thus, one can analyse the concerns over health and hygiene in the nineteenth century – which form the foundation of 'social' housing – as both a project of government but also a way of inducing freedom. As Osborne (1996: 115) notes in relation to the new techniques of sanitation,

> What was at stake was not just a Victorian fetish for cleanliness, but a strategy of indirect government; that is, of inducing cleanliness and hence good moral habits not through discipline but simply through the material presence of fast-flowing water in and through each private household.

This represented a shift from quarantine and confinement to interventions which sought to tackle society itself (Walters, 2000: 51); a shift which also marks the emergence of a distinctive housing policy, although at this time related to health.

The emergence of statistics and expertise

These shifts in techniques of government became possible as a result of twin developments of expertise and population. Changes in the art of government were brought about by an emerging 'problem of population', highlighted by the rise of statistics ('the science of the state'). Foucault (1991: 99) states this concisely:

> Whereas statistics had previously worked within the administrative frame and thus in terms of the functioning of sovereignty, it now gradually reveals that population has its own regularities, its own rates of deaths and diseases, its cycles of scarcity etc.

It was this discovery which changed the frame of government away from government *by* the family to *through* the family – in other words, the family was no longer a model of government but its instrument. This discovery also heralded a shift in the ultimate end of government towards the welfare of the population in all its possibilities. In this process, the norm was born. And the norm is productive of rule through emphasising both similarity and difference:

> The norm is equalizing; it makes each individual comparable to all others; it provides the standard of measurement. ... But the norm can also work to create inequalities. This is, in fact, the only objectivity that it provides: the norm invites each one of us to imagine ourselves as different from the others, forcing the individual to turn back upon his or her own particular case, his or her individuality and irreducible particularity. (Ewald, 1990: 154)

This focus on statistics was particularly productive during the early to mid-nineteenth century when, as Hacking (1991) observes, there was an avalanche of statistics which enabled a certain knowledge of populations and their regularity. Yet, the *techne* of rule did, and does, not need to work within this frame of expert knowledge. As Valverde (2003b) shows in her study of licensing, common sense is a powerful tool in the process of governing through the self:

> The legal technology of the licence allows governments to ensure that certain spaces, activities and people are under constant surveillance and are subject to immediate disciplinary measures, but without state officials or centralized state knowledges being involved in this micro-management. (236)

Nevertheless, the term governmentality is, at heart, about knowledge – or attempts to know – and ensuring the wealth, health and happiness of populations.

Disciplinary power and 'bio-power'

This is ensured through two different types of power which hinge on the subjectification and linked objectification of persons. First, there is disciplinary power operating through the techniques of selection, normalization, hierarchical observation, training and pyramidal centralization. This is combined with a new form of power – what Foucault terms 'bio-power' – which arises out of the recognition that population has its own regularities, but works on subjects in different ways. Biopower works on the population as a whole, through statistical projections of the future, and involves power over life and death:

> And their purpose is not to modify any given phenomenon as such or to modify a given individual insofar as he is an individual, but, essentially, to intervene at the level at which

these general phenomena are determined, to intervene at the level of their generality. (Foucault, 2003: 246)

In his powerful analysis of bio-power, Foucault links this notion to racism – not only does it involve power over life but also over death (as a metaphor for all forms of exclusion). As he puts it (ibid: 255), 'the death of the other, the death of the bad race, of the inferior race (or the degenerate, or the abnormal) is something that will make life in general healthier: healthier and purer'.

The problem of the 'social'

The problem of population also gave rise to the development of the 'social'. We should note that the social way of government is, from this perspective, a distinct problematization which 'set[s] the terms for the way in which human intellectual, political and moral authorities, in certain places and contexts, thought about and acted on their collective experience' (Rose, 1996: 329).

The social became framed in relation to a range of problematizations about birthrates, anti-social behaviour, problem families, health and community. Experts became interrelated with the state in that the calculations of rulers concerning health and wealth were 'more or less directly transcribed from the views of experts into the machinery of rule' (Rose, 1993: 295). And the state, in combination with the private sector, took a key responsibility because it had the relevant knowledge and resources to deal with the structural problems presented (O'Malley and Palmer, 1996: 140). Nevertheless, the state continued to act through the freedom of the subject. So, for example, Walters' consideration of the various social laws enacted at the turn of the twentieth century is that they offered hope and, as a result, 'social insurance was to activate the springs of self-reliance' (2000: 67); they acted on a particular ethical vision.

And Beveridge's adoption of the notion of a contract between citizen and state, the latter insuring the former against certain evils, emphasises both the binding together of individuals through social insurance as well as the individualization of the subject. Beveridge (1944: 6–7), for example, linked his second principle of the attack on the 'five giants on the road of reconstruction' with the third principle of co-operation between the state and the individual such that the state 'does not stifle incentive, opportunity, responsibility'. The notion of governing through freedom comes clearly from his emphasis on thrift and household management – as he puts it, 'management of one's income is an essential element of a citizen's freedom' (12).

Rose (1993) suggests that the 'social' has been reconfigured by a shift to 'advanced liberalism'. Drawing on Foucault's observation that neo-liberalism has been more innovative than it has been credited, he asserts that there has been a 'more durable transformation in the rationalities and technologies of government' emphasized in the phrase 'advanced liberalism'. This form of government 'entails the adoption of a range of devices that seek to recreate the distance between the decisions of formal political institutions and other social actors, and to act upon these actors in new ways, through shaping and utilizing their freedom' (ibid: 295). The various techniques of New Public Management are key here as they transform welfare bureaucracies 'from one dictated by the logics of the system to one dictated by the logics of the market and the demands of customers' (Rose, 1999: 150). Perhaps the most vivid expression of this change has been the 'audit explosion', which entails new ways of thinking about, translating, and producing knowledge (Power, 1997). Neo-liberalism involves a new relationship between strategies for the government of others and techniques for the government of the self summed up by the use of 'community' (Rose, 1996: 331). Important in the make-up of community is an ethical character: 'the subject is addressed as a moral individual with bonds of obligation and responsibilities for conduct'; the subject becomes an 'active and responsible agent' (Rose, 1996: 332).

Yet, just as there is this kind of regulated, ethical freedom, there are also those who do not live up to the ideal. That is the risk of liberalism (as well as its inevitability), against which it insured through the creation of confined spaces such as the prison and the poor house, and more recently projects such as the 'Dundee Families Project' designed to re-train households. Thus, Valverde (1996: 361) argues:

> The justification of 'good despots' by reference to a defect of the will, a failure of desire, is the key to 'workfare' programmes aimed at the remoralization of the long-term unemployed and others whose 'habits and whose very souls are perceived as requiring some combination of liberal-therapeutic, disciplinary and morally coercive techniques to bring them up to the level of liberal subjects.

This form of despotic liberalism or, as Dean (1999: ch 7) refers to it, 'authoritarian governmentality' seems crucial to our understanding of the dividing practices of governments in the administration of welfare, and thus at the heart of the policing role of welfare (Cowan and Lomax, 2001). As Rose (1999: 258) puts it, the question relates to the 'circuits of exclusion' – it is exclusion which 'has become the organising term for welfare reform in British and European rationalities of social democracy. Social Problems are recast as "the problem of the excluded" '. A distinction is drawn in welfare programmes between those who are willing to adhere to the core values of the moral community and thus 'form the object of scrutiny of new moral authorities in the benefit agencies and elsewhere'.

One final, pivotal point to make concerns a particular technology of government which is operationalized in different ways in these different mentalities of government. The technology of risk, and its close relation insurance, is one way in which we are exhorted to self-governance. The current ubiquity of practices in and around the notion of risk has caused some profound transformations in government. Partly, this is because risk offers a way of dividing, classifying and monitoring populations (see, for example, Ericson and Haggerty, 1997; Garland, 2001). Risk enables new methods 'of ordering reality, of rendering it into a calculable form ... It is a component of diverse forms of calculative rationality for governing the conduct of individuals, collectivities and populations' (Dean, 1999: 177). However, risk also implies a new relation between state and individual, state and expert, as well as a retreat from the subject. The expert becomes a foot soldier at the whim of the manager. As Castel (1991) argues, a shift from 'dangerousness' to 'risk' implies new modes of anticipatory surveillance when certain risk factors are present. Technologies of risk provide one tangible way in which the 'social' has been reconfigured by a shift to 'neo-liberalism'.

Governmentality, regulation and social housing

It is Rose's understanding of the development of the 'social' that is to us the key, linking governmentality, regulation and social housing. For, our view of social housing is that it is first and foremost a site of *governance*. It is through the mechanism of 'social housing' (or whatever terminology our predecessors would have used) that various authorities have sought to exercise rule. To paraphrase Rose (1996), the creation of a sector termed 'social housing' has set the terms for the ways in which moral, political and intellectual authorities have thought about and acted upon those who inhabit this particular 'social' space.

We referred in our discussion above to the ambiguities surrounding tenure and social housing – that most academics would choose to exclude owner occupied housing and the private rented sector (excluding housing associations) from their definition of 'social housing'. At times, those agencies seeking to regulate social housing have also sought to limit social housing to housing for letting; it was considered possible to regulate the rented sector because housing providers could be regulated through their interests in property. The state's support for a social rented sector could be safeguarded by controlling the disposal of property by social housing organizations.

This characteristic of a social sector, for example, was integral to the new map of social housing created by the Housing Act 1974. The architects of that legislation stated that the 'prime purpose of the proposed legislation [was] to stop up any leaks in the control of equity of housing associations' (PRO HLG 29/1097)[1] and so the definition of 'housing association' in the 1974 Act was limited to those organizations providing housing for *letting*. The control of the assets of organizations of people with an ownership interest – the old co-ownership societies – was thought to be too problematic (Waddilove, 1970). Equally, the social sector sought to create a dividing line between itself and the *private* rented sector because it wanted to build an image of a sector that could be trusted – by both governments and tenants. So dividing practices have operated in the regulation of social housing, to create a space that is capable of being regulated.

However, as we have suggested, our view of the 'social housing' sector is considerably broader. We argue that the private rented and ownership sectors are essential to the functioning of the social sector, either as constituent elements of it or as refractions of it. It is the capacity for regulation that, arguably, becomes the distinguishing factor, because 'social housing' brings with it a recognition of the need to regulate to achieve certain ends. However, as we have also suggested, what these 'ends' should be is highly contested – a number of different rationalities pervade social housing thinking. Here three ideal types, 'three discourses of social exclusion', developed by Ruth Levitas (1998) can be helpful in identifying different rationales.

The 'moral underclass discourse' (MUD), has been the driving factor behind the interventions of Victorian philanthropists and the Octavia Hill housing managers. This rationale identified the 'underclass or socially excluded as culturally distinct from the "mainstream" ', and focused on the behaviour of the poor underclass (ibid: 21). Within this rationale, mechanisms to regulate the morals and behaviour of the poor were critical technologies, but so too were technologies to control the providers of social housing so as to ensure that they only housed those households deemed amenable to moral regulation. Moral regulation has always been embedded in social provision, and we return below to current trends which might be termed the 'retraditionalisation' of moral regulation (see Hunt, 1999).

The second discourse, the redistributionist discourse (RED), 'emphasises poverty as a prime cause of social exclusion'; posits 'citizenship as the obverse of exclusion [and] goes beyond a minimalist model of inclusion' (ibid: 14). Its application to housing identifies the social provision of housing as one mechanism for the redistribution of wealth, by making good quality housing available to all, regardless of income (see Marsh, 2004). In its wider sense, this discourse would recognize the importance of social mechanisms of control of such housing provision through for example, co-operative control over housing, or control by the local community through local councillors. Arguably, this redistributive agenda has been a motivating factor for many municipal authorities to develop large stocks of council-owned housing: Labour's housing manifesto for 1985 posited that '[l]ocal authority housing has substantially improved housing conditions and weakened – although not broken – the link between poverty and bad housing' (Labour Housing Group, 1985).

However, a redistributive agenda did not have to restrict its focus to publicly-owned housing provision. This perspective would include the regulation of those landlords whose housing was available for the relief of poverty; it would also encompass mechanisms, such as improvement grants and area improvement strategies, designed to provide resources and support to communities of poor owner-occupiers. During the 1970s and 1980s some urban authorities such as Leicester and Birmingham, with inner city wards occupied by very poor, largely ethnic minority populations housed in the worst quality owner-occupied housing, developed area renewal strategies as mechanisms for the redistribution of resources. Integral to the 'social housing policy' of these councils was a strategy of providing improvement grants to owners in a targeted manner.

The third discourse of social exclusion – a social integrationist discourse (SID) – is narrower than the first two, and focuses on the ability to participate in paid work. Levitas argues that the New Labour government has developed an 'inconsistent combination of SID and MUD' (ibid: 28). The social integrationist discourse can be seen in housing policy in the emphasis on the need for mixed tenure provision, for affordable housing available to those whose occupations are 'key' to the community, and for the promotion of home ownership as the tenure of choice through extending the possibilities of the 'right to buy'.

These three broad rationales for social housing all require regulatory technologies, but they will be *different* regulatory technologies. An RED agenda demands high levels of regulation of providers of housing, particularly in terms of quality of provision and allocation policies, to ensure that housing is used to alleviate poverty. The MUD agenda implies technologies for regulating the occupiers of housing, but also requires the regulation of providers because housing managers and occupants become jointly responsible for improving the targeted community. The third agenda – social integration – arguably implies less prescriptive regulation, because it is numerical outcomes that become important, not quality, or the nature of recipients. Certainly this is the attitude the Housing Minister has adopted in relation to the government's latest attempt to increase the volume of 'affordable housing' by enabling developers to access social housing grants (Housing Act 2004, s 220).

Nevertheless, we would agree that the MUD and SID discourses are apparent in the present government's social housing policies. Indeed, because our perspective on the state is that it is one of a number of centralized sites through which power can be exercised, what we are interested in is the way that these government policies are not just actively supported by the social housing professionals, but have arisen at least in part out of the changing practices and identity of the social housing providers over the past two decades. Here we return again to the importance of Foucault and the governmentality literature to the analysis, and to Foucault's focus on the subject and the power. As Foucault put it, to govern 'is to structure the possible field of action of others' (1983: 221), and it is this statement that encapsulates our understanding of regulation – that it operates on the acting subject, utilizing the subject's capacity for action, and provides an intimate link between the governance of the self and others. Social housing providers have not changed simply because they have been told to do so. Rather, they have altered their policies and practices to align with rationalities that they have themselves internalized, rationalities that have arisen because these bodies have been central to problematizing existing modes of governing and creating allies around alternative programmes (Callon and Latour, 1981).

Moral regulation and 'retraditionalisation'

One particularly pertinent strand of the governmentality literature has been Alan Hunt's development of the idea of moral regulation. 'Moral regulation' schemes are those 'which involve practices whereby some people act to problematize the conduct, values or culture of others and seek to impose regulation upon them' (Hunt, 1999: ix). Many of Hunt's examples of moral regulation operate at the boundary between external moral codes and processes of ethical self-control (1999: 12–15). Moral regulation can be regulation from below or above, can be seen in different techniques and practices of government, and involves processes of contestation. An example of a campaign of moral regulation was the health and sanitary campaigns in the mid-nineteenth century discussed above. These were inherently moral, requiring the division of particular sub-populations into categories of poor or pauperized.

As Osborne and Rose (1999: 745) note, it was not just squalor which so concerned the Victorians, but also sexual promiscuity and 'by the 1880s, this had stabilised into a novel question: overcrowding'. Out of this came a recognition of the social as a 'kind of anti-individualism: the need to conceive of human beings as citizens of a wider collectivity who did not merely confront one another as buyers and sellers on a competitive market' (Rose, 1999: 118). It is through this analysis, for example, that we believe it is possible to see the impact on housing management of the social work approach developed by Octavia Hill and her followers.

The new moral agenda embraced by the Conservatives and New Labour in Hunt's term is 'retraditionalisation' (1999: ch 6). Moral regulation, associated with the Victorian campaigns against alcoholism and other vices, is 'alive and well' (216). Its tone is less prescriptive, 'but rather seeks to engage in a reflexive project of the self which harnesses self-monitoring and introspection to the production of a personality in which authenticity comes to displace conformity' (218). All housing associations have become central to this project, as estates of social housing are constructed as problem sites, communities of the 'socially excluded', the 'flawed consumers' who cannot afford to buy their own homes. Crime control has become an explicit part of the role and practices of housing managers and social housing agencies have become actively involved in the shift towards the *responsibility thesis* (Cowan and Pantazis, 2001).

As with the nineteenth-century philanthropic housing societies, social housing agencies today are required to actively govern the moral character of tenants. Tenants are encouraged to become 'responsible' neighbours; behaviour, and particularly the behaviour of their adolescent sons, is expected to conform to the 'proclaimed commonly held "community values"' (Flint, 2002). 'Both housing practitioners and the newly empowered tenants play complex governing roles in this utilisation of techniques based around the construction of moral communities within this new governance' (Flint, 2003: 623). This new political rationality requires new technologies of governing to make it operable, but technologies which carry strong memories of the old.

We hope that in this chapter we have demonstrated the possibilities of our project – of weaving together elements of regulation studies with governmentality. We would modestly suggest that those who believe this to be an *impossible* project do so because they are taking a particular view on the meaning of 'regulation'. Parker *et al* (2004: 2) argue that at least some neo-Foucauldian research is simply not about regulation. In their study they draw on Black's definition of regulation as 'the intentional activity of attempting to control, order or influence the behaviour of others' (2002c: 1). As we discussed above, a more expansive definition would refer to a range of activity, from authoritative rules and their enforcement through to more nebulous forms of social control, including unintentional forms of regulation and non-state-based forms of regulation (Baldwin *et al*, 1998: 3–4). Thus, a variety of unintentional or unconscious regulatory activity, including those which harness self-capacity, as well as different types of regulatory instruments become relevant.

However, the other possible criticism of our project is that it is *incommensurable* arising from a difference in views about the role of the state. This too, we suggest, can be overcome, but requires us to engage in a small modification in tone more than anything else of some of the post-Foucauldian governmentality literature. It is to the position of the state and sovereignty that we turn in this final section.

Law, sovereignty and social housing

Let us expand on the problem. Most regulation literature retains a strong concept of the state and sovereignty; but some of the governmentality literature makes the important observation that regulation (as we use this term) occurs 'beyond the state'. This takes up Foucault's perceptive comment that, in political thought and analysis, we have yet to cut off the King's head (Foucault, 1981: 88–9). In *Discipline and Punish*, Foucault begins by counterposing two forms of regulation – 'a public execution and a timetable' (1977a: 7). First, he recounts in all its gory detail the way in which Damiens, a regicide, was punished; and then, he switches to the rule book drawn up for some young prisoners in Paris. He uses this rhetorical technique to demonstrate how sovereign power, an essentially negative repressive mode, had become displaced by disciplinary power, a more positive set of micro-techniques which sought to engage the self-regulatory capacities of the subject. In so doing, the subject was conceptualized in new and different ways.

While we acknowledge the importance of this set of techniques of governance beyond the state, our understanding and approach requires us to engage with notions of sovereignty. Foucault, himself, in his lecture on governmentality similarly acknowledged the importance of sovereignty even after its eclipse. He makes the point that sovereignty did not cease to exist when a new art of government based around population came to dominate; rather, 'the problem of sovereignty was never posed with greater force than at this time, because it no longer involved ... an attempt to derive an art of government from a theory of sovereignty' (1991: 101). Indeed, he goes on to say that one form of government does not replace another for 'in reality one has a triangle, sovereignty–discipline–government, which has as its primary target the population and as its essential mechanism the apparatuses of security' (102). This neat triangle, and the re-positioning of the sovereign in Foucault's work, provides an explanation for the apparent dichotomy noted by Garland (1996) between, on the one hand, the failure of the state to control crime combined with strategies for devolving crime prevention; and, on the other, an almost hysterical (in the clinical sense) denial of the failure of sovereignty combined with the assertion of punitive force.

Nevertheless, it must be admitted that Foucault was ambiguous on the relation between sovereignty and discipline, suggesting in some of his work a historical transition from one to the other. This problem at the heart of Foucault's work is also law's problem because Foucault probably equated law with sovereignty, as punitive forces. Thus, subsequent scholars (for example Ewald, 1990; Fitzpatrick, 2000; Hunt, 1992; Hunt and Wickham, 1994; Rose and Valverde, 1998; Stenson, 1999; 2000) have sought to resurrect, or at least problematize, the relationship between law, discipline and government. We do not need to summarize this literature for our limited purposes in this book, but let us summarize the messages from this literature which are important for us.

First, the growth of bio-power can be associated with the rise of law – as Ewald (1990: 138) suggests, 'normalization tends to be accompanied by an astonishing proliferation of legislation. Practically speaking, legislators never expressed themselves as freely or as extensively as in the age of bio-power.' Laws are derived from norms and are often framed as norms, as well as providing the basis for government in the name of the norm. Thus, for example, the 'retraditionalisation' of society, a concept used by Hunt (1999) to frame various crises in recent times in moral regulation terms. This gives rise to an important observation about reading case law. Case law is the interpretation of law and, as such, provides a base for all of the knowledges which are represented by law and run through it. Thus, when reading cases, we follow Valverde's focus on 'the deployment of knowledges within and in relation to law, wherever that occurs, prioritising questions of epistemological authority and sidelining doctrinal questions' (2003a: 21). What is of interest to us in this study is the way in which the spectacle of the trial exposes aspects of activities by regulators and other actors, activities that are often otherwise hidden from the public gaze. Equally of interest is the way in which the courts 'ventriloquize the "national" community' (ibid: 47). Second, law and government work together but apart from each other, being both separate but inseparable. Law's truth is an oversight of the processes of government, intervening only occasionally, and the truth of administration is left largely untouched. As Fitzpatrick (2000: 17) observes:

> In the outcome, the vast bulk of decisions in administration are left beyond the reach of a law which is qualitatively different to it. Such a contrary law, by intervening occasionally to correct aberration, confirms the massive normality of administration, confirms it as the nature of things.

Third, liberalism and neo-liberalism *need* law, and they need it particularly to demarcate spaces requiring control – 'between the spaces of consumption and civility and the savage spaces on the margins' (Rose and Valverde, 1998: 549). Kevin Stenson (1999: 50) makes a similar point when he refers to the way in which governmentality studies should have an 'emphasis on *the establishment and maintenance of sovereign control over territory* as a core principle of liberal rule.' The mentality of housing policy has been to separate off social from private housing in a self-fulfilling prophecy; and it has done so through a variety of techniques including law.

This attempt to re-place sovereignty into our own analysis has tremendous significance in this study of social housing. It requires us to be sensitive to different forms of governance, and to involve formal legal mechanisms of control, interwoven with the informal. We do not suggest any hierarchy between sovereignty, discipline and government, but some interrelation that is both context and temporally specific. And finally, since regulation may be regarded as a technology of government, it enables us to integrate notions of regulation with mentalities of government.

Chapter 2:
Constructing the Domain

The purpose of this chapter is to set out the context for the rest of the book by providing a historical survey of events and problematizations in the history of housing policy. We make no claims to writing the history of housing, nor even to create a linear progression of historical events. Like Foucault, we are not searching for an 'essences', but 'the myriad of events ... the accidents, the minute deviations – or conversely, the complete reversals – the errors, the false appraisals, the calculations that gave birth to those things that continue to exist and have value for us (Foucault, 1977b: 146), that have created the conditions under which modern housing policy became possible. We seek to construct the *domain* of modern housing policy – the terrain in which the social has been imag(in)ed in housing – through the consideration of four perspectives: poverty, pauperization and the concern for public health; the necessity of state intervention; expertise and the development of housing management as a profession; and legal and economic boundaries constructing the public/private divide.

These divisions are largely for our narrative convenience – what arises in one perspective appears in a different guise in another. So the emergence of expertise is first seen in constructing a public health paradigm through which the regulation of housing took place. Professional power condensed in the state and used its mechanisms; additionally, expertise constructed and reinforced those legal and economic boundaries of the public/private binary divide. Different understandings provide different lash-ups. We use our last section as a case study – of the housing association sector – to amplify the themes of this chapter and the book.

The five themes identified in our introduction are interplayed throughout this chapter. In particular, the shifting understanding of the social, and its impact on the development of a set of understandings about the housing question are prominent, as is the shift which occurs over time. Equally, one might say that the need for social housing grew out of concerns about the moral regulation of the poor and the desire to work through their potential for self-control. What is particularly important in this chapter is the shift, which occurs as a result of the concern about certain occupiers, to expertise in management.

Poverty, pauperization and the concern for public health

Interest in housing as a social problem was not an independent growth; it had sprung from [concerns with sanitation]. ... The reformers would have swept the towns clean, if they could: they rampaged destructively through the congested centres of the industrial town tearing down the rookeries. ... The forces of law and order and the churches were behind them. It had been noticed that, as well as disease, crime and vice accumulated in the labyrinths of the slums. The police and the priest were as unable to penetrate as the sunshine (Bowley, 1945: 2).

One of the several lines that were later to converge on the birth of housing policy was a series of problematizations in the nineteenth century concerning the relationship between the health of the public and its housing. These problematizations were specifically related to various crises of sanitation and epidemics (cholera and typhus), as well as being an offspring of the emerging divide between poverty and pauperism. Acting as a catalyst to these problematizations was a range of statistical and more qualitative publications which emerged during this period related to the 'housing problem'. Practically every city had such a publication and, in addition, there were those influential publications which sought to capture the national picture. Indeed, one might say that nowhere was the 'avalanche of statistics', to which Hacking refers, more prominent than in the link between public health and housing. There were, as Gauldie (1974: 147) suggests, 'a long succession of works whose literary merit and statistical accuracy may have varied, but whose cumulative influence was considerable'. What becomes clear from these publications is an articulation that 'the task of good government of urban space is actually to promote health' (Osborne and Rose, 1999: 742).

What seems to occur gradually is a shift in focus from the external structures to the internal structures of the family and immorality. The concern for 'health' was not simply for the elimination of physical disease, but encompassed the moral and social health of the 'dangerous classes' (Harloe, 1995: 16). There is a concern about the ungovernability of the occupiers. In these publications, the 'fear of the moral descent of poverty into pauperism' (Dean, 1992: 241) is palpable. The concern was that pauperized households were congregating together with the impoverished, each feeding off the other, as the cause of social danger. So while poverty was regarded as an inevitability – indeed, something that was useful and necessary in the project of wealth – pauperism symbolized 'a series of *different forms of conduct*, namely those which are not amenable to the project of socialization which is being elaborated' (Procacci, 1991: 160). Indeed, the 'poor', in this scenario, were 'virtuous examples of renunciation of pauperism and adhesion to the values of well-being' (ibid: 159).

These linked concerns come clearly out of the series of reports. Chadwick's 1842 report on the sanitary conditions of the working classes (see Flinn, 1965 – references to the report below are taken from this publication). This report occupies a crucial moment in the development of housing policy as the question of housing standards and conditions mutated into a more concerning question about the development of regulations for 'public health' based upon the miasmatic theory of the causes of epidemics. And the report provided a convincing case for change through the citation of evidence from a series of reports from around the country (even though it was not signed by the Poor Law Commissioners themselves, but by Chadwick, their secretary).

Chadwick's report was made possible by a combination of different factors – the impact of cholera and typhus epidemics, the developing medical profession (principally coming out of Edinburgh), concerns over the costs of poor relief, and the development of 'vital statistical' studies as well as the census. The report grew out of the work, published for the Poor Law Commission in 1838, of Kay, Arnott and Southwood-Smith. What is immediately apparent about Chadwick's report is how he weaved concern about the sanitary condition of property with the moral condition. This conjunction of public health and sanitation (the external), with the morals of the working classes (the internal) provided a link between housing, health and pauperism. Overcrowding, for example, was said to be the cause of 'promiscuous sleeping'; and the state and condition of properties 'of inferior construction had manifestly an injurious operation on the moral as well as on the sanitary condition, independently of any overcrowding' (Flinn, 1965: 194). There were telling examples of the pauperization of previously 'decent' persons as a result of the state and condition of property. And there was a view expressed of the pauperising effect of charity: '… by this pecuniary aid they have only added fuel to the flame; that is, they have enabled the inmates to purchase more ardent spirits' (p 201). Equally, the report draws a divide between 'the economy of families' – those kept in good order, clean and comfortable are less predisposed to sickness and death (see especially the report of a Mr Mott, pp 206–7).

James Hole, for example, in his influential study of *The Homes of the Working Classes* (1866), equally links the physical structure to 'moral evils'. By so doing he makes sites of housing for the poor criminogenic. In a telling footnote (p 21), Hole reminds his audience of 'one of the frightful consequences of the horrible conditions under which vast numbers of the population live there is a vast amount of illegitimacy and infanticide'. Similar links are made by Andrew Mearns in his pamphlet (1883):

> Ask if the men and women living together in these rookeries are married, and your simplicity will cause a smile. Nobody knows. Nobody cares. Nobody expects that they are. In exceptional cases only could your question be answered in the affirmative. Incest is common; and no form of vice and sensuality causes surprise or attracts attention.

Although these were cast in moral tones, there was also a recognition that individuals were part of a broader collectivity (Rose, 1999: 118). Thus, new spaces of government emerged which provided a shift in focus from quarantine and confinement to interventions which tackle society itself (Walters, 2000: 51). This is also the appropriate juncture for the birth of housing policy, as the focus on external sanitation became linked with the dwellings of the poor.

In this sense, the birth of housing policy – the need for ways of thinking about and acting on housing – was not just a question of the social but linked inextricably with the moral regulation of the poor.

Some scholars of social housing tend to hark back to the Housing of the Working Classes Act 1890 as the foundation of housing policy, but this Act was in itself a consolidation of the welter of public health legislation which already existed. The police had been given a role in regulating lodging houses, and used their powers to divide out the 'infamous brothels, harbours of criminals' from the industrious (Gauldie, 1974: 245, citing the 1853 report of Captain Hay of the Police Commissioners). Slum clearance powers and improvement schemes had been created in the Cross and Torrens Acts (1868 and 1875 respectively) about which Gauldie (1974: 267) makes the following observation:

> The acknowledged purpose of the new Act, the 'improvement' of our cities, the creation of better public health by the removal of the focus of disease, was almost unanimously approved. It was, in fact, for most people, if not for the immediate instigators of reform, not the real reason why they were prepared to suffer bureaucratic interference with private property. The first and most sweeping improvement schemes were deliberately driven through the most criminal areas, with the dispersal of criminals from their haunts, and the suppression of crime as the first motive. The fact that these haunts were in most cases also the most insanitary parts of the cities was a secondary consideration. The frequency with which the emotive phrase 'dens of vice' crops up is some indication of attitude.

This suspicion was, perhaps, confirmed by the lack of replacement housing built.

The response to fears of the 'moral evils directly traceable to the wretched dwellings of the poor' (Morris, 1998: 38) by some nineteenth-century philanthropists was to set up 'model dwelling companies'. Their aim was to demonstrate that model housing for poor people could be provided as an alternative to the overcrowded squalor of the slums, and still provide a return on investment (Merrett, 1979). It was not their objective to house the very poorest sections of the population, but as one financier for the Improved Industrial Dwellings Company put it, the objective was to 'meet the wants of that portion of the working classes most worth working for, those earning from £1.5s to £2 per week' (quoted in Merrett, 1979: 16), or what Hobsbawm terms the 'aristocracy of labour' (1971: 154). When it became necessary that they should provide for the poorer working classes, the Labouring Classes Dwelling Houses Act 1866 enabled them to access to preferential rate loans from the Public Works Loans Commission (Malpass, 2000: 35).

The Royal Commission on the Housing of the Working Classes

From the start of their enquiry, it was overcrowding which concerned and inflamed the passions of the *Royal Commission on the Housing of the Working Classes*. This was not a novel problem – indeed, it had exercised

Chadwick and others – but what was really concerning to the Commissioners was the fact that the march of progress had failed to dim the problem. They fixed on this as the housing question from the outset of their collection of the evidence and subsequently linked it back into the sanitation question. The failure of local authorities to respond to overcrowding through the use of their powers relating to nuisance and fitness (especially as a result of the alleged corruption of local vestries) particularly worried the 1885 Royal Commission (see Reynolds, 1974).

The question of overcrowding was also explicitly linked in with the moral condition of the working classes, although it was admitted in the Report that overcrowding and the single room system might not be the immediate cause of immorality (Royal Commission, 1885a: 24). The evidence suggested links between overcrowding and incest ('I can only remember one case of incest in which I did not trace it to the parties living in one room': evidence of Rev John Horsley – Royal Commission, 1885b: 87). And Lord Salisbury, who had campaigned and legislated on the issue for over 60 years, observed that 'If I were to go into the details of the consequences of overcrowding, particularly in single rooms, very few people would believe what I said' (1885b: 2). Nevertheless, what appeared to the Commission established beyond doubt was the link between overcrowding and the single room system and health – the former were said to be 'most destructive to bodily health' (Royal Commission, 1885a: 24) causing a considerable amount of labour to be lost (p 25).

The committee focused initially on a part of London, Clerkenwell, known for its overcrowding. The evidence adduced suggested a link between the landlords and the vestries, responsible for the regulation of overcrowding. Specific questions were asked about the 'demoralizing' effects of the conditions of the housing, and whether there was cause and effect. So, in their evidence to the Royal Commission, two police inspectors who had been concerned with the regulation of lodging houses, were asked questions about the minutiae of overcrowding in certain houses in certain streets of London. And the dialogue between the Commissioners and the inspectors was conducted in explicit moral tones, particularly about the rationale for issuing summons against lodging house landlords (Royal Commission, 1885b: 135–42). There were clear concerns about the occupying habits of certain groups of outsiders expressed during the interaction.

Although these concerns with overcrowding and sanitation, reflecting the failure of half a century of legislative intervention in the public health system, were hardly novel, the solutions prompted by them were in the main highly controversial. Indeed, so controversial were they that there were a series of minority reports where members of the Commission either expanded points or questioned them. Chief among these was the suggestion made to trial an expansion of the provisions of Salisbury's Acts to enable local government to provide housing (Royal Commission, 1885a: 68–9). The concern of the Marquess of Salisbury in his additional memorandum was that such building should only take place in London because of the particular circumstance of the capital. He also argued that the rents of such houses should reflect real costs because otherwise 'it would destroy the market of the speculative builder, and its liberality would only have the effect of driving everyone else out of a field of enterprise which it would itself be capable of entirely occupying' (p 98). Similarly, concern was expressed in the memorandum of two MPs, Goschen and Stanley, that 'the action of private builders and private companies will be proportionately discouraged' (p 104). They preferred municipal action in relation to the replacement of clearance areas. Richard Cross similarly believed that local authority building should only occur 'under exceptional circumstances' linking such circumstances to those unable to provide for themselves. For Jesse Collings MP, the central problem was 'competition rents' for which local authority provision was required to ameliorate – indeed, local authorities were regarded by him as the most appropriate body because they act 'without profit' but were a profit to be made, it would benefit the whole community (p 126).

Although there were differences in the detail, the 1885 report provides, in many respects, *a* key moment in which the collective became implicated to some degree or other in the individual housing of the poor. Of course, this was subject to the concerns about the pauperizing effect of state involvement and differences in degree and/or location. But, the Commissioners themselves seemed mostly to be convinced of some local government involvement. This was not necessarily a reflection of the evidence before them – Lord Salisbury made clear his belief that 'by private effort in London everything could be done that we require to be done' (Royal Commission, 1885b: 3); and Octavia Hill made clear her belief in the importance of private individuals being responsible as house management 'seems to me to want a knowledge about the needs of the people, and the habits and desires, and the rental and the locality, and the quantity' (p 306).

Origins of state provision

The intervention of the state in the provision of housing was seen my many Victorians as an intrusion into the private sphere, a sphere in which philanthropy had a role, but the state should stay out of. The Charity Organisation Society, which had championed a social work intervention into the lives of the poor, was not prepared to accept the state stepping into that sphere (Finlayson, 1990; Thane, 1996: 21–4). Octavia Hill objected to the role the London County Council came to play in providing housing for the poor which, she said, would discourage private enterprise (Owen, 1965: 387); and Sir Richard Cross (of the Cross Act) and Lord Shaftesbury were both concerned that state provided housing at below market rents would 'destroy the moral energies' of the working classes (Merrett, 1979: 20–1). From 1851 to 1914 a number of Acts of Parliament enabled local authorities to build housing, but this was not through the direct application of state (local or central) subsidy.

However, there came about an understanding that in order to make housing affordable for the working classes, state subsidies would be essential.

Some scholars argue that the introduction of state subsidies for the building of working class housing can be directly attributed to the failure of the MDCs attempt at 'philanthropic capitalism'; by demonstrating the impossibility of providing decent housing for poor people in a capitalist market, they made an effective case for state subsidy of working class housing (Gauldie, 1974; Merrett, 1979; Owen, 1965). However, programmatic changes are rarely the result of one single cause, but rather emerge from resistance to, and the problematization of, existing practices. Daunton (1983; 1987) and Malpass (2000: 46) both argue that this supposition of direct causation is an oversimplification; the necessity for state subsidy to make housing affordable was the outcome of debate and struggle at the time, much of which has become silenced by the presentation of the outcome as inevitable.

It has also been argued that state provision of housing was an inevitable result of the failures of the private rented sector from the late nineteenth century, and in particular the Glasgow rent strikes which forced Lloyd George to introduce legislation to control rents (Damer, 1980; Melling, 1980). Others suggest that the Boer War had identified the 'disastrous physical condition of the urban working class' (Damer, 1980: 79) and that the First World War provided a break in housing policy which decisively led to state intervention (Merrett, 1979: 31). Swenarton (1981) argues that it was primarily the threat of Bolshevism which motivated Lloyd-George combined with the economic problems in the immediate post-war period of high building costs. On this view, it was 'the uses to which housing could be put for wider political and ideological ends' (p 67) which mattered. Similarly, Bowley's (1945) version of truth was that housing policy became a national issue after the war in a 'sudden' and 'accidental' way. Holmans' version (1987: 39–49 and 292–4), however, tends more to the evolutionary perspective, suggesting that the failure of the private sector in the decade before the war, together with the failure of the Housing of the Working Classes Act 1890 (under which just 20,000 properties were built in over 20 years) as well as a realization of the ability of the state to mass production during the war, were all factors. The political rhetoric of building 'homes fit for heroes' was a message that housing should not be a cause of insurrection.

Nevertheless, state provision of housing was necessarily thought of as a contingency, to be used while the private sector was in abeyance. Indeed, in the inter-war period, the private sector received considerable state subsidy for the production of housing in attempts to revive it and state provision of housing was almost always through the private sector. It was during this period that the boom in housing construction for ownership began as a result of a conjunction of interest between speculative housebuilding and the building societies (Ball, 1983; Craig, 1986 and Chapter 8 below). However, as Bowley (1945: 41) observed:

> The job of providing houses could once more, if the local authorities or electors liked, be developed as a social service. The door to at least partial socialisation of the field was definitely propped open. It remained to be seen whether the threshold would be crossed.

The three different phases of council provision of housing in the inter-war period were then supposed to be temporary – Bowley (1945) refers to them as 'experiments' – until the private sector could again take up the mantle of provision.

The three experiments involved, first (1919–23), a survey of housing need combined with a subsidized building programme; the second experiment (1923–33) was central subsidy of local authority and private provision; and third, the slum clearance and replacement schemes. In the first phase, local authorities were required under the Addison Act of 1919 to survey their areas and provide evidence to the central government of the need for additional units of housing in their areas. Given the lack of credibility attached to local authorities' performance of their housing obligations during the nineteenth century, it was perhaps odd that they should be chosen for this function in the immediate post-war period. Part of the explanation for this decision must be the paucity of available alternatives against the need to move quickly on the massive building programme then envisaged (see Malpass, 2000: 74–7).

The contingent involvement of councils in housebuilding can perhaps be shown by comparing the completions of new properties under different subsidy systems – for example, under the 1923 Act, which sought to create a level playing field for public and private provision: 74,000 had been completed by the local authorities, while 350,000 new private sector properties had been completed (Committee on Local Expenditure, 1932: para 73); on the other hand, the more generous subsidies under the 1924 Wheatley Act, lead to 505,000 new properties being completed by local authorities, although the measure of subsidy was moved around during this period (Holmans, 1987: 309).

The Wheatley subsidy was removed in 1933 as a result of the report by the Committee on Local Expenditure. This report was necessitated by the major, global recession; and in a classical economist's response, it clearly indicated areas where public expenditure could be cut. In so doing, it made apparent its author's own rationality about the relative value of public and private. The report noted that, although local authorities may have found it necessary to build new properties 'where they are satisfied that a clear need remains to be met', 'we look forward to the return of private enterprise to the provision of working class houses to let' and were 'strongly of the opinion' that no new subsidies should be introduced and the previous subsidies phased out (paras 80–1). There were other strong indicators of support for the private sector from official reports, which assumed that public provision would be for a limited period only (see Chapter 7). Malpass (1990: 37) notes that the withdrawal of local authorities from building general needs housing was 'specifically to remove competition' and to enable the market to recolonize an area of demand it had withdrawn from before the First World War.

It is the third housing experiment which was productive of a new problem. Up until this point, as Power (1987: 66) suggests, councils became landlords without commitment or forethought. From this time, however, a novel problematization became apparent, one which transformed understandings about the purpose of public provision of housing – for those *in need* (a theme we take up in detail in Chapter 3) – and which also necessitated the creation of expertise in its management. Rehousing the slum dwellers was seen as problematic because of concerns about the ethico-moral capacity of those households to syncretise their habits with those of the earlier generation of council housing occupiers. We discuss the effect of this new problem – of expertise in housing management – in the next section.

Post-Second World War

The development of council housing in the aftermath of the Second World War followed the path developed in the post-First World War era. Indeed, as Malpass observes, although relatively radical solutions of universalism were being developed for certain services such as health and education, the development of housing was regarded as a recurring need. The key criterion was building as many new properties as possible over as short a period as possible. The conceptualization of the housing problem was, then, a quantity issue; it was assumed that the local authorities would lead the way, subsequently to be supplemented and overtaken by the private sector (Malpass, 2003: especially 594). Indeed, '... if the construction of the welfare state is associated with the reform, reorganization and extension (as distinct from simple growth) of key public services, then housing barely qualifies for inclusion' within the welfare state matrix (Malpass, 2004: 215). Cole and Furbey (1994: 64) expressed this same conclusion by a different avenue, arguing that if the welfare state was about the creation of universalism and a minimum subsistence level, housing certainly was not aimed at either: 'Adolf Hitler proved a more decisive influence than William Beveridge in shaping the housing requirements of post-war Britain' (p 60).

This tension between public and private provision was, according to Malpass (2004), resolved decisively in favour of the private by 1954, as the housing question mutated into playing 'the numbers game' with more limited resources. Housing's subservience to economic and political demands is apparent in this period. Local authority house building was shifted at this time back into the rehousing of slum dwellers, thus returning to the 'third experiment'; the role of the private sector was talked up, and restrictions on its housebuilding role were removed. This was combined with shifts towards higher rents and the use of rent pooling to facilitate and pay for further building programmes. Although local authority building programmes did take off in the following two Labour governments, this was aimed in part at slum clearance. High rise blocks and system building were the products of this shift, not necessarily as an economy but in response to limits on available land and appropriate labour (see Holmans, 1987: 116–17). Merrett's explanation (1979: 130–1) suggests that the domain of expertise altered decisively during this period towards architects:

> [W]e can say that the state's switch to a high-density redevelopment strategy took the shape of high flats because of the formal hegemony in local authorities of architects who were zealots of the modern movement, and that simultaneously this sea change in the

form of public sector housing was underpinned by the material interests of big capital in raising its degree of monopoly in the competition for contracts.

This critical role of the expertise of architects also echoes another of our themes – the blurred divide between the public and the private. The professional organization of architects is dominated by higher paid private practice architects Malpass (1975). And so, as Dunleavy (1980: 113) points out, the influence flows are likely to be asymmetric, from private to public. Once again, it was private sector innovations, culture and ideology that had become highly influential in the design of public sector policies.

The problems experienced by those living in high-rise (which were being increasingly documented by social scientists), combined with their labelling as 'sink estates' because of whom they were designed to house (largely slum dwellers), and a number of exogenous factors came together to produce the negative image of council housing which appears on the front cover of this book. In particular, the discovery of unpopularity in the 1970s (see, for example, Bottoms and Wiles, 1986; Damer, 1974) and the IMF loan in the mid-1970s raised questions about the continuing commitment to building by local authorities. The promotion of the private sector, the increasing residualization of the council sector and marginalization of its occupants, were processes in train well before the arrival of the Thatcher government (Murie, 1997a). The demise of local authority house building, and the promotion of other tenures was, in other words, already in train, to the extent that the Housing Green Paper of 1977 became a rather muted document – little could be done to salvage council housing's tarnished image.

1979 – present

The questions raised by the public/private binary were answered in favour of the private by the Thatcher governments which set in train the enhanced processes of privatization (discussed in Chapter 8) through the right of individual households to buy their housing, and the restrictions on new building imposed on local authorities. The attack on state provision veered from the early privatization agenda through to an attack on council housing management itself. An important discursive shift occurred here – from dividing off the slum dwellers from the respectable occupiers, to an attack on the tenure itself.

More than any other part of the post-war social settlement, the public provision of housing by the state was indelibly altered by the approach adopted at this time. Local authorities became managers of an increasingly residual stock of housing which provided accommodation for an increasingly marginal population (see Forrest and Murie, 1990). Forced into this situation, with their performance compared with other providers, management has adopted an increasingly entrepreneurial attitude and approach upon which succeeding chapters of this book amplify. When, in 1994, the then Department of the Environment espoused the belief that council housing was 'for people whose overall needs were substantial and enduring' and that people should not 'expect the state to provide for them on demand' (DoE, 1994: paras 1.1

and 1.2), they were building on these twin themes of residualization and marginalization. As one of us noted, 'council housing, ironically, has been more closely aligned with the dismantling of the welfare state than it was with the rise of the welfare state' (Cowan, 1999: 144). However, as we demonstrate in our case study at the end of this chapter, for the housing association sector, those other providers of 'social' housing, the increasing focus on the private located them squarely at the forefront of the re-envisioned sector – not public, not quite private, but 'iN Business for neighbourhoods'.

Expertise and the management of housing

Expertise is a key development in the social, in that it fragments one central problem into a series of discrete social problems which can then be solved (Rose, 1999: 123). Until the early 1930s, not much thought and attention had been given over how the properties being built with state subsidy were to be managed. Annual reports of the Ministry of Health, for example, refer to 'administration' at the end of the 1920s (for example, Ministry of Health, 1930), but this mutates subsequently into a crucial set of understandings about *management*. Management was not necessary – or, at least, expertise in management – before this time because the occupiers rarely needed attention as they were the better-off; after this time, the intense campaigns of slum clearance demanded the creation of expertise and professionalization.

It was at this time that experts became integrated into the process of governing households. Hitherto, the role of experts had been in the planning, design and construction of properties (Tudor Walters, 1918). In the Housing Act 1935, the government created the Central Housing Advisory Committee (CHAC), a group of the great and the good who employed sub-committees of experts. In their first report, this committee of experts considered the question of expertise in relation to housing management. The models of housing management available at that time were thin on the ground – perhaps the best known was that developed by Octavia Hill and taken on by the Association of Women Housing Managers.

What emerged from this period was an apparently neutral schema of management (CHAC, 1938: 9–10). Management was demanded 'to prevent waste'. There were two sides: the 'business side' – 'the application of skill in caring for the commodity'; and education – 'skill in treating the person who is paying for the use of the commodity ...'. The rehousing of slum dwellers particularly required the latter as 'a form of social education and aims at teaching a new and inexperienced community to be "housing minded" '. The essential question for the 1938 committee was whether this was a role for women or not, and it was one which they essentially fudged leaving it to the local authority.

The Octavia Hill system

At this point, it is worth dwelling on Octavia Hill, a key philanthropist in the invention of housing policy, often cast as the founder of housing management.

In fact, two 'approaches' to housing management developed. One approach originated in the model dwellings companies and charitable trusts (such as Guinness), and was then taken on in local authority estates. In this 'system', largely promoted by the male-dominated Institute of Housing, management was carried out mostly by men, with the functions of property allocation, rent collection and maintenance carried out by different departments (Laffin, 1986, ch 5).

However, the 'system' developed by Octavia Hill was promulgated by her many acolytes and disciples principally in the housing societies to such a degree that it became understood as the principal – perhaps *only* system – of expertise. The success of history could be said to be Octavia Hill's, for it was she who succeeded in seizing the rules (see Foucault, 1977b: 151). Her expertise and 'system' became the foundation for the Association of Women Housing Managers, which authorized its expertise through developing training and a qualification in management. The Association – later renamed the Society of Women Housing Estate Managers – exercised some discursive influence over housing policy, if perhaps less influential in practice after the First World War (due to concerns about the role of women in housing management). There was considerable disagreement between the Institute and Society – in 1936 the Institute decided that membership of the Society was incompatible with its own membership, leading to the resignation of a body of its members (Brion and Tinker, 1980: 74).

What one might say was that Hill was the first person to develop *expertise* in housing management of the poor. Hill's system of housing management initially involved the purchase of properties using private capital, lent to her by John Ruskin. Her method involved what we might today call 'tough love'. In an essay in 1866, she described her approach as follows:

> ... my strongest endeavours were to be used to rouse habits of industry and effort, without which they must finally sink – with which they might render themselves independent of me, except as a friend and leader. *The plan was one which depended on just governing more than on helping.* (Hill, 1875: 15; emphasis added)

She explicitly linked the social and moral in describing her 'system' of improving the living conditions of the poor. This system sought to harness the forgotten capacities of the poor for self-government through the provision of better quality housing only after they had proved themselves worthy of it. Indeed, the provision of better quality homes was a potentially pauperizing event: 'Transplant [the poor] to-morrow to healthy and commodious homes and they would pollute and destroy them' (ibid: 7).

Sanitary reform was essential, but must come from within; education of children was also essential. She describes the way in which she sought to evict a regular rent-payer from his accommodation because he did not send his children to school, requiring him to 'do what you can to teach the children to be good, and careful, and industrious' (p 25). The 'intimate knowledge' of her occupiers gave 'power to see the real position of families ... to keep alive the germs of energy; to waken the gentler thought; to refuse resolutely to give any help but such as rouses self-help; to cherish the smallest lingering gleam of self-respect ...'. (p 31).

Crucial to her system was her process of selecting occupiers and their ongoing supervision. She required 'a sense of duty, and demand[ed] energetic right-doing among the poor themselves, and so purifies and stimulates them' (p 31). In her evidence to the 1885 Royal Commission, she described her system in relation to drunkards:

> I do not say that I will not have drunkards [in my properties], I have quantities of drunkards; but everything depends upon whether I think the drunkard will be better for being sent away or not. It is a tremendous despotism, but it is exercised with a view of bringing out the powers of the people, and treating them as responsible for themselves within certain limits ... you cannot get the individual action in any other way that I know of. (Royal Commission, 1885b: 297)

Her system was intensely moral and Christian, seeking the reform of the 'destructive classes'. Her practice was to provide such persons with poor quality accommodation and, if they 'improved' (as judged by 'the clergy and other gentlemen at work there': p 295), to improve the quality of the housing. Those who did not improve were summarily evicted. It is also clear that there were certain people who she would not have selected in the first place. The division, then, was between poverty on the one hand and pauperization on the other, and the aim was to save the poor from pauperization. Clapham (1997: 29) notes that 'her visits to collect rent were seen as opportunities to develop personal respect and friendship, to offer support and advice, and occasionally offer material help where this would not pauperise the recipient'.

These features of Hill's practice – expertise and social citizenship – are continuous, albeit mutated, themes in housing management as it developed during the twentieth century. It was at the level of political rationality and problematization that these mutations began. As already observed, Hill was set against state involvement in housing provision believing it was the proper realm of the individual. In this, however, she was already out of step.

The 1938 CHAC report

The problem for the 1938 CHAC was twofold – it was assumed in their terms of reference that management was required, but what did this involve; and second, which system was better designed for the purpose. The twin demands of management – business and education – linked the public and private. The business side was required for the purposes of public audit, but education facilitated the business; education of the household made business possible. Household education occurred before the move took place: the manager visited the household in their current accommodation 'in order to be able to foresee the family's probable future behaviour and to consider where it may best be placed' (p 19). 'Many will be grateful' for an educational induction (p 25). Although a large number of new tenants would be capable of adapting, the committee made a division of others:

> ... the remainder must be taught a new mode of living. Much can be done by education alone to improve social standards; ... Bad habits are not easily broken .... The bad tenant will learn more readily by eye than by ear: example is better than precept. (p 20)

Aftercare was another important role of management but this was generally to be undertaken by resort to 'suasion by a tactful appeal to reason' so that occupiers were 'masters in their own home' (p 23). There was a small minority who 'may be termed the hard core of the problem of management' for whom continuous surveillance was required (p 24). This group was effectively written off by the committee, in the hope that their children might be more orderly (for the different conceptualization of this 'problem household', see Chapter 3).

As to the second 'all important' question, the committee concluded that women were best suited to the management role as the 'housewife' was the person with whom the manager would have most contact. Whether the Octavia Hill system – which combined business and education in the one person – or the Institute of Housing's system – which separated them out – was most appropriate was left to the local authority (although some doubt was cast on the ability to combine both in the same person (p 28)).

This report, then, signals another key moment in the development of expertise. First, the report sought to define a role for expertise, both for the committee itself and for housing management. The Ministry of Health Circular which accompanied the report requested that local authorities respond to a questionnaire about their housing management, as the 'Minister is anxious to collect information' (Circular 1740: 7). And the report itself noted the different qualifications required for members of each professional association (although, in contra-distinction to the Society of Women Estate Managers, no qualifications were required for membership of the Institute until 1946 (Brion and Tinker, 1980)).

Second, the notion of housing management, probably from this point on, was constructed with a certain neutrality in official texts – 'the surface image fostered by local government that management activities are orderly, fair, neutral and apolitical and that "each receives according to need" ...' (Gray, 1976: 84). The centrality of the notion of need – implying a neutral, expert set of assessment criteria – assisted this process. Kemp and Williams note that, after the Second World War, 'the more intensive styles of management were themselves subjected to criticism' (1991: 130), and it is noticeable that subsequent CHAC reports employ more neutral terminology, and, indeed, relegate the education role almost to an after-thought. The 1958 committee report emphasized the business element almost from the outset (CHAC, 1958: para 4). The justification for this shift was said to be the need in 1938 to focus on housing as a social service because of the decanting process (para 6); the 1958 committee emphasised that the 'welfare role' now belonged to other experts, to whom households could be referred. The 'unsatisfactory tenants' were to be the subject of co-ordinated teams (para 120). By this stage, housing management had become technical, facilitated by the growth of professionalization and the development of qualifications for the role (though very few housing managers actually had any professional training at this time). It was now possible to provide a list of the tasks of housing management:

> Advice at the planning stage on estate layout and house design
> Administration of the waiting list
> Letting the houses
> Transfers and exchanges
> Rent collection and advice on rent schemes
> Maintenance and repairs ...
> General care of estates and their amenities
> Housing welfare and liaison with the statutory and voluntary social services. (para 134)

This should not be taken to deny the important role which 'education' schemes were still assigned (see the discussion in Chapter 3, for example) but the point is that their role and importance were quietened by this professionalization process.

The use of the descriptive list of activities is interesting for it tended to obscure the wide-ranging knowledges required for each separate task created a difficulty in establishing 'a coherent professional identity' (Laffin, 1986: 83). All of these knowledges were encapsulated in the same person (under the Hill system) and, at times, different knowledges have assumed greater importance in the public imagination than at others. More recently, there has been a fragmentation of these knowledges into discrete expertises exercised by different professionals. So, for example, today, the principal expertises of design have been translated into the expertise of crime control through the 'defensible space' metaphor (Newman, 1974). This fragmentation is also a preface to the measurement of management, and also its privatization – the specification of management is very much the condition precedent of that development.

Third, although the 1938 report re-produced the already bifurcated the role of the manager, it was clear which aspect was in the ascendancy. Management was regarded as 'the concern of the local authority for protecting and preserving what is seen as a piece of public investment rather than someone's home' (Bedale, 1980: 67) – hence, the justification for education and ongoing supervision of tenants was to facilitate the business side.

Fourth, the 1938 Committee report marked a shift in the techniques of government away from the carceral towards governing through freedom, a shift which has been contested over time and remains a key problem. However, the report proposed a rather different form of government – through the family and through community. It explicitly employed the nineteenth-century technique of 'familialization' through the housewife 'and added a number of tools and allies for her to use', the main instrument of which was ' "social" housing' (see Donzelot, 1979: 40).

Expertise and entrepreneurialization

The Thatcher governments' attack on welfare bureaucracy, and specifically housing management, was based upon their paternalistic approach, inefficiency, and incompetence. As Cole and Furbey (1994: 212) put it, one of the key successes of the Thatcher governments was their ability 'to consolidate the move from a crisis *of* council housing to a crisis *in* council housing'. Shifts through to comparing the performance of council and RSL housing management, the further specification of its tasks, approaches to risk, crime and contract, together with the various processes of CCT and Best Value have all indelibly altered the terrain of the government of housing management (discussed in Chapters 3 and 4). The turning point in this process was probably 1987, when the housing White Paper (DoE, 1987) diverted attention from the right to buy to a more full-frontal assault on the values of council housing management. An event of equal importance was the subsequent research conducted by a team from Glasgow University which compared the performance of councils and RSLs in the emerging environment of LSVT and CCT (Centre for Housing Research, 1989). The specification of housing management in this report made measurement possible, and, indeed, the subsequent processes of tendering and value-laden assumptions of entrepreneurial efficiency themselves. The actual findings of that report – that councils performed well compared to RSLs – were less important than the process of mapping the terrain of housing management itself.

A case study in constructing the public/private divide

In this last section we focus on story of the housing association sector. In part, this is to illustrate some of the themes from the earlier sections – the influence of concepts of poverty on housing policy, the necessity for state intervention, and the role of developing concepts of expertise. However, what this case study brings sharply into focus is the highly constructed nature of the public/private divide, and in particular the ways in which legal and economic boundaries have been used – and shifted – to sometimes enhance, at other times blur, this bifurcated version of housing policy.

Philanthropy and charitable interventions

The state has not been the only means of addressing the 'housing problem'. As municipal councils began to develop a significant landlord role, other institutions also intervened.

What is generally termed the 'housing association' sector developed from a myriad of responses to the ill-housed. Significant in this development was the role of Octavia Hill and the 5 per cent philanthropists, but earlier influences came in the almshouse movement, where the giving of alms provided housing for the poor and assured the alms-giver's passage to heaven through the regular recitation of prayers. The Victorian era saw the establishment of significant charitable trusts – Rowntree, Guinness, Peabody and William Sutton are all significant providers of housing today. The inter-war response through state subsidy provided resources to the public utility societies established by Raymond Unwin and other enthusiasts for the Garden City movement, who were attempting to provide working class housing while also promoting the ideals of garden cities.

Our purpose here is to demonstrate and expand on one of our key themes, the ever-shifting boundaries of social housing (further detail on their history can be found in Malpass, 2000). In particular, this body of organizations that set themselves up as distinctly *not* the state, as bodies that were 'independent' (but not always clear about being independent from *what*), have had a complex, sometimes ambiguous relationship with the border between public and private, wanting to establish room for a third space, a third sector – some called it a (the?) Third Way. Their *independence* has been central to their self-image, but also – and frequently in tension with this – has been their desire to be key players in housing policy.

One of the principal routes followed by this other sector was the pursuit of charity. The first part of this section will follow some of the difficulties and complexities that evolved from this particular form – a form that developed its own legal and bureaucratic rationalities. However, during the 1960s the charitable route became too constraining for many who sought to expand the housing association sector into the 'third arm' of housing policy (a term coined by Anthony Crosland, see Malpass, ibid.). In seeking expansion, they created the necessity for closer ties with the state to access public funding, and increasingly casting-off the 'voluntary' image which had been one of the sector's binding rationales. The 'voluntary housing movement' label, however, stuck until the 1980s. As associations sought private funding for their development, it was the public/private divide that created a new, and particularly critical boundary. Our concern with finding the 'social' in housing is partly created by the sector's desire to discard the 'public' image. We can do little more than ask questions about where concepts such as 'social' and 'public interest' go to when associations now want to 'brand' themselves (like Coca-Cola) as (social) businesses. So this second section on 'The limits of charity' will examine the ways in which the housing association sector has at times sought to differentiate itself *from* the 'public', at others become identified *with* the public domain. And in its most recent history, has critically 'bumped against' the public/private divide, bringing into the foreground some inherent ambiguities in its campaign for 'independence'.

The limits of charity

The housing association sector is made up of a diverse range of organizations that arise out of an equally diverse range of rationales. Some of these associations approached their role through the mechanism of charity: indeed, the charitable distinction has been at times held out as having special qualities. When, in the 1940s, some associations proposed to convert to charitable status to avoid excess profit taxation, the chairman of the National Federation of Housing Societies (an organization established in 1935 as the representative body of housing associations) wrote to its members warning of the dangers of 'posing' as charities (NFHS, 1945: 12). Other associations entered into the debate, defending the sanctity of charitable status and arguing that recovering tax revenue was not charitable funding but state funding (NFHS 1946a: 5). What quality it was that required such protection was never really explained by the defenders of the charitable ideal, but what this debate managed to demonstrate was that housing provided by charitable bodies was *different*.

One clear difference that Octavia Hill and fellow members of the Charity Organisation Society (COS) wanted to accentuate was that the 'charitable spirit' would be threatened by the intervention of the state. The journal of the COS commented that 'voluntarism and the state would be unable to coexist' (quoted in Finlayson, 1990: 185). Octavia Hill objected to the role that the London County Council came to play in providing housing for the poor which, she said, would discourage private enterprise (Owen, 1965: 387). And some of the charitable housing trusts viewed state subsidies with extreme suspicion: the Guinness Trust, opposed to any attempt by the central or local state to govern its affairs, chose not to use public subsidy, and only built one scheme with central government subsidy until after the Second World War (Malpass, 1998).

Particularly as they attempted to expand their role, charitable housing associations and trusts hit boundaries established by *law*. Charity law had never recognized the provision of housing *per se* as being a charitable purpose. The definition of 'charity' arose from an Elizabethan statute, the Preamble to the *Statute of Charitable Uses 1601*, interpreted and reinterpreted through case law; housing could only be charitable if it was intended to relieve *poverty*. In fact, those who have most ferociously 'policed' the boundaries of charity law have been the tax inspectors and local authority treasurers, not the state regulator of charities, the Charity Commission. Charitable status brought with it considerable financial gain in terms of relief from a wide range of taxation, local and national. Housing associations seeking such financial benefits of charitable status had not only to ensure that their objectives (as set out in their constitution) fell within one of the 'heads' of charity. They had also to demonstrate that their continuing activities were also charitable (Luxton, 2001). It was this that brought the day-to-day activities and decisions of associations within the fiscal regulatory sphere. In the 1950s the Borough Council of West Ham contested the eligibility of the Guinness Trust for relief from local rates arising from the provisions of the Rating and Valuation (Miscellaneous Provisions) Act 1955. Section 8(1)(c) of the Act enabled organizations that were neither 'established for profit' nor 'conducted for profit' to obtain relief from local rates. The Borough Council challenged the practice of the Guinness Trust and other charitable bodies of investing in stocks and shares and letting out land or property for profit; these were, it argued, profit-making activities, and the Court Recorder of West Ham agreed.

The Court of Appeal in *Guinness Trust v West Ham Borough Council* [1958] 1 WLR 541 overturned the decision, arguing that:

> The making of profit by the Guinness Trust is part of the machinery by which it achieves its charitable purposes. The making of profit, which can never be distributed, is not an object or purpose of the Trust. It is a means for the expansion of the sphere of charity. (NFHS, 1959: 31)

A decision against the Trust would have called into question the activities of organizations that had become essential to the delivery of housing for the 'poor'. The court could justify qualifying the 'common sense' reading of 'making a profit' so as to produce a particular outcome, in a turn that makes perfect 'sense' in legal terms. Nevertheless, as Moody (2000) has pointed out, public perceptions are just as important as fiscal advantages – charities benefit from public goodwill because they are understood to operate under ethical principles concerned with the 'public good'. The court's decision that such 'profit-making' activities did not infringe the particular tax law could not displace the commonly understood meaning of the term 'profits', associated with acting for private interests. Such connotations could call into question the motives of charitable associations. Present-day associations no longer refer to making profits, but to 'surpluses' that are applied for the objectives of these 'not-for-profit' organizations.

It was the policing of the charitable boundaries by the Inland Revenue that, probably inevitably, brought the housing association sector to consider breaking the charitable bind. The 1960s can be seen as one of those points in the history of housing policy of significant transformation. The problematization of municipal authorities as the principal providers of rented housing arose from attacks and resistance from a number of angles. Community activists in the inner city became vocal about the policies of clearance and the relocation of tenants into tower blocks on peripheral estates. Notting Hill Housing Trust was formed along with a number of other associations working in inner London and other cities. In London the London County Council (which became the Greater London Council), and a number of Tory-controlled councils, were providing significant funding for the associations, partly as a mechanism for reacting to community pressure without providing more municipal housing. The charity Shelter was launched in 1966, and very rapidly began to raise considerable amounts of funds which were channelled into associations leading to their development and expansion in a number of cities (Seyd, 1975). Housing associations, and charity, were becoming an alternative, a possible 'third arm' to government housing policy (Malpass, 2000: ch 7).

However, such re-imaging of the housing association sector hit against new boundaries. This new wave of philanthropists had expansionist intentions. Their rationale for forming as charities was principally to provide comfort to the local authorities – the 'political risk' of investing in non-municipal rented housing was high following the exposé of Rachman's activities by the Profumo affair (Cowan 1999: 63–4; see Chapter 7). Charitable status provided a badge of respectability along with a regulatory framework which would make it difficult for public funds to become private property (though see Chapter 5 concerning the scandal with Omnium association and others). But the interpretation of the Inland Revenue, that charity law required that *all* the activities of associations be for the relief of poverty, put very restrictive boundaries around them. Did this mean that when tenants were no longer 'in poverty' they had to be evicted? – the Revenue said 'yes'. Despite the Charity Commissioners' willingness to move these boundaries, their attempt to act as broker between the National Federation of Housing Societies and the Inland Revenue failed – resistance to change that was no doubt as much a product of the threat to fiscal income as an unwillingness to alter centuries-old norms. The Federation's Chairman, Lewis Waddilove, concluded in a memo to one of the Commissioners, that 'we avoid any attempt to redefine charitable status in relation to housing. The consultations which you kindly initiated have shown how sterile this to be' (PRO/CHAR 11/205).[1] Waddilove, however, had another avenue – he had been asked by Peter Walker, Secretary of State for the Environment, to prepare a paper on 'principles that might be included in a Housing Bill dealing with the Voluntary Housing Movement' (ibid). Expansion and transformation were to be facilitated through establishing new boundaries in the form of a regulatory and funding agency for the housing association sector – the Housing Corporation, through the provisions of the Housing Act 1974. Charity's boundaries were problematized from other directions too. Des Wilson, the first Director of Shelter, wrote in 1966 that the organization

> ... has to be more than just a fundraising organisation. It must raise money and work for what people can do. But it must uncompromisingly publicise what it can't do. Shelter can't just be a conventional charity, it must be a campaign to call for change. (quoted in Wilson, 1997)

So while a 'third arm' was considered necessary, charity was seen to be too prescriptive and restrictive in both a normative and a formative sense. What associations began to push up against was the boundaries of the public domain.

Housing associations and the public/private divide

Housing associations have had a complex relationship with the public/private divide. We have already noted that Octavia Hill wanted to preserve housing for the poor for the private business of philanthropic entrepreneurs. And the attempt in the 1930s to set up a national housing corporation to fund the expansion of the work of the public utility societies and others was grounded in the promotion of housing associations' *difference* from municipal authorities – their particular expertise in 'reconditioning', the improvement of older housing (see Malpass, 2000: ch 4; McDermont, 2005: ch 5; Moyne, 1933). In this case, it was an alignment of public and private interests that led to the failure of this proposal. The Moyne Committee's recommendations could not withstand the vigorous opposition of the local authorities, who allied private landlords and house-builders to their own cause, a grouping that had considerable lobbying power within the Ministry of Health (Garside, 1995).

Post-Second World War, it was the public side of the divide that was attractive to associations, as the Labour government restricted state subsidies to the public sector, and the private builders were required to have a license for new construction. In 1946 lobbying for the non-private status of associations achieved partial, but significant success: the Housing (Financial and Miscellaneous Provisions) Act 1946 put housing associations eligibility for subsidy on the same terms as local authorities (Malpass, 2000: 121). Nevertheless, the sector, despite (or perhaps, because of) its diversity and divisions, continued to assert its difference from municipal authorities as its advantage. They were 'in a more favourable position to experiment and take the lead in the continued effort for improvement in standards and new and better management ... Local authorities had to be more conservative in practice' according to Lewis Silkin, one-time trustee of the Sutton Dwellings Trust and Minister for Town and Country Planning in 1946 (NFHS, 1946b: supplement).

However, it was the desire to expand the sector in the 1960s that began to shift thinking on this boundary. With the 'independence' of charity becoming a burden, the prevailing view became clear that only a significant injection of public funding and state regulation could achieve this. The Housing Act 1964 had established a national Housing Corporation to promote and fund housing societies to provide co-ownership and cost renting; the Housing Act 1974 expanded the role of the Housing Corporation, making it the regulatory body for all housing associations in receipt of public funds. It was partly through the claim to hold specialized knowledge and skills in urban renewal that the housing association sector was enabled access to significant public funding its development programmes. The Housing Corporation became the channel for the comprehensive state funding of inner city renewal through the modernization of street properties, and new build housing. New housing association properties were in effect funded entirely from *public* funds, through a mix of grant (around 90 per cent of scheme costs) and loan from the Corporation and local authorities. So although the sector continued to see itself as different from public provision – it still called itself the Voluntary Housing Movement – its role in the 'social' was becoming re-imaged. Associations sought to shake off the amateurish image of voluntarism through the employment of professional staff. However, it was almost as if the public/private divide no longer mattered. The courts could declare, in *Peabody Housing Association v Green* (1978 P&CR 644) that they had no doubt that the association 'can fairly be said to be a public body' (p 660), but it was not willing to regulate Peabody *as if it were* like a local authority and providing *public* housing.

Indeed, it could be said that the public/private divide only came to matter again when it became important to be imagined as *private*.

Housing associations, public functions and private money

We can view the next (and current) 'phase' in the housing association narrative as a very deliberate attempt at *re-imaging* themselves. It has now become important to the sector, the Housing Corporation *and* the New Labour government, that associations are placed firmly within the *private* sphere. This is at the same time as the old distinctions between housing associations and local authority housing are becoming blurred, as council housing becomes 'privatised' through the right to buy and transfer into the housing association sector, and as Murie (2005) and others now argue, the increasing irrelevance of the old boundaries of tenure. What is the meaning of this new attachment to the private identity? What new ways of thinking are requiring such a re-imaging – if indeed they are 'new'?

One way of thinking that attaches importance to the 'public' label is the framework of public law, because the public label implies (now, but not always) the possibility of using the mechanisms of the courts to regulate. Ever since Court of Appeal in *R v Panel on Take-overs and Mergers, ex p Datafin plc* ([1987] QB 815) judged that the City Panel on Takeovers and Mergers fell within the jurisdiction of public law, it has been accepted that this 'public' label can be applied to bodies other than the bodies of central and local government, to include those bodies that are exercising functions of a *public nature*. With the increasing contracting out and privatization of the functions of the state, some flexibility in the view of 'public' by the courts was necessary. But the courts have been unsure how far to take this flexibility, generally considering that they cannot go too far without legislative backing. Now when issues of the 'public' nature of housing associations came to court, the judge considered that the court's response to the collapse of the public/private divide, and the increasing contractualization of government was 'one of the most important questions in public law today' (*R v Servite Houses and another ex p Goldsmith and another* [2001] LGR 55: 67b) as he could not find that the association was anything but a *private body*. It has been the Human Rights Act 1998, however, that has brought this question once again to centre stage – for under the Act the obligation not to infringe 'Convention rights' is placed only on public authorities, and those bodies performing public functions. We return to this issue below, p 54 in our discussion of the case of *Poplar HARCA*.

The second group for whom the public/private distinction matters are those concerned with rules relating to 'public spending'. In this category we would place, the Treasury, and all those bodies for whom the rules of the Treasury matter – that is government departments, local authorities and those who are spending public funds. What counts as 'public spending' is what is critical to this group. The rules of fiscal policy are highly complex – one might say deliberately so in order to preserve the policing of these rules to a limited expertise – but the essential point is that for any body considered as a public body, *all* of its expenditure counts as public spending, even if raised through borrowing from 'private' sources such as banks, or flotations on the stock exchange (Garnett, 2000). (The Treasury has recently enabled local authorities considered to be exceptional performers to become involved in *prudential borrowing*, where borrowing is not counted as public expenditure – but this has limited application to housing.) It was this 'rule' that motivated housing associations in the 1980s to find ways of casting off the 'public' label, to become understood within fiscal terms at least as 'private'. Critical to this assessment became the capacity for associations to be 'risk-bearing' – that is, to themselves bear the risk of their development projects, and not be reliant on public funds should things go wrong. It is partly this association between riskiness and the 'not-public' space that comes to be a cause for concern, for example see Cowan *et al* (1999) on the impact of financial risk assessments on allocation of housing according to need. Now is not the time to continue this exploration of risk, only to point out that such assessments of risk are always taken from a particular point of view – the point of view of business risk of private capital. Such assessments cut across functions that would otherwise be considered as public – the assessment of housing need. Returning to our chapter title, 'imag(in)ing the social in housing', the impact of this interrelationship between private capital and public functions appears to raise a clash of values. As long as the private finance initiative and other privatization initiatives are portrayed as being for the improvement of public services, this clash of values, a clash in the ways of thinking about governing, is hidden from view, or perhaps just unacknowledged.

The third perspective from which the public/private divide matters is the perspective of the *political*. Bauman argues that the public domain

... has been stealthily yet steadily colonized by private concerns trimmed, peeled and cleaned of their public connections and ready for (private) consumption but hardly for the production of (social) bonds. (Bauman, 2001: 190)

It is in Baumann's words that we see the connection between concepts of 'public' space, 'public' housing, and the 'social', and our search for the 'social' in housing. With the collapse of public housing the fear is that housing intended to meet collective, social needs becomes threatened. Certainly the tenants of the 35 councils who have so far voted against stock transfer believe that there is something to be defended in council housing, despite negative experiences of the lack of repairs, long waiting lists and bureaucratic log-jams (see the national Defend Council Housing campaign: http://www. defendcouncilhousing.org.uk/dch/). Council housing has provided some guarantee (vague, qualified and frequently thwarted, as we show in the following chapters) of primarily being aimed at meeting collective social needs, not the private needs of capital; and of being governed by mechanisms that (at least theoretically) are open to scrutiny, accountable through public fora, and ultimately accountable through the ballot box. For all the private sector has been heralded as being the only route for innovation (see below, p 53) the fears that the public interest is secondary to the private interest have not been, and cannot be assuaged. And even where private initiatives are carried out in the name of the 'public interest', as Mike Feintuck argues, the 'public interest' is ill-, or un-defined:

> [C]onstructs of the public interest currently in play can be viewed as insubstantial, ... a result of their reflecting almost exclusively *economic* considerations, and therefore containing inadequate recognition of the important *democratic* expectations. (2004: 7)

It was an *economic* set of rationalities and rules that required housing associations to take on a new form, of the private, risk-taking enterprise, and it was these rationalities that saw the re-emergence of the public/private divide as an *essential* boundary within housing policy. However, once the possibility of a new image emerged, it opened up new possibilities for existing actors within the 'traditional' public sector framework, as the story of the emergence of large-scale voluntary transfer shows.

Central/local relations and the search for entrepreneurialism

Following the election of the Conservative government under Thatcher in 1979, local government became increasingly subject to the unifying controls of central government. Constraints on the freedom and autonomy of local government cuts in public spending and legislative restrictions that meant local authorities could no longer build new housing, and had very few resources to allocate to improving existing housing, meant that the option of transferring *out* of central government control into the housing association sector became seen by some in local government as highly attractive. In 1988 Chiltern District Council took the pioneering and innovative step of achieving the first sale of an entire local authority housing stock to a housing association. The LSVT programme has since that time become the principal vehicle for achieving change in the social housing sector. By 1995, 67 local authorities had balloted their tenants and 40 had transferred their stock (Mullins *et al*, 1995: 25). The New Labour government elected in 1997, did nothing to slow down this programme of privatization, but rather gave it added impetus, particularly evident in the Green Paper on housing (DETR/DSS, 2000). Through their business plan the new association is able to raise private funds for improving its newly acquired housing stock and building new 'social' housing.

While local authorities have justified the transfer of housing on grounds of the inability to replace social housing lost through RTB, and their inability to deal with the increasing level of disrepair in the housing stock (see DETR, 2000a: 60–5), there is considerable evidence that impetus to transfer arose from the desire of local government officers for more autonomy – LSVT has been seen as a way of freeing the entrepreneurial self in local government staff:

> Transfer brings the prospect of working for a growing, rather than a declining, organisation; of greater autonomy in being able to plan over the medium term, rather than on a strictly annual cycle; of less interference by elected politicians; and of improved working conditions ... In general, officers may see greater opportunities in the more entrepreneurial and innovative atmosphere of a new organisation than in the bureaucratic, scrutinised approach of the local authority. (Kleinman, 1993: 169)

A decade and a half on from the first housing transfer, LSVT is no longer the pioneering approach it appeared in 1988 – the impetus now comes from a central government intent on a programme of 'modernising' public services and local government. Under New Labour the private sector has been valorized to an extent even the previous Conservative governments did not reach. The transfer programme is a central element of the government's social housing policy, as part of a regime of re-imaging the provision of previously public services as most efficiently, effectively and innovatively delivered through private sector mechanisms. According to Treasury doctrine, as set out in *Public Private Partnerships: the Government's approach* (HM Treasury, 2000: 16):

> The private sector can compensate for the higher price paid for its borrowing in a number of ways:
> - it can be more innovative in design, construction, maintenance and operations over the life of the contract;
> - create greater efficiencies and synergies between design and operation;
> - invest in the quality of the asset to improve long term maintenance and operating costs; and
> - underlying all this, the discipline of the market place ensures the private sector can manage risk better – it has better incentives and is better equipped to deliver on time and within budget.

And once housing associations had adopted the idea of a new image, they became enmeshed in a whole range of new practicalities as well as value systems that were to re-shape and re-image them. The increasing importance of financial matters meant that voluntary committee members – now renamed 'boards' in emulation of private business – had to possess professional skills: business skills, legal skills and financial skills (ODPM, 2003c). So while boards remained voluntary (though with some adopting systems for paying some members) they began more and more to look like company boards. So too did their accounts. The accountants of the housing association sector sought to re-define housing association accounts in the image of companies so that they would be recognizable to the private sector. Housing association accounting principles were modified through the mechanism of sector-specific Statement of Recommended Practice, or SORP, approved by the Accounting Standards Board. In the words of the Board's Chairman, these are principles that 'appeal not only to judgment but to conscience' (*Guardian*, 2002). In 1992 the first SORP for the housing association sector was agreed, and in 1999 associations adopted a format very similar to company or plc-style accounts (NHF, 1999). This was not simply a matter of changing appearances, but introduced practices that could dramatically alter the fortunes of housing associations as headlines in the housing press demonstrated: 'William Sutton plunges into the red as new SORP regime takes effect' (*Social Housing*, 2000: 15).

So the move over the public/private divide into the private domain in response to one particular rationality, has impacted not only on the financial shaping of the housing association sector, but on the overall image of the sector. Research indicates that associations saw themselves as adopting a more commercial approach (Chaplin *et al*, 1995: 11), and today, some associations are likely to be seen benchmarking themselves with Marks and Spencers (Murray, 2002) and are considering conversion to public limited companies (Randall, 2002).

This new image is not without resistance, and it is in the legal arena that some of these elements have become visible. As suggested above, while economic rationalities would direct associations into the private domain, the interests of tenants and other users of social housing may be considered best respected in the public domain.

The 'public function' and private finance

The issue that exercised the judge in the *Servite* case, could housing associations be considered as public bodies, has arisen most prominently in a case (*Poplar Housing and Regeneration Community Association Ltd v Donoghue* (2001) 33 HLR, 823–46) brought under the Human Rights Act 1998, concerning Poplar Housing and Regeneration Community Association (Poplar HARCA), a housing association set up to take the transfer of some of the housing stock of the London Borough of Tower Hamlets. The association was registered with the Housing Corporation, and was established with a board which included five members from the Tower Hamlets council. The issue arose as to whether this new association was a public body because one of its tenants, Ms Donoghue, argued that Poplar HARCA's intention to evict her form the association flat she occupied contravened her rights under the European Convention of Human Rights. The public/private issue arose because, under the terms of the Human Rights Act (s 6), only 'public authorities' or bodies exercising 'functions of a public nature' for whom it is unlawful to contravene Convention rights. It is an interesting observation that what started life as an attempt by a tenant to protect incursions into that most private of spaces, her home, has been reconstructed through the actions of lawyers, officials, economists and judges, into a case in which the central issue is the nature and identity of *public* space.

In fact, the Court of Appeal decided that, in the very particular circumstances of this case, the association's dealings with Ms Donoghue and its administrative practices were so 'enmeshed' with that of an obvious public authority (Tower Hamlets) (para 65(v)) that the association was acting as a functional public authority – that is, it was carrying out functions of a public nature. However, for our purposes here, it is not the court's *legal* reasoning about what constitutes a public authority or public functions that is of interest – there have been many articles written on this matter (see for example Alder and Handy, 2001; Craig, 2001; McDermont, 2003). Our interest centres upon the ways in which the issue became a critical one for the development of *housing* policy. This becomes apparent from the content of the government's intervention in the case, which came about due to s 5 of the Human Rights

Acts 1998. This section provides a right for the Crown to intervene where a court is considering whether to make a declaration that primary legislation may be incompatible with Convention rights. The Department of the Environment, Transport and the Regions (DETR) and the Housing Corporation both gave evidence in the case, and it was clear from their evidence that their primary concern was not a finding of incompatibility, but the potential impact of the court deciding that a housing association was a public authority. In their witness statements emphasis was placed on the *independent* nature of housing associations. Brushing aside its total irrelevance to an organization such as Poplar HARCA, considerable importance was placed on the voluntary and philanthropic roots of housing associations: '[h]ousing associations are the legal embodiment of the voluntary housing movement'.[2]

The essence of their argument was that associations are firmly embedded in the *private sector* and, to quote the Corporation's legal adviser:

> ... it is the very nature of this private sector status that has brought in the £20 billion from finance institutions, which monies might need to be added to the public sector borrowing requirement should RSLs be found to be public sector bodies. Such a finding would also put a halt to the whole stock transfer programme.[3]

So, despite assurances that the Human Rights Act 1998 should enable Convention rights to be defended against a wide range of institutions, the economic rationality requires that law interprets 'public' as narrowly as possible. What is not important is that citizens should have legal rights that are enforceable against housing associations and the other voluntary and private sector organizations that are becoming increasingly central to the delivery of welfare services. Rather, the public domain comes to threaten housing policy, as it could mean that the rights of tenants might take precedence over the interests of the private finance institutions.

However, it may not be the imperatives of the legal frame that most threatens economic rationalities, but an institution that is firmly grounded in the principles of the market, the European Union. It has long been a crucial stand of the EU's drive towards a Single Market that the processes by which public bodies procure and outsource service should be regulated within the Single Market framework. Public procurement has been seen as 'an obvious target for Community action' (Harlow and Rawlings, 1997: 247) as it represents a significant proportion of Gross Domestic Product in Europe. Public contracts have been, in the vast majority, awarded to national contractors, which the Commission considered arose through discrimination by national governments. Therefore a number of EU Directives have attempted to regulate the publication of contract notices and the various stages of tendering a contract. The Directives, and an extensive body of emerging case law, represent an attempt to structure the discretion of Member States or other contracting authorities (Lewis, 2001: 124). The 'contracting authorities' (those bodies obliged to comply with the requirements of the Directives) have been defined by EU law to include not only central, regional and local government, but also other bodies *governed by public law*. The Commission has recently ruled that the UK housing associations are to be considered as 'bodies governed by public law' for the purposes of the public procurement directives. This ruling calls into question whether associations' status as private sector bodies for the purposes of the government public spending rules can be sustained (Wilcox, 2005). For the government's housing policy and housing associations themselves this ruling could have the same dire consequences as the Corporation predicted in the *Poplar HARCA* case – a serious threat to the private funding behind the LSVT programme. There is a certain irony that, in defending a 'free' market, the EU may have erected a new public/private boundary for the practitioners and policy-makers to deal with.

Conclusion

The particular set of questions which we might now term 'the social housing problem' have been fairly constant since the early nineteenth century. The way we think about and respond to them, as well as our underlying rationalities, may have shifted in quite decisive ways. However, the path was never particularly clear and apparently decisive events more contested. For example, the 1885 Royal Commission report had a complex web of minority reports and memoranda, and the recommendations were not completely implemented (or implemented differently) in the 1890 Housing of the Working Classes Act. Similarly, although much attention is given over to the Octavia Hill system of housing management by academics and policy-makers, it is not clear how significant her system was on the housing management practices of the majority of municipal landlords. Nevertheless, her evidence to the Royal Commission occupied upwards of 20 pages of evidence, and her self-claimed entrepreneurial expertise in private housing, together with her middle class female disciples, all occupy an important discursive role in any housing history. This ethico-moral objective of housing management recurred but was silenced through subsequent debates about its content.

An important point for us is the mutating role of the binary between public and private. In its original incarnation of public health policy, the public regulation of health was closely linked with a private, internal ethico-moral cleanliness. The question about the link between external housing conditions and the condition of the occupiers was one which particularly animated the housing reformers of the nineteenth century; and was never conclusively answered, the 1885 Royal Commission simply arguing that the link had not been proved beyond doubt. The link, however, formed the bedrock of the Hill system and the interventions by Salisbury.

The issue of public intervention mutated after the 1885 Royal Commission report to the question of numbers – how to provide the extra units of housing required to meet the needs of the population. This question dominated the twentieth century, particularly the post-war periods. There were periods when the numbers question was dulled by other housing questions (such as about urban renewal), but the numbers question even infiltrated these debates because the question was about how best to improve run down areas. It was the local authorities which were chosen for the provider role in the early post-war periods (although the properties were generally built by using private capital and private builders). But commitment to public provision was regularly questioned and certainly was not a given. Other sectors – capitalist private and philanthropic private – have been equally prominent in policy, if not more so because the concern has been about their (re-)generation. This is a recurring theme in this book.

Chapter 3:
Needing Need

Need has become the defining tool of social housing. Not only does it operate to define who gets in, and who doesn't, but it has also come to define the purpose – indeed, the mission – of social housing. Thus, to adopt Rose and Miller's schema, need is both a rationality and technology of social housing. It has been a mantra, repeated again and again, that social housing is about meeting housing need; and, until comparatively recently, this mantra went unchallenged. It is also a wonderfully *obscure* device around which a variety of different expertise has coalesced. Yet, it is also the case that need, as an organizing principle of social housing, was a comparatively late entrant into the arena, only emerging in the late 1920s becoming established during the economic crisis in the 1930s. It was primarily a response to the assumed issues created as a result of the rehousing of households from slum clearance areas.

In this chapter, we develop this point about the way in which need became essential to social housing, and also how it came to operate as a regime of truth around which various technologies and experts coalesced. Yet, need also came to be contested from three different perspectives – criminological, post-bureaucratic, and welfarist – so that the truth of need has mutated into a rather different form, more consonant with the rationality of neo-liberalism and welfare reform, choice.

Need as purpose

If, as is clear, need did not provide a foundation for the development of social housing, what purpose did its introduction serve? Or, to put it another way, why did we need need? Walters' perspective on need is, we think, valuable in this regard. Need, he argues (2000: 76), constructs a 'manageable domain, and the basis for a political relationship between the individual and the state'. As Donzelot (1979: 64) suggests, 'need was made to operate as a means of social integration and no longer as a cause of insurrection'. Using normative need, which is bureaucratically constructed, the selection criterion gave the state an apparently objective basis for resource allocation. Yet, although it appears a neutral concept in output, the inputs were anything but neutral. Need acted as a key rationing device, but the parameters of 'legitimate' need, and hence the scope of the social, were open to renegotiation as the state's vision of social housing shifted. One only needs to think of those minority groups which, throughout the history of social housing, have been excluded from its munificence – from the current (asylum seekers) to the historical (the poor). Need also came to operate as the foundation of housing management.

Need as technology/rationality

The idea of need first appeared in official discourse on housing in the early 1930s during the depression. As for legislation, the word 'need' as a basis for allocation is nowhere to be found – rather, local authorities have been exhorted to give 'reasonable preference' to particular groups of persons, reflecting policy priorities as well as the history of central–local relations in the housing system, since 1924 (Laurie, 2002). However, in government publications by experts need became prominent during the 1930s; as we shall see, this was because of a new set of moral and ethical problems. As Anne Power memorably remarked (1987: 66), in the post-First World War period, 'councils became landlords without commitment, plan or forethought'. This came across particularly when considering to whom the properties, being built as 'homes fit for heroes', were to be let. The idea of heroism implied a process of categorization, division and exclusion. Before long, however, it was recognized that something different by way of management was required. Thus, Ministry of Health Guidance in 1920 referred to:

(1) The careful selection of tenants;
(2) The elimination of unsatisfactory tenants;
(3) Constant supervision of the property and its occupants by officials directly employed and paid by the owners;
(4) Systematic and punctual collection of rents. (p 2).

What one has in this statement is a fascinating pastiche of discipline and government – there is at its heart a process of division along a biopolitical line, implied in the 'careful selection' and 'elimination' process, coupled with the use of discipline through 'constant supervision'. The statement also identified the creation of a certain type of incipient expertise of management, an ability to make these divisions and to observe.

The guidance was silent on the need of those selected for this accommodation, because need was not the main consideration. The post-1918 campaign of 'Homes fit for heroes' implied the construction of *fit* properties for returning soldiers – that is, not necessarily those in the greatest need nor necessarily the provision of affordable accommodation. These homes were to be a step up from those constructed for the working classes in the late nineteenth century. The extent of state subsidy to underpin development meant that some of the cost had to be borne by the occupiers through rent:

> There is really no doubt about how rent policy worked out in practice. The market for local authority houses was largely confined to a limited range of income groups, that is, in practice, the better-off families, the small clerks, the artisans, the better-off semi-skilled workers with small families and fairly safe jobs. (Bowley, 1945: 129)[1]

Neither was this a mistake, for the purpose, perhaps silent in this period but prevalent in the late nineteenth century, was in part to facilitate the process of 'filtering down'. The rationale was that once households had moved to this new accommodation, their old accommodation would be free for those on lower incomes. The failure of this policy was partly a result of state controls on the private rented sector and partly also because of the increase in new households in this period (see Burnett, 1986: 242).

In part, it was the failure of this policy that the concept of need was designed to address. However, selection in terms of need was also introduced to settle an equally fundamental question – who was this mass building for. This problem became more and more significant during the 1920s as properties were being mass constructed and at a time of impending financial crisis. It was now that the welfare role of council housing was given prominence. In a succession of Ministry of Health annual reports, beginning in 1929–30, the problem of administration of council housing came to be constructed as a problem of need, requiring the development of new techniques of management. It was said that the purpose of local authority housing was to provide for those 'who are least eligible in the eyes of the private owner' and made reference to the statutory 'reasonable preference' to be given to those with larger families. Although this was said to produce difficulties in rent collection, the Ministry advised on the use of differential rents (requiring better-off households to pay more, to offset the rents of those who were less well off (Ministry of Health, 1930)).

In the subsequent report, the question of rent was linked with need – there were those tenants who could afford private sector rents 'and whose continued occupation of the houses at subsidised rents means the exclusion of those whose need is unquestionably greater' (Ministry of Health, 1931a: 97). Thus, in identifying need as an organizing problematization, the Ministry of Health were also identifying the role of council housing: it was the provision of property at a subsidized rent for the short term until the household could afford to exit the tenure for private renting. The limited, residual role envisaged for municipal landlordism mirrored the prevalent belief that the private sector would soon be able to provide for all.

The Committee on Local Expenditure (1932), set up in the wake of recession, gave just two paragraphs to the 'management and allocation of accommodation' and echoed the Ministry's view on targeted assistance: 'subsidies should not be wasted by being given to those who do not need them'. The Committee thought that tenants who could afford to should pay higher rents 'to increase the revenue obtainable to reduce the loss arising from housing estates';[2] or vacate their properties which could then be sold on the open market or let to poorer households (para 95). Thus, in this period the notion of need mutated into an organizing principle not only of who should get council housing, but also how long they should get it for. Indeed, as noted in Chapter 1, the London County Council wrote to 300 tenants in 1933 suggesting that they vacate their properties in the interests of those persons whose need was greater.

By this time, the emphasis on need as the selection criterion was also required because the focus of council housing had shifted away from new building for the better-off working class to slum clearance and the rehousing of slum dwellers. This was accompanied by a discursive shift in focus towards more intensive 'management'.

Slum clearance devalued the tenure in the popular consciousness: slum clearance estates were 'stigmatized as "rough" and their occupiers sometimes shunned' (Holmans, 1987: 178). Some local authorities were also concerned at the slum dwellers' 'bad influence on other council tenants' (Schifferes, 1976: 66). Thus, councils experimented with methods of dealing with this pauperised population, of discipline and normalization by cutting them off 'in special blocks under close supervision until they proved themselves capable' (Kemp and Williams, 1991: 130), the social housing equivalent of Foucault's description of the treatment of towns afflicted by plague (1977a: 195–9).

This development necessitated the growth in expertise of housing management (see Chapter 2). It was this technique of government which fostered and supported a growing practice of pre-visits by a local authority officer to the applicant's current accommodation to 'ascertain their circumstances ... and the domestic standard and financial resources of its members' in the manner of Octavia Hill and others (CHAC, 1938: para 25). The forms used by housing visitors tended to translate Victorian labels into everyday life, and inscribe them on to forms to be completed by the expert visitor. Damer (1976: 73) draws on the forms used in Glasgow which required the visitor to differentiate from 'very good' to 'unsuitable' the type of person, cleanliness and furniture. Such judgements were largely based on the 'detective work' of these employees who were specifically employed because of their experience as middle-aged married women (Damer and Madigan, 1974: 226). This was constructed as a practice of expertise (Macey and Baker, 1965: 215, cited in Power, 1987: 97). The apparently neutral notion of need was thus anything but neutral. Although it had become technicized and institutionalized through the forms, which created their own form of knowledge, designation as being 'in need' was conditional upon being seen as conforming to a barely articulated norm of good husbandry.

After the Second World War, the discourse of need became further grounded in technicality and expertise, which only served to enhance the claim to neutrality and expertise as well as silence the ethico-moral grounding of management. So, for example, in their 1949 report, a CHAC sub-committee considered that properties should be let to those 'in the greatest housing need', which implied a hierarchy of housing needs and which were subsequently specified (overcrowding, ill-health, lack of a separate home, condition of dwelling, exceptional cases and other factors) (CHAC, 1949: paras 7 and pp 15–24). These categories of greatest housing need did not reflect the categories of household to which 'reasonable preference' was statutorily required to be given, which might plausibly be presented as dissonance between the expert management systems in place and law (see Rose, 1999: 286–7). The committee deprecated the general use of other factors to override the technical housing need criteria (although regarded such factors as reasonable when distinguishing between households with equal housing need) (para 32). Hence, it would appear that at the level of policy discourse the dominance of housing need over other factors such as behavioural or housekeeping standards was complete: allocation should be on the basis of objective criteria. This is not to say that standards were not relevant – far from it – but that in official discourse, objectivity and scientificity was maintained. As Holmans (1987: 181) points out, the more technical schemes were still favouring the same type of tenant as in the 1930s.

The technicization of need by this stage can be illustrated by the CHAC discussion of the methods of selection used by local authorities. There were points schemes, under which households would be given points for the housing need, and, in some areas, other factors such as war service and length of time on the list (paras 30–5). There were priority schemes, under which households would be placed in broad groups of priority on the basis of their housing need (the equivalent of today's banding schemes). These were regarded as requiring further analysis within the groups to determine relative housing need (para 36). Then there were other technical schemes (allocation on date order or by ballot) which were deprecated for not taking account of housing need (paras 38–9). The technical was clearly favoured over the lottery.

In 1949, legislative reference to council housing being for the 'working classes' was removed. Housing need, thus, became the sole criterion, a matter which a subsequent CHAC sub-committee regarded as important in defining the proper role of management:

> ... tenants today are much more representative of the community as a whole and are, for the most part, independent, reliable citizens who no longer required the support and guidance which was often thought to be necessary in the past. *Local authorities must recognise that this is a major social change which is likely to become more marked in the years ahead: and that this recognition must be given positive effect in their management practice.* (CHAC, 1959: para 7; original emphasis)

Not only did this redefine the task of housing management – away from its social services 'aftercare' role – it also suggested a hegemony of the technical.

This hegemony was reflected in the 1969 CHAC sub-committee report – the influential Cullingworth committee. This report played an important part in demystifying the role of the housing visitor, suggesting that the emphasis of housing management should be on what households want rather than what a housing department itself thought was suitable (CHAC, 1969: para 91). In so doing, the expertise of housing management was subjected to the expertise of the individual household. However, the notion of housing need itself was not questioned – indeed, the proper role of housing management was regarded as selecting those in the greatest housing need. Yet, with the broader political agenda starting to move against the 'indiscriminate' subsidy of council tenants, the proposal that the assessment of housing need should be conditional reasserted itself. The committee regarded an expanded role of need, to take account of economic and social needs, to be essential; thus, housing management once again was required to be experts of the social: 'It is good financial policy as well as good social policy to ensure that priority in the allocation of council houses is given to the most socially needy groups' (para 61). This time, the Committee did not regard any particular allocation scheme as more appropriate than another; but schemes that combined factors were the only method which escaped direct criticism.

By this stage, a number of factors had altered the terrain. First, a further major slum clearance campaign had created a new demand from older households; second, the steady rise of owner-occupation meant that more households with stable incomes were opting for that tenure. Holmans (1987: 196) remarks on a striking change in the age and financial circumstances of the population of council housing between 1960 and 1976. Thus, even before the advent of the right to buy in the 1980s, 'social housing' was already catering for the poorest households, 47 per cent of which were in the lowest three income deciles by 1979 (Murie, 1997a: 449).

Needing need: RSLs

The role of RSLs as 'community builders' has often come into conflict with their role as social landlords. In particular, this has led to conflict with local authorities over arrangements for councils to nominate tenants to RSL properties. These *nomination agreements* have been the tool through which local authorities have sought to influence the make up of RSLs' communities, and have been the site of conflict between RSLs and local government on many occasions. This process of responsibilization of RSLs into meeting the priorities of local authorities was, and is premised on the level of public funding given to them. In effect, they became the *licensees* of rehousing priorities. From an early period, this lash-up was reflected in the creation of new sites of management – for example, the National Federation of Housing Societies (1946) developed model agreements in the 1940s under which RSLs would notify vacancies to, and accept nominations from, the council.

In part, the local authority view appeared predicated on a desire to be seen to be controlling the 'public goods' in their locality. Nomination agreements not only controlled tenants (through restricting their access to this resource); they also exercised dominion over the RSLs. As far as the RSLs were concerned, the implications of rule were far-reaching in that their apparent autonomy could be overridden through the simple expedient of nominations. As the Federation warned:

> mutual agreement on the *proportion* is a matter for careful and tactful arbitration between the housing society and the local authority, as the latter may exercise its right of nomination for the *full*. (NFHS, 1946d: 1)

Thus the tension here was over the potentially different operationalization of housing need. Creating communities was seen as a matter of ensuring that the right persons were chosen, and then of creating the circumstances under which they would be acceptable members of the community, able to conform to the norms of that community.

Thus, housing associations needed need: it justified their purpose – building communities – as much as it provided the foundation for local authority housing activity. What differed was the different way in which they defined it. The concern for RSLs was that local authorities nominated 'unsuitable tenants' (LHAC, 1970). Families at the top of council waiting lists, 'may well be facing less severe housing difficulties than many others known to a housing association for whom there is no hope of decent accommodation for many years' (ibid). The argument was concerned with the prioritization given to the local authority assessment of housing need, not to the question of need itself. As RSLs became more confident of their own 'expertise' in meeting housing need, they sought to contest the councils' expert knowledge.

Underlying this debate about need was the issue of control and freedom. While the position of RSLs was marginal, and they had access to charitable funding as well as other voluntary resources, they had relative freedom to decide on the nature of the communities they created and 'serviced'. Their concern for local authority definitions of housing need did not dominate their activities. In being able to control their allocations, and provide additional resources to support their communities, they had little need to resort to despotic forms of regulation. They were in the business of providing 'judicious and economically-minded assistance to the poor' (Osborne, 1996: 110), but only those poor they chose to help.

This autonomy/control dyad broke down during the 1970s and 1980s, when RSLs became the focus of attention and the recipients of considerable amounts of public money. At this time, they were also criticized for the limited role they played in meeting housing need and for the closed allocations policies (Noble, 1981; Audit Commission, 1989). The response of the London Housing Association Council (part of the National Federation) and the London local authorities was to commission research into the existing nomination arrangements and produce a code of practice for associations and councils. *Partners in Meeting Housing Need* (Levison and Robertson, 1989), contained 'recommendations of good practice ... taken from examples set by housing associations and council housing departments who work well together'; the intention was to produce 'a fairer and more efficient nominations system' (ibid).

Partners was an attempt to use bureaucratic structures to implement a normative agenda: associations should be housing those in greatest housing need (as determined by the local authority), and should not be able to pick and choose those tenants to minimize their own management problems. It 'recognised that each housing association will have its own selection criteria ... [but] recommend[ed] that housing associations should generally accept the local authority's prioritization of housing need' (ibid: 25). It acknowledged that most RSLs would want to make a home visit to all nominees prior to allocation (a procedure that local authorities had had to cut if only because of budget constraints), but the purpose of the visit was purely to check the information supplied by the authority and give information to the nominee – it was '*not* to make assessments of the housing need or to check housekeeping standards' (emphasis in original) (ibid). Similarly, the reasons for an association rejecting a nominee were very specific and limited to changes in the circumstances of nominated households, unsuitability of the property to the households needs or inaccuracies and changes in the information supplied by the council (ibid: 26).

Contesting need

We have so far demonstrated that from the 1930s through to the 1960s housing need came to dominate the allocation of council and housing association accommodation. Need became needed and accepted as a neutral basis for allocation and the subject of expertise. Yet, not far below the surface of this apparent objectivity lay an ethos which sought to divide the population on the basis of a moralizing ideology. Households could not deviate too far from an implicit norm related to behaviour and housekeeping in order to be accepted as being needy, let alone more needy. Although this moral filter was gradually removed from policy pronouncements at the national level, central government's desire to move council housing towards a more clearly welfare role introduced criteria other than 'objective' housing need into the selection process.

For some time, need had also been the subject of contestation at the level of technology as well as rationality. There has been a coalescence of concern, which has operated to forge new links between social housing and broader problematizations of welfarism. In this section, we consider two particular challenges to the notion of need as a technology, and link these up with the gradual emergence of a central problematization – need could not do the job(s) any more.

The problems of bureaucracy

From the 1960s the operationalization of housing need came under a sustained critique on a number of grounds. Undoubtedly, the Cullingworth committee report formed part of that critique, not only in seeking to generate criteria concerned with social need but also on more specific grounds, such as the imposition of residential qualifications and the treatment of black and minority ethnic households (CHAC, 1969: ch 9). The critique was not housing need itself, but that, whatever might be set out in policy about allocation according to need, the wrong households were being prioritized because of systems or local policy failures.

The first part of this critique concerned the use of discretion. The open-ended obligation prescribed by legislation – that 'reasonable preference' should be accorded to certain types of households – provided a discretion which was too broad:

> ... discretion was depicted as the bug in the system – a source of deviance which allowed short-term management goals to compromise the principle of social justice. It was the smokescreen behind which housing departments infused an agreed hierarchy of needs with a range of other, more dubious, allocative principles. (Smith and Mallinson, 1996: 341)

The solution, on this view, was to provide closer attention to rules, the supposed binary opposite of discretion (c.f. Sainsbury, 1989). A further problem with discretion was opened up by a more discrete research enquiry into the role of selection and allocation systems in the systematic direct and indirect processes of discrimination against black and ethnic minority households (classically exemplified by Henderson and Karn, 1987; also Lambert *et al*, 1978). Smith (1989: 36) summarized the impact of this discrimination in the following terms:

> Even if black people prefer segregation, it is hard to understand why they should pursue this in the more run-down segments of the housing stock, rather than in areas where they could secure the symbolic and economic benefits associated with suburban life.

Yet, as subsequently transpired in research, more formally bounded rules did not alter these effects because of the impact of broader socio-economic disadvantage (Jeffers and Hoggett, 1995). Indeed, what emerged from the abundant research into council house allocation was the way in which the operationalization of need was dependent on a system of 'political influence, by possessing a bargaining counter, or by articulacy and social acceptability' (Jones, 1988: 98). Political influence was not just a question of individual households being assisted, but also of the more systematic way priority was given to households wishing to transfer within the sector (Clapham and Kintrea, 1986). This could be justified in a number of ways – as rewarding long-standing tenants, as opening out the accommodation they were leaving for new tenants, as being a rational use of available accommodation. Broadly, however, its effect was that those who could 'afford' to wait longest were rewarded with the best properties. Despite the ethos of social housing management, which emphasized the role of need, it relied for its efficacy upon bargaining instincts in the same way that the private sector does, and that leads inevitably to inequity.

A consequence of these debates about allocations, particularly that opened by Cullingworth and emerging from the rule: versus discretion debate, was increasing the complexity of the schemes themselves. Complexity was also made possible by the development of technology:

> Allocations systems seemingly have become ever more complex, designed to reflect the range of nuance of housing need, a trend made possible by the development of the first computerised allocation administration in the late 1970s and early 1980s. Computerisation is now universal, except among the smallest housing associations. (Pawson and Kintrea, 2002: 648)

A by-product of that level of sophistication was an increasing reliance on risk as a housing-management tool, although it was not named as such until the late 1990s. An early recognition of the relevance of risk was provided by Cullingworth himself, as academic, when he wrote (1973: 51): 'Unfortunately, the truth of the matter is that local authorities, like sound business enterprises, tend to reject "poor risk" applicants: and, incredibly, social work departments often acquiesce in this.' To some degree this represented a return to themes prominent in the 1920s.

It is possible to think of housing management in terms of risk management and avoidance with one option being to screen high-risk households out of the sector through the selection and allocation process. Fred Gray (1979: 207) summarized the rationale for the concern with attracting the 'good tenant':

> This preoccupation may influence the local authority's views on who should be offered a council house, and what sort of dwelling it should be. Rather than being based solely on

the 'need' of households (however this is defined) selection and allocation may reflect, in part at least, the desire of the local authority to minimise management tasks.

As this type of risk management became more prominent – or at least more widely recognized – it is plausible to portray need not as the organizing criterion but largely as window-dressing: the overriding factor was that new tenants should not be a burden on housing management – what Cowan (1997) refers to as 'tenantability'.

The selection process provided one method of insuring against that potential burden. Even the homelessness legislation – supposedly the apotheosis of need – could be analysed as an exercise in risk management (Cowan et al, 1999). In this, there was a neat *inversion* of the welfare relationship: the notion of insurance is at the heart of that relationship, whether or not it is named 'social', and the relevant concept is insurance of the self. However, in the context of housing selection and allocation, the insurance is of the bureaucracy. This insurance scheme divided its populations into good risks and bad risks, filtered out some of the bad risks (for example through the notion of 'intentional homelessness') and subsequent management practices 'engage in "close watching and masterful inactivity" to weed out the bad who slipped through and the good who succumbed to the insurance temptation' (Baker, 2000: 570). To complete the insurance analogy, in contrast, the quote from the 1959 CHAC report presented above, p 63 can be construed as indicating that in a mass tenure risks are manageable because they are effectively pooled across the population.

Insurance also operates against a rather different set of risks. These are the risks that the wrong people are getting through the system. This set of risks can be expressed both programmatically and operationally. Programmatically, it can best be seen through the periodic concerns, which might be 'moral panics', over welfare fraud (see, for example, Golding and Middleton, 1982). As regards social housing selection, these concerns were raised most notably in the early 1990s as a central plank in the Conservative Major government's 'back to basics' campaign. Despite its ill-fated nature, it raised controversy about who was getting social housing. The 'wrong' households, in this context, were so-called 'single mothers' who were 'jumping the housing queue' ahead of 'married couples'. A Green Paper and subsequent White Paper made clear these concerns (DoE, 1994; 1995); for example:

> Allocation schemes should reflect the underlying values of our society. They should balance specific housing needs against the need to support married life, so that tomorrow's generation grows up in a stable home environment. (DoE, 1995: 36)

Although these kinds of motivations did not appear on the face of the 1996 Housing Act, similar statements did appear in early drafts of the Code of Guidance (to which local authorities were required to have regard).

This political risk of social housing selection policies also has an operational dimension, although one which has a different set of undercurrents. The risks here are generated from the assumption that welfare applicants *know* the law and how to circumvent it. Such a perception gives a purpose to bureaucracy and discretionary decision-making – to weed out those who abuse the system. It is combined with an uncertainty as to who is actually abusing the system (everyone or just a few) and this uncertainty is probably responsible for generating the importance of 'gut feeling' in decision-making (e.g. Cowan, 1997; Loveland, 1995). Despite the existence of internally and externally imposed criteria, there can be what Simon Halliday (2004: 55–9) refers to as a 'culture of suspicion' about applicant households among the personnel, which can be fed by experience. As Halliday puts it:

> A general culture of suspicion existed in relation to the openness and truthfulness of homelessness applicants. This might also be described as a siege mentality, whereby the homeless persons units were being subjected to bogus applications. This was reflected in how caseworkers interpreted applicants' behaviour in interviews. (p 56)

Halliday locates his discussion in the context of Lipsky's groundbreaking work on street-level bureaucrats (1980), but the data also supports the point being made here about the risk/insurance interface. Although bureaucracies may resist, often creatively, the implementation of policies they wish to avoid (particularly the stereotyping of single mothers – see Cloke *et al*, 2000), there are other dividing practices going on at the sharp end which reflect concerns about the purpose of the system.

Criminological perspectives

A further problem for and of housing need was the 'discovery' of unpopular estates and their links with allocation schemes. The crime problem and social housing allocation thus became linked. The creation of such 'problem estates' (as they were labelled in policy terms) was related to the stigma which slum dwellers carried with them to their new properties and to complex, localized sets of circumstances (classically, Damer, 1974). Certainly, labelling an estate in this way could create a self-fulfilling prophecy in that properties on such estates were often matched with the more desperate (see Bottoms and Wiles, 1997). These areas then became the focus of a series of criminological studies, and were constructed as criminological problems: Bottoms and Wiles (1986), for example, referred to 'residential community crime careers'. Some academics and policy-makers tended to see unidimensional causes and solutions – the architecture, the management – to these multidimensional issues. The result was an attempt to 'embed' the governance of security into social housing itself (Johnston and Shearing, 2003: 26–7). Thus, for example, during the 1980s, the Priority Estates Project employed a decentralization approach to housing management to cure the ills of the worst estates (to less than emphatic evaluations – see Cole and Furbey, 1994: 213–15).

The problem of crime on social housing estates, and the link with processes of housing allocation, lead to a new fixation: the creation of communities. This was memorably captured in the title of a pamphlet issued by the Joseph Rowntree Foundation in 1993, *Building for Communities* (Page, 1993), which became know as the 'Page Report'. The Page Report concerned housing association estates but it is undeniable that it also caught the mood in the sector more generally. The report took a very different stance on what RSLs should be doing now that they had become key providers of housing. It was highly critical of the direction some RSLs had taken, building large estates in 'remote and difficult locations' (ibid: 13) which would house 'a segregated income stratum of uniformly poor tenants', and will 'almost certainly be difficult to manage and ... likely to gain a reputation as a 'poor' housing estate' (ibid: 12).

The Page Report brought a perception into the world of housing professionals that these changes were leading to a crisis in the sector (alternatively, the crisis had already arrived). The Foundation's position as a neutral funder of research, together with its ability to attract media and political attention, meant that the report had 'influence far beyond its readership' (see Levitas, 1998: 41). In fact, *Building for Communities* was not research, nor had the Foundation intended it to be so. It was, in effect, a 'position statement', designed to further the legacy of Seebohm Rowntree and his inquiry into poverty in York.

The Page Report could be said to reflect RSLs' rediscovery of the idea of community. It advocated a form of 'social engineering' in the building of 'balanced communities'. In so doing, associations should either return to building smaller developments, or buy up and improve street properties 'using skills they have developed over the last century' (ibid: 50). Alternatively, if large estates had to be built, they should mix rented housing with housing for sale or shared ownership, producing 'balanced communities' with 'renters and owners living in adjoining houses' (ibid).

In creating inclusive communities, the need to exclude those who could not be expected to conform to the community norms, became paramount. '[C]ommunity is not simply the territory within which crime is controlled, it is itself the *means* of government' (Rose, 2000: 329), and so the report advocated attention to estate security. And significantly for the RSL/local authority relationship, it advocated that associations should exercise exclusionary practices in order to ensure the security of their estates. Criticizing the approach of *Partners*, the report advocated that 'housing associations ... have a good and valid reason to enquire about the tenancy history of each applicant and to refuse a nomination from a local authority where the nominee is known to have a history of seriously disruptive behaviour' (ibid: 36).

But it was not only the security of members of their newly made communities with which RSLs were concerned. The Housing Act 1988 had exposed RSLs to financial risk through requirements to raise a proportion of their development capital from private lenders. Under the Act, 'associations became inherently risky operations. ... In order to sustain themselves, they are reliant on rents being paid. The allocations process presents a critical opportunity to weed out bad payers' (Cowan *et al*, 1999: 411). RSLs' dependence on private funders created a need to distance themselves from rule exercised through local authority nomination agreements in order that they could meet the requirements of their new 'partners'.

Despite (academic) challenges to many of the assumptions of the Page report (see Cole *et al*, 1996; Griffiths *et al*, 1996), its effect has been far-reaching. Cowan (1999: 257–8) argues that the focus on allocations policies as causing decline on RSL estates led to the Corporation revising its *Performance Standards* on selection policies:

> RSLs selection and allocation policies for new lettings should give reasonable preference to those in greatest housing need, except where this would lead to unsustainable tenancies or unstable communities (Housing Corporation, 1997: para F2.1)

For the housing association sector, Page had been instrumental in creating a paradigm shift in ways of thinking about social housing provision, a move from needs-based allocations to policies intent on creating sustainable communities. Yet, the report was equally influential on the sector more generally. Many of the subsequent developments in allocation policies – council and RSL – can be traced back to this document.

Indeed, one product of these various reports and studies – both of bureaucracy and criminology – was a new problematization, which enjoined assemblages of risk and uncertainty in the name of need. The desire was to create communities (usually prefaced with the word 'sustainable' or 'stable'); more than this, though, the desire was to create moral communities, in which households would be self-regulating. Need, thus, became used as a tool to weed out households who are, or might be, anti-community. So-called problem tenants were discouraged from making an application for a social housing tenancy through requests 'for references, offer[ing] trial tenancies and insist[ing] on tenant contracts' (PAT 7, 1999: para 4.36). Risk assessments were common in respect of certain problem tenants, such as sex offenders, with housing professionals becoming key 'stakeholders' in multi-agency assessment processes (Cowan *et al*, 1999, 2001).

The knowledge being drawn upon in these processes is both statistical and clinical. It is both precise and common sense knowledge; it is inexact, more so because it can also be the target of practices of resistance by housing officers themselves. The questions being asked are predictive: the likelihood of further housing deviance, and the degree of dangerousness to the community. These questions lead to a bureaucratic imperative for 'information bingeing' (Halliday, 1998) and reliance on databases of housing deviance, which themselves create uncertainty as a result of known errors (Cowan *et al*, 2003: ch 3). The selection process then becomes prophylactic. This explains why there are areas with empty housing next to households apparently in need. Need as a technology has outmanoeuvred need as a rationality. Given the use of need as an exclusionary device, when there is no requirement to ration the resource, need as a rationality itself becomes problematic.

Choice and neo-liberalism

The emergence of the problem of need coincided with broader shifts to neo-liberalism. To an extent, this was a coincidence, although there were also clear links between the contestation of housing need and welfarism more broadly. The problematization of housing need as a rationality of social housing fits neatly with the shifts in the welfare state. The discovery of an inactive 'underclass' combined with 'social exclusion', and the re-discovery of 'community' in the works of the communitarians, operated to disrupt the welfare consensus. New Deal policies, welfare to work and the like, work on a different vision of the subject of welfare. As Deacon (2004: 911–12) puts it:

> The idea that those claiming welfare should be required to fulfil conditions regarding their own behaviour and that of their children has been extended across a swathe of social policy; from welfare to work, to education, health, and, of course, housing. The primary purpose of such welfare conditionality is not to determine entitlement or to establish need, but to change behaviour. It is to reaffirm and enforce the responsibilities and obligations of those in receipt of welfare, as job seekers, as parents, and as tenants.

Welfare is thus used to work through the freedom of the subject, and becomes conditional on their activity (Carr, 2005a). The relation between the self and the expert shifts in the process signalling also a change in the role of the expert.

Nowhere is this more apparent than in the 'new' systems designed for the selection of households for social housing which have been labelled choice-based lettings (CBL). These systems provide a wonderful example of the neo-liberal method of governing through freedom. As Rose (1999: 87) suggests, 'modern individuals are not merely "free to choose", but *obliged to be free*, to understand and enact their lives in terms of choice'. Choice makes the subject of housing management active in their own housing 'solutions' – it fits neatly with the re-discovery of the ethical, self-aware citizen, and it works broadly on a market principle of desire, advertising and bidding for property. Choice also works to enhance communities, particularly their stability, because only those who want to be housed on an estate – in that property – will bid for it.

A new rationality

Choice-based lettings was the highly publicized solution to the problems of 'need' provided by the New Labour government in their 2000 housing Green Paper. It was based on methods developed in Delft, and subsequently brought to Britain through incorporation into Harborough District Council's selection and allocations process. Between 2001 and 2003 the government ran 27 CBL pilots (see Marsh *et al*, 2004) and has stated as a policy objective that all local authorities should be running some form of CBL by 2010. There is considerable encouragement to, and pressure on, the RSL sector to engage in CBL at the level of research reports (see Winn, 2001).

The details of CBL schemes can differ, but the key characteristics are: households are given an amount of currency to bid with; properties which are available are advertised in newspapers or on the internet; households bid for them; housing management rank the bids for particular properties by currency level; the person at the top of the list for the property is offered it; feedback is then given, often in the newspaper or on a website, on the length of time the 'winner' had been on the waiting list and their band. The currency each household is awarded can take a number of forms, but most commonly households are placed in broad bands related to housing need. Then if two households from the same band bid for a property they are ranked by a second criterion, such as length of time registered.

Choice-based lettings implies a radical alternative rationality for social housing. There are at least two implications of this – first, there is a radical questioning of *who* social housing is for, and second there is the equally radical shift in model. As regards the former, the Green Paper makes a series of observations (paras 9.11–12) about the residual role of social housing – it is for those who could not afford private sector housing or who are just too vulnerable to live in such housing. Nevertheless:

> We do not believe that social housing should only be allocated to the poorest and most vulnerable members of the community. However, if social housing was available to anyone who wanted it, there is a risk that it could be denied to those who had no other choice. In order to prevent this, we believe that priority for social housing should generally continue to be given to people in the greatest housing need and for whom suitable private sector housing is not an affordable option. However, we recognise that there may be occasions when it is necessary and desirable, for some wider community benefit, to allow exceptions to this.

Choice-based lettings schemes were being drawn upon to divide certain households into social housing 'for some wider community benefit'. Thus, the category of who social housing is for was expanded. Indeed, this came through explicitly when the Green Paper discussed 'local lettings policies' designed not to assist vulnerable households access social housing, but 'to give priority for housing in defined areas to households who could help create more sustainable communities. These might include key workers, for example, even if this meant some degree of underoccupation' (para 9.30). At the same time, although these paragraphs are less than explicit on this point, certain vulnerable households are divided out because they are not community-minded or community builders. Thus, powers were promised to suspend the anti-social from the housing list or have their priority reduced – a disciplining mechanism with the possibility of redemption held out for such households who were to 'be given a clear indication of what they needed to do to get the restriction lifted' (para 9.13).

Second, there was a shift in the model used for social housing selection, a shift from bureaucratic processes to something rather different.

> Even in the private sector, people cannot always live exactly where they would like. They must make choices. Choice implies a trade-off between people's needs and aspirations on the one hand, and the availability of housing they can afford on the other. Those who cannot afford housing in one area may have to look elsewhere, and are free to do so. But the more opportunity people have to decide these things for themselves, the more likely they are to feel ownership of the decision and to be satisfied with the outcome. And the more information they have on which to base their decisions, the better those decisions are likely to be. (DETR/DSS, 2000: para 9.6)

Choice-based lettings, then, is a market-based model of social housing selection and allocation. Its basis is an analogy with assumptions about the ways in which the private sector works; as well as the benefits of the private sector approach. Thus, for example, under CBL, households are entitled to refuse accommodation they bid for, on the basis that they would be able to do so in the private sector (see Marsh *et al*, 2004: para 10.17) For this marketized model of the process, so the claim runs, will allow people more ontological security as they have chosen their property: they will feel ownership of *their* decision and get satisfaction with that. This links in with a further set of claims about the benefits of choice – and here some quite amazing claims are made for it:

> Applicants for social housing who are more involved in decisions about their new homes are more likely to have a longer term commitment to the locality. This will promote more sustainable communities at village, town and city level. It will increase personal well-being, and help to reduce anti-social behaviour, crime, stress and educational under-achievement. (para 9.7; cf the more toned down version in DETR/DSS, 2001: para 6.4)

Choice-based lettings is about the creation of governable communities; or, to put the claim another way, communities which are better able to govern themselves. Such communities will be sedentary, sustainable and ontologically satisfying. Not only all of that, but CBL assists in the responsibilization of those communities into the self-government of education, stress, crime and ASB reduction policies.

Implications of choice: the subject and expertise

Choice is constructed as an empowering process, equivalent to the private sector, and one which individuals manage themselves through flows of information. Individuals, it is assumed, become self-determining, responsibilized and entrepreneurial in their choices. They are aided in this by a new role for experts who, rather than 'panoptically sort' through the bureaucratic allocations process, manage the 'letting' of the property. As the Green Paper made clear,

> Under a lettings service that puts decision-making in the hands of customers, the role of housing professionals becomes less one of gate-keeper and more one of advisor and advocate. This would help households to make informed choices about their housing options, be it with regard to meeting needs within their existing home, or the opportunities available for re-housing. A more proactive service should be offered to those in urgent housing need in order to reduce the risk of homelessness. (para 9.33)

Readers should note that the discussion here is closely linked in with the discussion in Chapter 4 about the increasing marketization of social housing.

Subjects

Choice-based lettings schemes harness two different versions of the objects of the schemes. They build on the notions of customer/consumer which developed as a result of the shifts through CCT. These shifts meant that, rather than thinking and talking of 'clients', we now refer to 'consumers' or 'customers' of a social housing 'product'. This shift was more than rhetorical, implying a new sovereignty of the individualized, 'aggressive and self-interested' subject – the customer-/consumerization of the housing service thus implied activity on the part of the housing applicant in pursuing their claims to an efficient and effective service (see generally, O'Malley, 2004: 68–71). As O'Malley and Palmer (1996: 141) suggest, 'conceptions of expertise still remain very much in place, but the rhetorical question of who is understood to be "on top" becomes more open as the consumer/customer, contractual imagery is extended'. The notion of a consumer or customer challenges the expert domain of housing management, but it is a challenge which has effectively been confined to certain domains. The various customers' charters in social housing challenge certain bureaucratic practices, but leave judgement intact elsewhere – for example, the determination of need is still a management domain.

Choice-based lettings employs a new specification of the subject – although the language of consumer and customer retains importance, under CBL we now also think of 'home seekers'. The services run by the CBL pilots were labelled using variations on the theme of 'home' and 'search', 'choice'; 'finder' or 'hunter': the expectation of activity on the part of the individual is clear. This is constructed by some as a moral imperative – the problem with the previous system was that applicants simply applied and relied on the bureaucracy to provide. Choice-based lettings requires activity on the part of the homeseeker, both as a moral requirement and a condition of access. This came across clearly from interviews with some of those managing the CBL pilots

> We want them to be more proactive, to behave more maturely and to replicate the way people might behave in ... the market if they're looking to buy or rent, really. So they have to go looking for the information. ... we want to try and get away from the dependency that they have at the moment. On sitting and waiting, and then being allocated a property, we want them to go out and find what they want. (quoted in Marsh *et al*, 2004: para 6.14)

Importantly, the search for the home is not related to any particular tenure – although CBL systems enable social housing allocation, the information provided to home seekers can also encompass low-cost home ownership and available properties in the private rented sector. Thus, the home seeker is part of a responsibilization process – they actively seek their accommodation – which is just as much about tenure and location. Thus, the private sector becomes implicated in choice. And home seekers are encouraged to transfer to other areas or look to other areas for their housing solution, emphasising the need for mobility in the search for a home. In those areas where there is still a shortage of social housing, disseminating information is designed to emphasize the paucity of available accommodation so that the home-seekers are able to appreciate the *true* housing situation in the area and hence make *informed* decisions about their housing options: including concluding that they are not going to access social housing any time soon.

Other interesting discursive shifts are evident. Prominent is a re-interpretation of 'vulnerability'. If social housing allocation had a core service, it was about providing a service for vulnerable households and much effort was spent specifying this category. Case law, for example, defined such households as those households which would otherwise have had difficulty in finding and keeping accommodation in the private sector (*R v Waveney DC ex p Bowers* [1983] QB 238); an almost impossible assessment of difference which additionally focused attention on the private sector.

However, in the CBL regime, 'vulnerable' home-seekers are those households which are unable to access the different sources of information, such as media advertising, or are unable to bid. These home-seekers remain the subject of intervention by the provider, but the intervention reflects the activity implied in the search – rather than bureaucratic direction of the process, it more typically focuses on providing information in a manageable form or a discussion of whether to bid for a property. Housing need forms of vulnerability are typically embodied in the currency given to a household rather than being important to the process of allocation, unless that vulnerability has links with the search for housing.

Expertise

Not only is there a new specification of the subject, there is also a new specification of expertise – from allocators/gatekeepers to advisor/advocate. It is a process which appears to make the expertise of the housing manager subservient to that of the consumer. Peter Somerville (2001: 122), drawing inspiration from the work of Clarke and Newman (1997) on the new managerialism, has argued that CBL 'marks a deliberate attempt to move away from a politically contested system based on principles of equity and fairness to a more technically defined one based on managerial precepts such as those embodied in Best Value'. From this perspective, CBL offers a transparent, open, readily understandable system that is customer-focused, and which also consequently complies with new managerialist precepts of auditability and accountability. Housing officers are, therefore, able to provide information from the computer records which automatically and regularly are programmed to spew out the relevant data.

The challenge to expertise, in one sense, comes from the assumption at the core of CBL that the subjects are, or should be, the experts. It is their *felt* need which the old processes undermined but which becomes relevant when they decide whether or not to make a bid for a property. What is interesting here is the way in which the courts have viewed this new truth about expertise, or to pose the question like O'Malley and Palmer: who should be on top? The clear message from the Court of Appeal so far has been that the bureaucrat as expert must be on top.[3] In *R(A) v Lambeth LBC; R(Lindsay) v Lambeth LBC* [2002] HLR (57) 998, the Court of Appeal were faced with a question about the legality of Lambeth's CBL system. Lambeth is an area of London, which is one of the highest demand councils for its limited stock of housing.

Lambeth's policy essentially required households to self-assess their own housing need through their willingness and ability to wait. The longer households were willing to wait, the choosier they could be. This is an explicit, common element of many CBL schemes in that waiting time is the currency commonly employed, as suggested in the Green Paper. In an area where there is a high demand for social housing, but low supply, the Court of Appeal recognized the difficulties of designing a defensible allocation scheme (it had taken Lambeth a couple of years to design their CBL system). However, they raised two concerns about including a mechanism of 'choice' within the scheme.

First, the Court of Appeal made clear that the assessment of need is for the local authority to make. Lambeth's self-assessment approach was deprecated because, for Collins J, the individual has their own interest at heart and Lambeth's scheme was 'altogether too haphazard' (para 20). Similarly, Pill LJ made the following observation:

> I fail to see how permitting an applicant to assess his need so highly that he accepts inferior accommodation amounts to conferring a preference on him. The two concepts are different and the right to choose does not amount to a preference within the meaning of the section. (para 38)

This represents a significant problem for the rationale of choice schemes, many of which incorporate a self-assessment element. Yet, it is difficult to see how this element of self-assessment differs from previous, assumed lawful practice in which applicants chose areas usually knowing that some were more popular than others (and, therefore, they would have to wait longer). All Lambeth's policy did was formalize that process so that its applicant households made their judgements on the basis of full knowledge. What seems important after the *Lambeth* case is that the local authority makes a final judgement on the basis of its knowledge.

Second, the argument was put to the Court that 'choice' was a bureaucratically rational policy in that the average rate of refusals (that is, the average number of refusals for any particular property) had reduced considerably after the implementation of the self-assessment element of the allocations scheme, and thus impacted upon longer term community stability. Although there are assertions here about the importance of sustainable communities, the argument can be resolved to a purely financial one. Essentially, the more refusals a property gets, the longer it remains unoccupied which impacts adversely on the rental income stream (and has an adverse impact on the housing revenue account); furthermore, if a property proves unpopular, that can be a factor which tips an estate into being regarded as unpopular, with a more significant impact on rental income streams (see, for example, PAT7, 1999).

Collins J made a number of points to rebut the success of the scheme to CBL, in the course of which he made the following observation about the Lambeth scheme:

> What has helped is not necessarily choice but a greater knowledge of what an applicant was prepared to accept. Furthermore, in many ways the policy provides the antithesis of choice. A realisation that what would otherwise be regarded as substandard accommodation in an unwanted area can be the only way of avoiding an unacceptably

long wait is hardly what most would regard as a real choice. It is not the sort of choice which the Green Paper seems to me to be advocating. (para 13)

The final sentence can be disputed. The Green Paper makes clear that *'Choice should be well-informed*: People should understand what housing is available and what their chances are of getting it' (para 9.17; original emphasis). The sort of choice being advocated is one in which the lack of supply is made crystal clear to applicants. Providing this information can in itself lead applicants to seek housing solutions elsewhere. However, for the Court of Appeal, the problem with a greater symmetry of information is that choice is undermined.

Change or continuity?

Superficially CBL schemes appear to offer a major shift in the way social housing is allocated. Yet, they exhibit considerable continuity with the recent past. First, housing need remains prominent. The Green Paper (DETR, 2000: para 9.16) together with all the bidding guidance and news releases emphasized that 'meeting need remains the priority for lettings and transfers policies'. Indeed, since New Labour has taken office both the 'reasonable preference' categories and the definition of statutory homelessness have been broadened by the Homelessness Act 2002 (see also ODPM, 2002). Thus, need retains its hegemony – indeed, what is interesting about the shift to choice is that its hegemony has not been challenged in policy documents. It remains the key assumption underpinning social housing, even though it appears to have been undermined, and overthrown, by choice.

Yet, the undermining of need may be less significant than first appears. Under choice the pocket of expertise in relation to selection still remains: households must still have their housing need assessed. The role of gatekeeper thus remains important. It retains this importance because ultimately (like other systems of government in neo-liberalism) they must be able to be controlled as necessary. This is particularly true in higher demand areas where there are a significant number of households who are 'in need'. The particular innovation in choice, in this respect, lies in the home-seekers ability to choose a particular property. Yet, this is not a particularly big step away from what went before. Applicants for housing have always been able to choose the areas where they want to live – indeed, such choices were encouraged (see, for example, Cullingworth, 1973: 54 referring to LAC 41/67 in which the Ministry of Housing and Local Government suggested that tenants should 'so far as possible be offered a choice of accommodation at varying rent levels').

Equally home-seekers' choices are constrained by the provider's labelling of properties. Previously, providers had sought to meet the challenges of estates which had 'tipped' into problem areas or had issues around anti-social behaviour by developing 'local lettings policies'. These policies used the lettings systems to achieve ends such as a reduction in child density on particular estates or the encouragement of particular social groupings (key workers, the employed, etc) to live in them (and were welcomed in, for example, the Page Report). Choice-based lettings schemes cater for the diversity of management aims in relation to particular properties and estates by the simple expedient of advertising properties for a particular type of home seeker or with a particular level of assessed need only. The Green Paper (para 9.29), acknowledged this interaction: 'Labels could therefore be used to impose restrictions on access to a property under a local lettings policy, for example in order to correct a significant social imbalance such as an excessive child density on certain estates.' Hence, the impression that the consumer is in charge of the process under CBL is misleading: available choice is typically heavily constrained and shaped by housing management.

The innovation in choice is in providing a label for a range of policies and practices which were in any event becoming prominent in government policy. Thus, choice could plausibly be portrayed as an organizing theme for a series of unconnected developments which were already in action. Choice provided a label linking these developments together into a coherent strategy. Better housing advice, which seeks to govern the housing 'solutions' of 'home-seekers' through the provision of information about the availability of housing across the range of housing tenures and areas; working with the private sector to ensure that range becomes available to all; transparency in selection and allocation; better marketing of the stock; a service which is more responsive to anti-social behaviour. The choice label has allowed a certain creative space, however. A number of housing providers have set up independent companies, or arms-length units, to run their CBL systems and others compete to run them or offer their services as consultants. Thus CBL can be seen as part of the shift towards the marketization and entrepreneurialization of social housing.

Conclusion: a process in transition

The processes of change described in this chapter – and the shift from need to choice – are neither complete nor evenly distributed across the geography of social housing. There is clearly something going on as a result of the Green Paper, but whether it represents a paradigm shift or something rather more shallow is unclear. What has been argued, however, is that these developments can only be seen in the context of the bigger picture of developments both in the state of social housing and welfare. There has been a conjunction of the two, and in the process a possible locking together of their futures, although signs of resistance are apparent (in unlikely locales, such as the courts, as well).

We have argued that need was a relatively late entrant into social housing policy and procedures but came to act as a symbol for the sector; a kind of unifying purpose. In the process it became a powerful tool, through which those seeking social housing could be placed in hierarchies and around which considerable expertise developed. Yet, at the level of national policy, need only gradually came to supplant factors relating to the suitability of households as the principal basis for selection and allocation. In addition, the contested nature of the concept 'need' is apparent: the redrawing of its boundaries – particularly whether it is exclusively a housing issue or should encompass questions of social and economic disadvantage – emerges from our consideration of successive policy documents. Broader debates over the purpose of social housing were reflected in the repeated reconfiguration of need and its role in allocations.

Need proved problematic at an operational level. Research repeatedly demonstrated that the ideal of allocation on the basis of objective, comparative need was elusive. In practice, when demand outstripped supply, allocation systems operated with an implicit moral order which acted both as a rationing device and as a means of managing the risks to housing management. The dominant position of needs-based allocation was also unable to withstand the challenge of deviant behaviour, which it was portrayed as exacerbating, or the apparent unpopularity of parts of the social housing sector. Some new principle was required to fill the gaps in purpose, and choice appears to do that. Choice works through need, not necessarily supplanting it, again demonstrating the value of obscurity.

Choice also meshes with broader shifts in government towards neo-liberalism. There are some familiar concerns – about the anti-social and vulnerability – which have been repackaged in the process. The shift in process hinges on values of choice, marketing and media which have been imported from the private sector. The perceived need for such innovations flows from the conjunction of the unpopularity of the sector in some parts of the country and the pressure to deliver the results from an increasingly demanding performance and consumer-oriented culture.

Chapter 4:
On Money

In the previous two chapters, we discussed the derivation and purpose of the development of state provision of housing, as well as the attempt by philanthropic housing providers to fill the void opened by the failure of private enterprise. This chapter follows on from that analysis by taking a closer look at one of the central methods through which the various envisionings of the social have been translated into practice – finance. Housing finance is difficult – and it has deliberately been made so. Rather than to explain the minutiae of housing finance, the concern of this chapter is to reflect upon those mentalities of governing which have driven the mundane practicalities of housing finance. For it is in the application of the rules and procedures of housing finance, and resistance to them, that new mentalities of rule appear.

In telling this narrative, it is also our purpose to explain how social housing has come to be governed through the requirements of private sector lenders – the hegemony of the idea of the private in this space of governance. Such is this dominance that, in attempting to meet the eminently applaudable (though decidedly limited) 'decent homes standard', the options open to local authorities all require relinquishing autonomy and control to the private finance sector. In this respect, our critique echoes other fields of social policy, such as those who question the seemingly inexorable slide of the National Health Service into a fragmented, privately funded sector of health providers driven by financial incentives rather than assessment of health needs (Pollock, 2004).

The chapter approaches its subject through three central problematizations. First, we consider *affordability* – the need to devise technologies of governing that enable the less well-off to have access to housing that they can afford. Subsequently, we consider two other key problems which came to dominate the mentalities of housing – the need to control *standards*, and to ensure adequate *supply*. These two concerns work in continuous tension with affordability. In the hands of New Labour, these tensions have led to privatized provision with state subsidy – Social Housing Grant – becoming available to private developers; 'affordability' becoming defined in terms of affordable home-ownership; and the moralizing technology of the 'decent homes standard' becoming a 'Trojan horse' for the further privatization of municipal housing.

The central theme of this chapter is the shaping effect of money, through both direct governing and governing at a distance, and the interconnectedness between housing *need* and affordability. Indeed, it is argued that just as need is both a rationality and a technology, so affordability assumes both guises. But such is the opportunity for obscurity in the world of housing finance – technical terms, defining and redefining concepts – that the *work* that is done by affordability and need is often not understood except in backwards analysis.

The affordability problematization

The notion at the centre of governmentality – the security of the population – has put the provision of an affordable home to all the population at the heart of governmental concerns. In this sense, affordability could be said to be at the hub of our question in Chapter 1, 'what is "social" about social housing?'. It is the problematization of affordability that has dominated governmental policies on housing for at least the last century, since the philanthropists' scientific surveys into the measurement of poverty (for example, Rowntree, 1901). This interrogation of poverty and the affordability of rents charged by private landlords created the conditions through which governments became able to intervene in the lives of the poor, through benefits and *subsidies*. The problematic of how to provide affordable housing is therefore central to our understanding of the regulation of social housing. Yet it is obscure, not necessarily deliberately so, but obscure enough to create a contested space for governance, as we show in the following sections through an attempt to go behind the technical.

Affordability and the problematization of housing condition

Malpass and Murie (1999: 162) have pointed out that the term 'affordability' only became used in housing policy debate in the late 1980s. Nevertheless, as they acknowledge, 'the issue of what people could afford to pay for their housing has been at the heart of housing policy for decades'. If need has been a mantra of social housing, then one can say the same about affordability – the aim of housing policy has been to provide a decent home for every person within their means since the Second World War, if not before (Hills and Mullings, 1990). And like need, the term 'affordable housing' has been used by politicians and housing professionals as if it required no further explanation, despite its apparent malleability – an obscuring of purpose through the lack of definition.

However, in order to make decisions as to the necessity for, and extent of, subsidy, affordability required definition. It was this requirement for definition that demanded the creation of specialist knowledge. In its infancy, definitions were based more upon notions of common sense than on scientifically developed expertise. Rowntree's surveys of York and the many social surveys of the late nineteenth century had established the problem of the affordability of rent *in relation to* earned income. And it appears that a similar calculation was made in the inter-war and post-Second World War period of a maximum notional rent. In the inter-war period, Bowley (1945: 96–9) says that 'it was generally considered' that there was a maximum of 10 shillings including rates and 'that [this rent] formed a sort of dividing line between the really comfortably-off families and the rest'.

The specialist knowledge subsequently drawn upon was that of the housing economists and accountants who were able to create an apparently neutral, scientific understanding of affordability:

> Affordability is concerned with securing some given standard of housing (or different standards) at a price or rent which does not impose, in the eyes of some third party (usually government), an unreasonable burden on household incomes. A number of judgements and assumptions are made in putting the concept into practice, and, in broad terms, affordability is assessed by the ratio of a chosen definition of household income to a selected measure of household income in some given period (Maclennan and Williams, 1990: 9).

So, although this formulation acknowledges that the notion of affordability requires 'judgements and assumptions', it still attempts a form of scientific neutrality by reference to measurement and ratios. This apparent scientific neutrality is what is interpreted on a daily basis by the interlocutors, the accountancy profession.

This formulation also provides a link with a rather different question which becomes apparent through defining affordability – the *standard* of housing. Throughout its history, housing policy has enabled judgements to be made about housing standards which have been integrally linked to questions of affordability. This reflects a curative approach to private sector mentalities – to provide economic housing – which nevertheless feeds off these mentalities, requires a balancing act between the price that tenants can afford to pay for housing and a minimum acceptable standard. When viewed from the perspective of finance, standards must be balanced against overall supply – with a limited supply of resources (subsidy) the question is whether to provide greater quantity by reducing quality, or maintain quality at the expense of numbers. This is a problem that has recently gained new prominence in the 'decent homes standard' as we discuss at the end of the chapter.

From affordability to subsidy

Affordability, need and subsidy can be seen as three inter-dependent variables. What is affordable depends on the needs that are to be met; what is unaffordable, and therefore requiring subsidy to make affordable, is a product of whose needs are to be taken into account. All three concepts arise from the moral and ethical underpinnings of the need to provide secure homes for the population. So for example, the motivation behind charitable donations to housing trusts – a 'subsidy' from philanthropic sources – was integrally linked to ensuring the security of the middle and upper classes: they were 'an insurance policy of wealth [which] promotes social order and good feeling' (see Owen, 1965: 470).

Subsidies can be seen as a technological manifestation of a particular set of rationalities, but defining what a subsidy is becomes just as problematic as finding a definition for affordability. Here we are very much in the domain of economists. For example, Haffner and Oxley (1999: 148) suggest the following:

> A housing subsidy involves action initiated by government which, by means of an implicit or explicit flow of funds, reduces the relative cost of producing or consuming housing. In reducing the relative cost of housing the subsidy results in housing receiving favourable treatment compared with other commodities or investment goods.

Examples of housing subsidies would be: annual payments made to local authorities by central government to off-set the cost of borrowing to fund the construction and repair of council housing; and capital grants paid to individuals and housing associations to cover a proportion of the cost of carrying out a repair and improvements to older properties. From 1919, governments have intervened in the housing market chiefly through a variety of building subsidy mechanisms to encourage municipal authorities to provide housing for the working classes. The application of subsidies was to address both affordability and supply: the private sector on its own could not address the extreme shortage of housing (see also Chapters 7 and 8 below), nor provide at acceptable cost to certain occupiers. Throughout the history of state intervention in the provision of housing, levels of subsidy have been premised on a number of variables – acceptable levels of rent, building and land costs, design and space costs, costs of servicing debt, the state of the economy and costs of administration/management. Underpinning these variables has been an ethico-moral truth about the assumed 'just desert' of the occupiers.

So, for example, properties built in the immediate post-war periods reflected the policy need to build 'homes fit for heroes'. This required properties with high space and design attributes, for which state subsidy was required to be balanced by relatively high rents (certainly unaffordable other than to the better-off working class – see Chapter 3). As part of the 'great crusade' against the slums in the 1930s, subsidy was paid to municipal authorities under the Housing Act 1930, then suspended in 1932 due to the global financial crisis, and reintroduced in 1933 (Malpass, 2001: 235). The tenants to be re-housed were the poorer working classes, and so subsidy systems produced lower rent, lower standard properties. Levels of subsidy also reflected the greater management costs thought to be required in respect of those households; and an additional subsidy was available for the creation of undesirable flats for this group.

Perhaps the most significant economic innovation of the 1930s, which created the ability for further building, was the introduction of the technique cross-subsidizing between a local authority's new and existing housing schemes, known as 'rent pooling'. This technique enabled the setting of *all* rents to be conducted on the same basis rather than being determined by the subsidy allowed by a particular Housing Act, or the outstanding debt on the property. While in the 1930s local authorities used this technique to generate additional finance for building, rent pooling came to be used as a potent technique of governing the desires of occupiers, and generating demand for ownership (through increasing council rents thereby making renting less attractive), although rent pooling was not general practice within local authorities until the 1950s (see Malpass, 1990: 65–6).

The governing effects of subsidy

Money is a powerful tool of governing (Vincent-Jones, 2001). State subsidy would suggest a one-way process of governing, with the type and degree of service specified by the funder. By contrast, we suggest that subsidies enable two-way processes of governing, through mechanisms of 'direct governing' (Cooper, 1998) – clear and visible relationships between donor and receiver, governor and governed – as well as governing at a distance, where both sides come to internalize and normalize at least some of the priorities of the other. Money makes both the funder and receiver responsible to each other, creating a mutuality of interest. The receiver becomes responsible for delivering the demands of the funder, whether a particular rate of return or a specified number of new homes each year. The funder becomes responsible for ensuring the financial survival of the other by maintaining a flow of funds.

One way that subsidy systems govern is through the myriad of explicit rules and regulations defining what is permitted, procedures to be followed and who must carry out the various processes. These rules and regulations must be accepted in order to access a particular form of subsidy – a process of direct governing. For example, the Ministry of Housing and Local Government and its successors produced guidance in publications such as the *Housing Manual*, supplements and circulars; and housing associations funded by the Housing Corporation have been required to meet the Corporation's detailed requirements set out in the *Development Procedure Manual*, at times a file two inches thick. Central government has manipulated its systems of providing subsidy to meet particular priorities over the twentieth century (Gibb *et al*, 1999: 65–6).

However, to see the governing effect of subsidy systems as operating in only one direction is to ignore the impact of prior power relations, relations that are intimately bound up with the location of knowledge. For example, the 1919 state intervention was premised on the requirement on local authorities to conduct a survey of the need for the provision of housing in their areas. The evolution and design of subsidy systems form part of the process of governing, in which it is frequently less obvious to see who is the governor and who the governed. Subsidy systems have arisen out of particular problematizations, points at which the effectiveness of existing programmes and systems have been called into question, and perceptions of failure (that needs are not being met by existing regimes).

Financial expertise

The 'failure' of programmes has provided the impetus both for the questioning of government and for the formation of new programmes (Miller and Rose,

1990). Those actors who can articulate difficulties, deficits or inadequacies of their particular framework, and use the resulting uncertainties and concerns to promote their own form of expertise and definitions of 'truth', become able to suggest solutions, enabling new programmes and regimes to emerge. This requires the emergence of new actors creating climates in which their own truth representations become accepted as normal. Such actors align the interests of others by defining the problems of the latter and then suggesting that these would be resolved if all parties negotiated a new programme in which the new actor becomes an integral player. Central to this process of governing at a distance are the skills and expertise that allow one actor to have knowledge of, and understand, the problems of another (Latour, 1987a).

Those 'programmers' who design subsidy mechanisms are generally required to seek to achieve a number of goals at once. The mechanisms they choose are influenced by the alliance of interests that has come about from a particular problematization and perception of governmental failure. So for example, the Housing and Town Planning Act 1919 was heavily influenced by reports on working parties advised by Seebohm Rowntree (Joseph Rowntree Housing Trust), and Raymond Unwin, architect and pioneer of the garden cities movement. The Act for the first time enabled local authorities to provide assistance to the public utility societies (voluntary housing bodies provided a limited return on capital – Malpass, 2000: 77). Its subsidy mechanisms, which applied to both local authorities and the societies, enabled not only the construction of new housing provision, but also the promotion of the ideals of the Garden City movement – the standards it promoted had been considered too expensive before the war, but were adopted afterwards as 'proof of the government's commitment to producing a land fit for heroes' (Malpass, 2000: 76).

A similar story can be told with the rules relating to housing associations. The Housing Act 1974, a highly significant event in defining current housing policies, was primarily a piece of legislation that sought to end policies of clearance and new build, as well as promote the renewal of the urban environment. The expansion in the funding of housing associations under the 1974 Act emerged in part through the political networking of members of the National Federation of Housing Associations, and its championing of associations as experts in urban renewal (a field in which municipal authorities were seen as lacking in skills: Crook and Moroney, 1995). The associations, as the 'experts', became central to the formulation of the rules and procedures that surrounded this new form of funding, even setting the critical rates for allowances in funding formulae (see McDermont, 2005: ch 5).

Affordability governing citizens

Housing policies until the late 1950s were dominated by issues of subsidies to housing providers, supply subsidies which reduced the impact of the borrowing costs incurred in the provision of housing. However, an alternative, sometimes complimentary subsidy mechanism could be in the form of personal subsidies – state subsidy paid to individuals to reduce their housing costs. The Housing Act 1930 encouraged local authorities to establish means-tested rent rebate schemes or differential rent schemes, and subsequently governments sought to encourage such schemes through circulars and guidance.

The post-Second World War Labour government was resistant to income subsidies, as they were regarded as less efficient and unable to meet the demand for large number of new homes. Income subsidies also caused concern at the level of rationality because of their negative effect on individual dignity, as the functioning of such schemes required mechanisms for means testing household income. However, Conservative governments from the 1950s onwards again sought to encourage local authorities to establish rent rebate schemes for tenants who could not afford the rent levels charged for municipal housing (that supply subsidies produced). Such attempts met with resistance from the non-county boroughs and urban local authorities and their implementation was inconsistent (Malpass, 1990: 98).

Means-tested rent rebate schemes superficially appear to arise from a need to provide help to those tenants who could not afford to pay local authority rents – that is, rebates might be seen as a mechanism for supporting a redistributionary discourse (see Chapter 1). The Conservative government of 1970–74 actively supported and promoted such state intervention. It began with the introduction of Family Income Supplement in 1971, and followed that with a national rent rebate and allowance scheme in the Housing Finance Act 1972 (Robson, 2001: 329). The redistributive effect can, however, be subverted to enable alternative intentions to be realized. Although the 1972 Act was never fully implemented, the introduction of schemes of rent support to the poorest households enabled providers to *increase* average rents across the board and so realize a greater total rental income (Malpass, 1990: 99), while at the same time appearing to continue to provide for those in most financial need. Furthermore, they can also be manipulated to enable government to withdraw its subsidy, requiring occupiers to subsidize each other (in turn, creating an incentive for the better off to exit from the sector). Throughout the 1980s and 1990s, personal subsidies – now termed 'housing benefit' – became an integral mechanism for making the 'social' housing system work, enabling central government to reduce and eliminate its own element of income subsidy.

Governing affordability

In the previous section we have sought to demonstrate how the experts defining and re-defining of the technical terms of finance have themselves governed social housing. In this section we examine the impact of attempts to govern affordability, through governing rent setting policies, as well as manipulating subsidies. In doing so, we do not attempt to explain the divide between revenue and capital (c.f. Cowan, 1999), in part because this divide has always been contested and thus a space for creativity. In part, this is because our purpose is not simple explanation but to flush out the techniques of governance implied in the panoply of financial controls.

Determining price: controversies over rent setting

Social housing often appears to be a series of problematizations about affordability. This generally requires governing rent-setting policies and those responsible for determining such policies. Under what Malpass terms the 'old' system of housing finance, it was a fundamental principle that local authorities were responsible for rent fixing (1990: 65; though he comments that ministers made it very clear to local authorities 'what they were expected to do about rents'). Up until the Housing Finance Act 1972, the 'traditional' settlement between central and local government had allowed local authorities a wide discretion to govern within their own territorial boundaries (Loughlin, 2000). Central governments were concerned about the *total* spending of public authorities, but each authority had relative autonomy in how they balanced expenditure between their various services. They were governed through the need to set 'reasonable' rents but little else was formal.

A basic tenet of local authority housing provision was that rents should be set on a not-for-profit basis (Malpass, 1990: 65), marking out a fundamental difference between the private and public rented sectors. However, the development of the technologies of personal housing subsidy described above enabled the 1970–74 Conservative government to attempt to break down this divide. The Housing Finance Act 1972 fundamentally ruptured the traditional central–local government settlement, in seeking to create a 'standard, market-related pricing system for all unfurnished rented housing' (ibid: 52). All landlords would be required to set rents at 'fair rent' levels, determined not by the landlord but by the Rent Officer.

However, the 1972 Act – described as an 'abattoir for the slaughter of council house tenants' – Skinner and Langdon, 1972: 39 – attempted a too dramatic reshaping of central–local relations, and failed to survive the incoming Labour Government in 1974. Nevertheless, the Act does survive in housing folklore as the inspiration for popular resistance to central control, in images of marches to support the Clay Cross councillors who defied the Act. It was also a 'landmark' in other ways. Its themes of reform – controlling those who had previously governed affordability at the local level, through the central determination of rent levels and more widespread control over the local authorities' Housing Revenue Accounts (Cowan, 1999: 145) – became increasingly key aspects of housing policy.

Governing through knowledge: the HIP system

In 1976 central government placed limits on the total amount local authorities could borrow for new house-building (Gibb *et al*, 1999: 70). In 1977–78 the Labour Government introduced the Housing Investment Programme (HIP) system as a 'means of facilitating forward planning and local autonomy in capital spending' (Malpass, 1990: 18). This was to be 'a comprehensive assessment of the local housing situation' with capital allocations made on the basis of this assessment over a four-year period (see DoE, 1977: para 9.07). The HIP statement fell into two parts: first, a Local Housing Strategy Statement, and, second, a bid for resources, with local authorities also being required to state what their priorities would be if they were given the same allocation as the previous year.

However, such knowledge-based technologies of self-assessment are not just tools for self-governing. The HIP system proved a powerful tool through which central government could govern local authorities, providing both the knowledge required for governing, and the means through which governing could be effected. From 1979 onwards, the HIP system enabled the Conservative governments to impose direct central control of local authority spending on housing and privatizing the stock (Cole and Goodchild, 1995). The local authority's assessment of need played only a minor part in the allocation process; central government priorities impliedly, if not explicitly, took preference.

> The preparation of housing strategies is now, more than ever, governed by tactical considerations designed to please, or appease, the Department of the Environment and to demonstrate awareness of current political priorities at central government level. ... One [survey] respondent noted the need 'to follow government direction, or risk being penalised due to discretion.' (Cole and Goodchild, 1995: 54–5)

The HIP system had introduced an 'objective' assessment of need in the form of the General Needs Index (GNI). However, the makeup of the index was highly contested and political preference was consistently implied (Leather and Murie, 1986: 49). Additionally, allocations were made to authorities on the basis of a number of factors, one of which being central government's assessment of 'efficiency and effectiveness', which gave considerable discretion to the DoE's regional controller. The detailed knowledge about local authority priorities enabled central government not only to set limits on how much an authority could borrow and spend, but also to specify expenditure on targeted programmes.

An additional factor in the central government control mechanisms became the 'top-slicing' of the overall capital allocations for local authorities for government priorities, paid for through Supplementary Credit Approvals (SCAs). The Single Regeneration Budget (SRB) and City Challenge were examples of top-sliced allocations. These allocations were made through a competitive bidding process whereby local authorities, and frequently consortia of local authorities, housing associations and private developers, bid for resources in nation-wide competitions. This competitive bidding for resources was intended to tackle the perceived inefficiency of local government, as well as force local authorities into partnerships with the private and voluntary sectors. Malpass (1994: 307) notes the ideological drive of such programmes and their effect on local governance:

> The problem for some authorities was the nature of the strings attached to the funding, in the form of the competitive bidding procedure, requirements concerning the high

profile involvement of private, voluntary and community partner organisations, and in particular the way that City Challenge was to be managed outside the direct control of elected local authorities.

A further example of central control over local capital was the way in which governments have sought to control the money generated by sales under the right to buy. Rather than being used to cross-subsidize new building, the Local Government, Planning and Land Act 1980 limited the amount of capital receipts that could be included in the HIP allocation to 50 per cent of the total received in any one year, reduced to 20 per cent by 1985. Although strict limits were placed on the amount of capital receipts authorities could *spend*, they were encouraged to use receipts to pay off existing debts. Having paid off their historic housing loan debt, an increasing number of local authorities were thus able to evade central control: no debt meant no need for subsidy, and so central government could no longer apply its rules (Marsh, 2001). The Local Government and Housing Act 1989 Part IV rectified this problem. By amalgamating the subsidy paid to local authorities for rent rebates to tenants with the other forms of housing subsidy, and placing a tight 'ring-fence' around how authorities operated their Housing Revenue Account (Gibb *et al*, 1999: 80–94), all local authorities were brought back within the subsidy net, and therefore within the system's direct control mechanisms. These control mechanisms very specifically further constrained the councils' freedom to fund repairs to Council housing, and sought to force local authorities to increase rents to finance their existing housing service.

We can see, therefore, that the housing finance system shifted from an implicit to an explicit method of direct governing in accordance with a certain political rationality – from Keynesian welfarism through to a neo-liberal model of prudence, relying on the market. This transition was brought about over time, ruptured by strategies of resistance, but much enhanced by the Thatcher government's emphasis on ownership, the market, and the attempt at creating a 'mixed economy' of providers.

Resisting through expertise

The strategies of resistance devised by the financial experts merit comment here. Expertise is an interactive, productive process through which individuals produce new knowledge. As the Thatcher government sought to tighten the noose around local housing finance, the response of local government was to draw on their own accountancy expertise to expose loopholes and enable other methods of 'creative accounting' to deliver the required finance. It was the uncertain boundaries between revenue and capital spending that was particularly productive (enabling, for example, repairs schemes to become 'capital' projects and funded through leasing arrangements – some would say, mortgaging the future), but ultimately, councils were led into financial markets and 'swaps' transactions as ways for managing debt. During this period, as Stewart (1996) puts it, a game of cat and mouse developed, with local authorities opening up loopholes, and central government closing them down.

Some attempts at 'closure' ended up in the courts, producing a clash of expertises as the separate systems of law and accountancy attempted to rule each other. In *Hazell v Hammershith and Fulham LBC* [1991] 2 WLR 372 (HL) the 'swaps' transactions were ultimately declared illegal, but the House of Lords labelling of the swaps markets as 'gambling' rather than the everyday tools of financial management (Loughlin, 1996: 353) led to an unsatisfactory account of the local authority debt management systems in a decision that impacted across the entire system of local government (ibid: 354). As the accountancy profession attempted to subjugate law to its principles and practices, law responded by imposing its 'rules' of statutory interpretation to limit the 'creativity' of local government accountants (see *R v Secretary of State for the Environment, ex parte Camden London Borough Council* [1998] All ER 1 927).

Housing associations: private borrowing, competition and affordability

While local authorities were being directed and encouraged down one housing finance route, housing associations followed a different highway. As discussed in Chapter 2, the Housing Act 1974 was a highly significant piece of legislation in the development of the sector. In giving associations a leading role in the 'new' policy direction of inner city renewal, the Act also provided a subsidy framework that was intended to act as 'rocket fuel' for associations (in the words of John Baker, the civil servant who was one of the principal architects of the Act). Associations could claim grant and public loans to fund all the costs of both newly constructed housing, and improving older housing. However, unlike in the local authority sector, the rent regime from the Housing Finance Act 1972 remained in place – rents were not set by associations, but were 'fair rents' set by the local Rent Officer. The regime was designed so that associations only took out loans to the extent as could be afforded by an occupier paying the fair rent; the remaining costs were covered by a capital grant.

Such a 'generous' regime could not survive the assaults on public spending of the Thatcher administration. During the mid-1980s associations and the Housing Corporation could see that public funding to associations would not continue at the level they had become used to. They explored alternative funding through private loans, finally enacted through legislation in the Housing Act 1988. That Act allowed associations to take control of their own rent-setting and let new tenancies as assured tenancies. From this point, the housing association subsidy regime became known as 'mixed funding' – a mix of public grant (from the Housing Corporation or local authorities) and loans from private funders (banks, building societies, and increasingly through financial bonds and stock exchange flotations).

In terms of understanding the increasing importance that affordability came to play in housing policy terms following the introduction of the mixed public/private funding regime it is necessary to consider not just the technological changes – the new tenancy regime, and the requirement to raise private finance – but the rationale that surrounded these new technologies. The 1987 housing White Paper and consultation document that accompanied it clearly stated the intention to create a more cost effective housing association sector by 'bringing to bear the disciplines of the private sector' (Malpass, 2000: 201). The new regime was intended to ensure associations took on the risks of the business of developing housing. Not only were they required to raise private loans, but also schemes funded after 1988 were no longer eligible for grants to fund future major repairs and other generous subsidies which had permeated some of the period from 1974. In addition, the new grant system calculated grant before the scheme commenced, rather than on completion. The effects of these changes were that associations now had to calculate and plan for the risks of managing and maintaining their properties for their lifetime, with no recourse to public funds if their calculations went awry (see Randolph, 1993). The costs associations were expected to bear increased through these changes.

Perhaps more significantly, the competition ethos, greatly strengthened under the new regime, impacted most fundamentally in the long-term on the affordability of rents. Associations were forced to compete against each other to win allocations of grant. In an effort to make bids more competitive, associations had two broad choices – reduce building costs, or increase borrowing (passing the costs of that on to the occupier through higher rents). Reducing costs meant taking on less risky projects, so development moved once again towards new building and away from risky urban renewal. It also meant developing larger schemes to produce economies of scale, a strategy that was quickly called into question (see Page, 1993, and discussion in ch 6).

The sector's welcome of the new system was tempered with concerns that rents would become unaffordable to the poorest households (Randolph, 1993). Government would not accept the responsibility for defining what affordable meant (Malpass, 2000: 213), which in turn created its own governance effects. Once again we see obscurity as a device of convenience, which (in this case) generated more intense competition, required housing associations to negotiate the best possible terms with private lenders (Langstaff, 1992: 37) and led to increasing rents.

Governing through self-regulation?

It was the sector's national representative body, the National Federation of Housing Associations, that took on the role of attempting to define affordability and monitoring rent levels. The Federation's affordability campaign linked the *freedom* to set rent levels with the responsibility to set affordable rents. It attempted to define affordability through *affordability ratios*. The Federation's initial assumption was that rents would be affordable if they took up no more than 20 per cent of net household income, which was subsequently revised to 22 per cent. An extensive system for recording and monitoring housing association rents, called CORE (Continuous Recording) was established. Returns of CORE were compared against the definition of affordability, with periodic reports published in *Housing Association Weekly*, the in-house magazine – tables were presented showing associations' performances in setting rents as compared to target levels. In December 1993, the Federation's Council adopted a new policy:

> Rents are affordable if the majority of working households are not caught in the poverty trap because of dependency on housing benefit or paying more than 25 per cent of their net income on rent. (NFHA, 1993/94: 13)

The Federation was, in effect, attempting to govern its members through a form of performance monitoring, for it was competition *between* associations as much as government decisions to reduce subsidy levels that was forcing rents to increase. The Federation's attempts at inculcating a sense of responsibility in its members was not helped by ministerial interventions. In 1993, it was reported that the Minister for Housing assumed '35% of net income to be the affordable level of expenditure on rent' (Malpass and Murie, 1999: 162). Ministers had in effect been willing to allow rents to rise because personal subsidies to tenants through housing benefit would 'take the strain'.

'Making up' housing consumers: governing the price of housing

We discussed in a previous section the role played by the emerging regime of personal subsidies to households, as an alternative (or supplement) to supply subsidies. Until the 1990s, the focus of social housing policy had primarily been on supply subsidies to producers. However, at that point a concatenation of policy initiatives and events refocused thinking on affordability towards mechanisms for governing how much social housing tenants paid for their housing, and the personal subsidies paid to tenants. For one thing, the housing subsidy framework had been dramatically reshaped: in 1975, more than 80 per cent of subsidies were directed at producers; by 2000, more than 85 per cent were income subsidies for low income households, primarily through housing benefit (Stevens *et al*, 2005: 2). The spiralling of housing association rents – between 1988 and 1994 they had increased by 80 per cent, when the Retail Price Index increased by only 30 per cent (Malpass, 2000: 214) – had dramatically affected the proportion of public spending going into the social security budget and threatened to 'crowd out' other priorities (Kemp, 2000: 268).

The separate trajectories followed by the local authority and housing association financing systems led to a second concern about rents: the considerable disparities between rents charged by different landlords in the same geographical area, as well as disparities within a single landlords' stock (Marsh, 2004: 187). In one sense, this was the systemic failure in the process of competition, as rent-setting policies differed between landlords creating a seemingly illogical whole.

A third policy shift, the new 'consumerism' of social housing tenants begun by Thatcher and embraced and expanded by New Labour, was intended to put 'choice' at the top of the agenda. It began to become evident that the tandem policies of consumerization and choice were being compromised by, on the one hand, apparently illogical and unfair rent structuring; and on the other, the two-thirds of social housing tenants in need of housing benefit, a group the government regarded as not taking direct responsibility for 'purchasing' their own housing (Kemp, 2000: 265). Taken together, New Labour's housing policies contained in the housing Green Paper (DSS/DETR, 2000) of choice-based lettings, rent restructuring and reforms to housing benefit were all part of a wider policy agenda – to shift the way social housing tenants were 'made up', to re-make them into housing consumers. The policies were designed to incentivize tenants (Marsh, 2004), to make them responsible for the cost of their housing and so act as rational consumers, making choices about housing provision based on how much they could afford. Whether or not this programme operates successfully – and the evidence suggests that, in part, it will not – this operationalization of the vision of tenant-as-consumer is part of an ongoing process of change.

Reforming housing benefit and restructuring social rents

However, reforming housing benefit is seen as threatening key 'stakeholders' in the new social housing regulatory space, the private funders. Private funders lent money to associations on the basis of certain assumptions. A key assumption was that, if necessary, tenants' rents would be covered by housing benefit. Of course, this represented a political risk/uncertainty, which the security of the transactions hinged upon (in addition to the security over the properties themselves), because government could withdraw this personal subsidy. Such binding of central government to private lenders and central government illustrates the impotence now inherent in housing policy (Malpass, 1999a). It simply is not possible to withdraw this personal subsidy (because private lenders will exit the sector and there will be no new private money for building) (Kemp, 2000: 273). Indeed, tinkering with the system – to provide incentives for tenants to 'trade down' into housing they can afford – endangers continued rental income (more expensive housing would become vacant) and therefore ability of associations to meet their loan repayments.

Similarly, attempts to restructure social housing rents encounters obstacles in the private funding of social housing. The housing Green Paper proposed a uniform system of setting rents across Registered social landlords (RSL) and local authority housing (DSS/DETR, 2000: ch 10). The restructuring proposals had a number of aims: keeping rents below market levels; providing a closer link between the qualities tenants value in a home, and how much they pay; reducing what were perceived as unfair inequalities between rents set by different social landlords; and making landlords more efficient by reducing possibilities for using rent increases to cover up deficits arising from organizational inefficiencies (Marsh, 2004: 290–1).

The proposals for restructuring that the DETR settled on aimed to create even closer links between market mechanisms and rents, by setting out a rent setting system based on property values (seen as an indicator of the relative attractiveness of properties to tenants), and local earnings indices (as the indicator of affordability – Marsh, 2001: 190; DETR, 2000b). Significantly, this attempt to structure the choices of social housing tenants could only be achieved by controlling the actions of social housing providers. For the first time since the Housing Finance Act 1972, central government sought to impose a system of rent setting on all social housing landlords (Marsh, 2001: 292). Registered social landlords had already become used to centralized rent controls: once government had become concerned about the size of the escalating housing benefit bill, it had altered its conception of value for money in grant competitions to include a calculation of 'total public subsidy' – the amount of subsidy any new scheme would consume that included a calculation of the notional housing benefit input (Malpass, 2000: 217). At the same time it began to place expectations on housing associations, on their average annual rent increase across the whole of their stock, expectations that were 'enforced' through annual performance monitoring and the publication of performance reports.

Similarly the mechanism for implementing rent restructuring over all social landlords was not through primary legislation but through guidance backed up by annual performance monitoring, and modifications to the subsidy systems. Such a combination of techniques of 'midway governing' (Cooper, 1998) made it difficult for landlords not to comply with the new system (Marsh, 2004: 191). Associations that projected they would not be able to meet the target rents of the restructuring regime within the specified timescale of 15 years were required to apply for an extension. Such extensions would be considered necessary if the 'restructured' rent levels were likely to threaten their ability to meet loan repayments (see Marsh and Walker, 2004).

Rent restructuring, which has meant in most cases that RSL rents could not rise as fast as RSLs would have predicted in their business plans, appears to threaten their ability to meet private lenders' requirements. It might appear surprising that the 'privatization' agenda for social housing does not provide a neat fit with the 'consumerization' agenda. After all, they would both appear to be components of a particular political rationality. But here one is reminded of O'Malley's (2004) point that technologies do not always arise out of rationalities, and that frequently it is the other way round. So we find that the potential to implement a consumerization agenda has already bumped up against pre-existing boundaries, which emerged out of a previous reshaping of social housing finance towards the private. Marsh (2004) also suggests that there are internal contradictions within the rent restructuring system, between the consumerization agenda and the need to ensure affordability. The promotion of choice would suggest that there should be large rent differentials between the most desirable properties (with the highest property value) and the less desirable – particularly between the largest properties and the two- or three-bed houses and flats. However, the linking of rents to local earnings levels tends to pull rents in the other direction, to ensure affordability for the largest households who have relatively lower disposable income.

'A decent home for all': sustainability and housing condition

The 'action plan'

We have argued that housing need, affordability and housing condition are interlinked concepts, each with its own rationality, each dominating the concerns of housing policy-makers and practitioners at different times. Indeed, a 'decent home for all at a price within their means' has been a recurring aim of government housing policies since the Second World War (Hills and Mullings, 1991: 137). However, the political rationalities that have driven housing policies, particularly from 1979 onwards, have meant funding strategies which promoted under-investment in council housing, forcing councils to economize by deferring repairs to their properties and halting improvements programmes. The priority of 'decency;' has been subverted. In the twenty-first century it is once again the *condition* of social housing that has returned to dominate. Indeed, as we discuss in the final section, in some regions it has become recognized that new social housing is not necessary – social landlords have begun demolishing difficult-to-let housing – investment in existing housing is the priority. Such concerns have led to the government establishing (in 2000) its *decent homes* target: 'all social tenants should have a decent home by 2010' (ODPM, 2003b: 14). In *Sustainable Communities: Building for the Future* the ODPM set out an 'Action Plan for Sustainable communities' which marked 'a step change in our policies for delivering sustainable communities' (ibid: 4). The plan included £22bn to improve housing and communities, £5bn for affordable homes, at least £1bn for key worker housing, as well as support for home ownership and new growth areas.

The action plan has been presented as a common sense strategy – who could argue that all tenants should not have a decent home (but why did the target simply relate to social housing tenants?), or against the ideal of sustainable communities. However, it has been the use of the decent homes standard as a vehicle for governing – both housing providers and tenants – that has been of particular concern amongst politicians, practitioners and tenants. The first concern is with the *adequacy* of the decent homes standard. The decent homes standard – defined as above the statutory minimum standard, in a reasonable state of repair, possessing reasonably modern facilities and services, and having a reasonable degree of thermal comfort – has come in for much criticism. The ODPM Select Committee criticized it as 'set at too basic a level' (2004), their criticisms backed up by evidence from those who have traditionally been ascribed the status of 'experts' on housing condition, the environmental health officers. Evidence from the Chairman of the Health and Housing Group described its deficiencies in graphic detail:

> I fear that the definition of the Decent Homes as we currently have it is so full of holes that it fails the test of being a suitable minimum standard. ... some of the features we might be able to find in a house that would pass the Decent Homes Standard ... [are] that it was infested with cockroaches, rats, mice, fleas, bedbugs, we could find that it was

a fire trap or we could find that the noise separation of parting walls or floors may be so poor that we could hear the neighbours cough or use the toilet. We might find that the windows, even in a tower block, may not be of a safe design and lack basic child safety features or stairways may well lack safety features. It could be severely overcrowded or lack adequate bathrooms or provision for the number of people in the house. A poor standard of thermal insulation and the lack of extractor fans in bathrooms and kitchens may lead to problems of condensation and mould growth and the unsatisfactory situation of the dwelling being unsafe or unsavoury, or it may be that you are on the upper floors and there is no lift access to your flat. It seems to me there are huge holes in the minimum definition.

Once again, obscurity becomes a tactic of governing. In utilizing the language of *moral imperative* – all homes must be 'decent' – the inadequacy of the standard has been hidden. But a more prescriptive, higher standard would have compromised another policy aim, the increasing involvement of private capital in social housing. A more prescriptive standard would have enabled a more accurate calculation of the financial cost of providing 'decency', so strengthening arguments for much greater levels of investment.

This is the second, and more widespread criticism of the decent homes policy – the limitation of options open to local authorities in planning to meet the standard. To obtain investment to meet the 2010 target, authorities have only three options: stock transfer, usually under the LSVT programme; the private finance initiative and, for 'high performing authorities' only, Arms Length Management Organisations, or ALMOs (ODPM, 2003b: 16). There is no 'fourth option' of allowing local authorities to tackle the problems themselves, as Deputy Prime Minister John Prescott made clear in a letter to all local authorities in October 2004.

The Decent Homes Standard appears very much as *moral regulation*: the deployment of a distinctively moral discourse which constructs a moralized subject and an object or target which is acted upon by means of moralizing practices (Hunt, 1999: 6–7). The terms of the debate construct both local authorities and tenants as 'moralized subjects'. Local authorities are exhorted to act within a framework that places certain actions as right. Prescott's letter continued:

> We continue to believe the strategy we have in place remains the right one for delivering Decent Homes, providing all local authorities with a level playing field and the opportunity to improve their stock and *the lives of their tenants* (emphasis added).

Within the context of decent homes creating sustainable communities, tenants too are required to act, to become responsiblized within the communities in which the government – and, more importantly, the private sector – is investing. Being responsible means having choices, but these choices of tenants must also be constrained within the three ODPM options.

Although changes to council's powers to borrow without explicit government limits were introduced by the Local Government Act 2003, the Chartered Institute of Housing has warned that:

> Council housing could not benefit significantly from changes to borrowing rules without radical changes in the rent and subsidy regime. These are not on the cards.

The main option for councils wanting to retain their housing stock is still to create an arms length company and bid for extra government subsidy. (John Perry, CIH Director of Policy)[1]

Most damning of all perhaps is the view of the Commons Select Committee that the Decent Homes target is being used as a 'Trojan Horse by the Government in a dogmatic quest to minimise the proportion of housing stock managed by Local Authorities' (Select Committee, 2004). Even so, as with most policy interventions, the Decent Homes Standard appears to be having unexpected effects some RSLs are forced to sell part of their stock to raise enough money to meet the Standard (Weaver, 2004).

However, the regime of truth that central government is attempting to impose on local government – that it is only the non-public sector that can 'solve' social housing's problems – has also become a site of resistance, reflecting the need to account for the polyvocality of governance. Tenant participation is a *sine qua* non of social housing – see Chapter 6 – but this also has unintended consequences as some tenants reject the privatization initiatives (for example in Birmingham and Camden) leading to new votes. In Camden, the response was not to release the £283m required to bring the properties up to the decent homes standard, but rather to acknowledge that some council tenants' homes would not be able to meet the standard (Ambrosi, 2004).

Inverting housing need

And so this leads us to our final (but interlinked) problematization – that of housing supply. From the 1970s until the mid-1990s, the issue of supply was not the dominant factor in the financing of social housing. This changed in the mid-1990s as a result of the demographer's calculations of the need for new homes, variously estimated as between 4.4 and 5.6 million, arising from migration, and the creation of an increasing number of smaller households as people lived longer and single parent households became more the norm. A disciplinary shift occurred, however, in 2002 when the Treasury took a renewed interest in housing supply. They commissioned an economist Kate Barker to carry out a review. Her report (Barker, 2004) is (naturally) an economists' modelling of the housing problem. Affordability and housing need, in effect, became *inverted*: it is now an issue of affordable home-ownership, with housing for key workers, particularly in the South East/Thames Gateway corridor, as the policy imperative. The debate about affordability is now no longer about ensuring an adequate supply of social rented housing for those in need. The terms of the debate have mutated into how to enable first-time buyers to have access to owner occupation. This perspective views housing need as arising from the needs of the economy, not the needs of the household. As the secretary-general of the Royal Town Planning Institute explained '[w]hat's driving this is Gordon Brown's perception that the biggest threat to the British economy is the excessive volatility of the housing market' (cited in Birch, 2004: 19).

Housing policies are now portrayed, once again, along a north-south divide. Low demand in the North (and parts of the Midlands), low supply in the south, particularly the south-east and London. However, this message is too simplistic. In some of the Housing Market Renewal Areas, areas of intervention on low demand where demolition of existing stock is proposed, recent research demonstrates pockets of substantial *increases* in house prices (Nevin and Leather, 2005); and the extreme shortages of the south east in reality are shortages primarily in London. Indeed, from splinters within the disciplinary perspective of economists, there are concerns about estimations of demand may be too high (Blitz, 2005).

Centrifugal forces: towards further private sector involvement

However, it has allegedly been frustrations with the apparent inability of the housing association sector to use supply subsidies to deliver sufficient affordable housing, that have driven new initiatives in New Labour's Housing Act 2004; this Act contains mechanisms that for the first time allow developers access to social housing grant to produce affordable homes, a proposal originally made by the Major government (DoE, 1995). As discussed in the next chapter, this change in funding strategies is likely not just to influence the nature of social housing providers, but also the nature of the state regulation of the social housing sector. Developers have made it clear that they will not accept the detailed prescriptive rules and procedures that the Housing Corporation requires housing associations to adhere to in order to obtain grant.

It is the very nature of private bodies that are being held up as irresistible virtues. In *Poplar HARCA v Donoghue* (2002) the DETR representative claimed that

> ... the very nature of this private sector status [...] has brought in the £20bn from finance institutions, which monies might need to be added to the public sector borrowing requirement should RSLs be found to be public sector bodies. Such a finding would also put a halt to the whole stock transfer programme.

This valorization of private sector values is absolutely central to the State's thinking about the future direction of all that was once considered part of the welfare state. In the Treasury's policy document concerning *Public Private Partnerships* (HM Treasury, 2000), it is acknowledged that the private sector cannot borrow as cheaply as the State. However, claims are made that it can compensate for this in many ways: by being more innovative; creating greater efficiencies; invest for long-term improvement and 'manage risk better' (ibid: 16). This rhetoric goes largely unchallenged, and indeed many in the public sector welcome the entrepreneurial possibilities private finance appears to hold out.

Conclusion

Examining the ways social housing and money have been thought about and give rise to the deployment of new technologies raises all the five themes of this book: how do we understand the 'social' in social housing; the regulation effect of finance; the impact of moral agendas; the obscurity of policy through the lens of affordability and the shifting boundaries – between private and public, between the personal and the institutional, and between the tenures of renting and owner occupation.

A cursory survey of the housing press would seem to suggest that it is two 'personalities' who dominate the thoughts of social housing practitioners: Kate Barker, and 'decent homes'. The term 'personalities' is used intentionally, for although only one is in actuality a person, the other has assumed such importance that its presence becomes over-bearing. Both 'personalities' come with their own rationalities, and technologies. Both herald a shift in housing perspectives. One is an economist, appointed by a Chancellor of the Exchequer to bring the rational order of economics to the somewhat chaotic world of housing policy. Kate Barker's review has shifted the terminology of affordable housing. No longer do we consider how to produce affordable rents; the focus is on the need for affordable home ownership. Since regulation of the RSL sector has largely been ceded to the private funders, the desire for ownership appears more malleable to governmental control.

The other personality is a moral standard that has been deployed to bring about the economic domination of housing policy. The language of the debates that these personalities are creating may be 'decency' and 'sustainability', but the intended outcome is the immersion of the social housing stock of Britain in the values and technologies of the private business sector. As we shall demonstrate in the next chapter, even the regulation of social housing is now predicated by the overriding necessity of meeting loan repayments. Regulation too is privatized as funders look to Ratings Agencies to accredit associations along with the Housing Corporation.

Governing social housing through money has always been, and still is a complex mix of direct governing (rules and procedures), and governing at a distance. The agencies of social housing have themselves become so much part of discourse formation that it is often hard to see where policies originate, or end. Stock transfer, so central to the state's attempts to mould the social housing sector, appears to have emerged from the desire of actors in the social housing sector to create their own freedom – a freedom to become entrepreneurs (see Chapter 2). Similarly, changes in the technologies of governing – such as allowing developers to access social housing grant – influence and shape the rationalities of rule, as the new technologies are required to encompass the values of those they seek as allies as well as to govern.

Chapter 5:
Regulatory Truths

We began this book with an exploration of the question, what is 'social' about social housing. One of our conclusions was that social housing was always regulated housing – that the two concepts worked in tandem. In this chapter we take one aspect of that regulation, the technologies, rationalities and institutions that have been deployed in the regulation of municipal authorities and housing associations, the organizations considered to be the principal providers of social housing. The chapter explores the regulatory space(s) of these providers, considering how the providers have been shaped, and have themselves shaped, their regulatory environment.

Ever since Michael Power (1994; 1997) brought into focus the power of audit in re-designing and re-shaping organisations it has been impossible to take the view that regulatory technologies, and the professional expertises behind those technologies, are neutral tools. Power demonstrated how auditing and auditors have become central to our concept of regulation, shaping public perspectives of what makes a 'good' organization. However, this primacy of auditors has not always been the case. While the previous chapter sought to demonstrate how financial strategies have been central mechanisms for shaping social housing, in this chapter we demonstrate that other professional expertises have assumed regulatory capacities.

Indeed, the questions 'who is interested in regulation? and what background of expertise do they bring to the process of regulation?' can provide much insight into the development of regulatory spaces, and how particular regulatory understandings have become 'regulatory truths' at any moment in time. That, in essence, is what this chapter is about. Creating a division between the previous chapter and this one has not been easy, and in some respects, decisions about what goes in which chapter may seem arbitrary, given the linkages between regulatory and financial strategies. This chapter seeks to cohere a discussion of financial regulatory strategies into an overall interrogation of the various strategies of 'regulating through freedom'. We do this through two broad sections. First, we discuss the development of technical regulation of housing associations. We then move on to more generic questions raised by the techniques of regulation. In that section, we consider the methods of regulatory controls implied by contract and performance management, as well as private actors such as credit rating agencies. We demonstrate the diverse provision of regulatory control, from the state through to private actors.

Controlling housing associations: technical regulation

Local authorities as governors

Whereas present-day scholars of regulation are faced with a deluge of practitioner and academic material about how to regulate, why regulate (and why de-regulate), regulatory tools, technologies and theories, locating any similar archive for early years of this century is difficult. As Prosser (1997: 1) has pointed out in relation to industry regulation, 'until the 1980s regulation was little discussed ... public ownership, it was assumed, was the main way of making key industries reflect the "public interest" '. Prosser's view can equally be applied to 'social' housing – although we have said that social housing has always been about regulation, the regulation of the production and producers of social housing has occurred primarily through its provision by public bodies, the municipal housing authorities. It has been the central–local government relationship that has controlled the vast majority of social housing provision, a relationship in which local authorities have acted within a framework of legislation and conventions that have allowed for a wide discretion to govern (Loughlin, 1996; 2000).

At the same time that central government Ministries were shaping local provision through subsidy rules, local government was also the route through which other providers – the charitable trusts and housing associations – were to be controlled. For local government, issues of freedom have been at the heart of strategies of governing. Local government has sought and, for much of the twentieth century, gained the freedom to govern by structuring the actions of citizens and organizations within its geographical boundaries. Being able to demonstrate control over local affairs has been a critical factor in structuring their relations both with central government and other bodies, such as voluntary housing organizations, which may seek to encroach on this freedom. For much of the twentieth century local government had the advantage over other housing providers of legitimacy and expertise, at least in the rhetoric of central government. In 1933 the influence of local government was strong enough to ensure that Ministers rejected the option set out in the Moyne Report of establishing a central funding agency for housing associations (see Garside, 1995; Malpass, 2000: 95–102), choosing to continue the channelling of subsidies to associations through local authorities. Government ministers and civil servants considered housing associations to be 'totally inadequate organisation[s] with which to replace' local authorities (PRO HLG 29/213: note dated 6 December 1933), a view that local authorities could use in structuring power relations. If diversity of housing provision was a policy objective (and Malpass (2000) would argue that the housing association option was never high on the agenda until the 1960s) then it was local government that would be central to the delivery mechanisms.

What this provided were local governable spaces of housing activity. The Housing Acts gave local authorities a wide arena for exercising discretion. The Housing Act 1935, s 27, for the first time local authorities to put in place agreements with housing associations as a condition of granting subsidy. Nevertheless, the Act simply specified that these agreements should detail the type of houses and rents at which they were to be let, leaving to the discretion of the local authorities the inclusion of other terms they 'may think expedient in view of the needs of their district in relation to the housing of the working classes'. The primacy of local authorities in the central–local relationship meant that, even where subsidies were paid by central government to the local authority to pass them on to associations, it was the local authority which had to agree upon scheme details. The role of the Ministry was one of suggesting good practice, drawing up model agreements (NFHS, 1946c: 11).

In common with many spaces of governance, a hybridity of governing techniques can be seen to be operating (Rose and Valverde, 1998). Local government professionals operated a range of modes and procedures, and particular claims to 'truths'. Housing was influenced heavily by medical and public health discourses: housing issues were frequently dealt with by 'Housing and Public Health Committees'; for authorities like the London County Council, the council's Medical Officer always provided observations on the development of any association site, as they did for all Council developments. However, regulatory control was at the level of detailed intervention on technical matters: the concerns expressed by the council's committees were about the layout, design and standards of building of housing societies' proposed schemes. Frequently scrutiny was about minutiae: approval for one Housing Trust's plans was 'subject to consideration being given to the arrangement of bathroom fittings so as to provide easy access to the window' (LCC/MIN/7552 and 7553 – Housing and Public Health Committee, 29 May 1935);[1] another to changes being made 'regarding windows in to bedrooms not being on the street side' (LCC/MIN/7554 – Housing and Public Health Committee, 26 June 1935).

This attention to detail, the contingency of subsidy based on professional judgements of medical officers and architects, was a potent mix of 'governing at a distance' through professionalism and expertise, together with direct forms of governing through subsidy and loan agreements. The gaze occasionally extended beyond these technical professional concerns, with for example, a concern with the associations' conditions of employment for their staff, asking for 'a further report on the wages and conditions of domestic staff' before approving another application for financial assistance (LCC/MIN/7772 – Housing Committee, 8 July 1964).

The subsidy/loan arrangements between housing associations and local authorities in effect created a long-term contractual relationship between the two bodies. In return, the housing association could be required to house tenants nominated by the local authority in properties in which any rent increases could also be determined by local government. Even in 1934, the limitations of this relationship worried the London County Council (LCC) – associations who could repay loans early would no longer be bound by conditions that housing should be let to the working classes at rents approved by the council. The council's Finance Committee asked the Housing and

Public Health Committee to devise the means to continue controls once loans were repaid (LCC/MIN/7293 – Minutes of the Housing and Public Health Committee, 18 April 1934).

That relationship was based around control of a *scheme* – controlling scheme design and standards, and the people who were to be housed – with very little, if any, focus on matters relating to the *nature* of the provider or the riskiness of their operations. This was primarily the exercise of a very *technical* form of control, by professionals with training that focused on particular aspects of detail – building standards, levels of rent, the nature of tenants. While local authorities were keen to use their relationship with associations to extract specified advantages, there was little indication of a desire, or need, to be regulators. Municipalities looked elsewhere for confirmation of the 'genuineness' of housing associations – to the Registrar of Friendly Societies (the London County Council expected societies to be registered Industrial and Provident Societies – LCC/MIN/7550) or to the Charity Commission (Waddilove, 1970). So while the LCC's rate fund contributions to housing associations, secured through legal agreements, gave the council 'substantial nomination rights' (GLC/DG/SCR/1/3: Housing Department Report to Chair of Scrutiny Committee), as well as considerable control over association rents and levels of rent increases (LCC/MIN/7767 Housing Committee 5 February 1964), there was no attempt at monitoring or scrutinizing the overall activities of associations. In 1979, the Director of Housing for the Greater London Council (GLC) claimed that 'our housing association operation is subject to closer control and scrutiny than anything else we do' (GLC/DG/SCR/1/3 – report to Scrutiny Committee 9 November 1979). However, this system of *technical* control was seen to fail spectacularly at the end of the 1970s, when a Yorkshire TV documentary alleged misuse of funds by a number of housing co-operatives and the Omnium group of housing associations, all funded by the GLC, leading to a reference to the Director of Public prosecutions (GLC/DG/SEC/1/86(2)).

Such failures form part of the genealogies of regulatory technologies and rationalities (Rose and Miller, 1992). The local authorities' attempts at governing were attempts to create a certain type of subject, moulded from knowledge of the professionals *doing* the governing (O'Malley, 2004: 26). Failure of technical, scheme-based regulation would eventually create conditions in which other forms of professional expertise would come to the fore in regulatory strategies. Perhaps their reluctance to become regulators arose from the disparate nature of the modes of control operated by local authorities, through the knowledges of those professionally trained to focus on detail – the detail of health, design and repayment of loans. These governors would only understand governing as a matter of structuring the minute daily decisions of associations as they designed housing, built it and let it.

Establishing a state regulator

Local authorities are hybrid bodies: administrative bodies focused on service delivery agents controlled by professional norms; as well as *political* organizations controlled by diverse political rationalities. In the 1930s, they had successfully defended themselves against the encroachment of centralized control by a national Housing Corporation (Garside, 1995). By the 1970s, political attacks on municipal housing from both right and left meant that a centralized state regulator and funder of housing associations had become the acceptable strategy for dealing with then current perceptions of the 'housing problem' – the state of the inner cities, as well as the perceived failure of the local authorities' solution of demolition and new building in outer estates (Crook and Moroney, 1995).

The Housing Act 1974, primarily concerned with strategies for urban renewal, also converted the Housing Corporation into the centralized regulator/funder of housing associations. As the local authorities had feared in the 1930s, a centralized regulator/funder implied a marginalization of their role. While the GLC was happy to accept a withdrawal from what it described as 'paternal' control, instead adopting the role of 'banker', it was concerned that there was little or no role for local authorities in programme decisions about housing associations and, in particular, the allocation of Housing Corporation funding. This could lead, as the GLC suggested in evidence to a review of Housing Corporation practices, to

> ... housing associations operating in an area ... feel[ing] that it is *their* responsibility to decide the amount, location and type of housing needed by the local community as a whole. (GLC, 1979)

Local authorities identified their loss of freedom to govern housing association activities with an assumption of responsibilities and duties by the regulatees, as well as a shift in power to the central state regulator. Local authority fears were largely borne out. The Housing Corporation imposed housing associations on local authorities without consultation, and until the 1990s capital programme allocations to associations continued to be made with little, if any, reference to the local authority. Programme agreements were more a reflection of the Corporation's perceptions of associations' abilities to meet delivery targets than local housing need (Wolmar, 1982: 13).

The Housing Corporation was probably the first UK attempt to establish a centralized state regulator. Given its innovative status, there was little to draw upon in terms of institutional design. That vacuum gave considerable scope for the regulatees to be involved in the design process, both of regulatory strategies as well as the centralized funding arrangements for associations. Indeed, the housing association sector was closely involved in the design of the 1974 Act itself, primarily through its representative body, the National Federation of Housing Associations (NFHA). The Federation's chairman was asked by the Secretary of State for the Environment to prepare a paper 'on principles that might be included in a Housing Bill dealing with the Voluntary Housing Movement' (PRO CHAR 11/205). The proposals in this paper were largely imported into the design of the 1974 Act. The Act converted the Housing Corporation, a body established by the Conservative government in 1964 to promote particular types of co-ownership and cost rent housing societies (reflecting the then political will that ownership and market renting should be stimulated) into a body that would promote, fund and regulate *all* housing association activity. Given the primary focus of the 1974 Act of promoting urban renewal, the critical point was that *expertise* in inner city housing development was seen to rest with the associations. In creating a new regulatory and funding sphere for this activity, the regulator and the regulatees both 'grew up' together into a regulatory community in which many of the rules were designed by the *experts*, the associations (McDermont, 2005: ch 5).

Even the principal means of regulation, a register of associations eligible for public funding to be kept by the Corporation, was designed with the involvement of the associations. The rhetorical argument for registration may have been that it would ensure the protection of *public* resources. Nevertheless, the Federation succeeded in influencing a number of strategic decisions concerning both the principles and the processes of the registration system, as well as the interests of the dominant group of members, through its representatives on the Housing Associations Registration Advisory Committee. That body had been set up by the 1974 Act (s 14) to advise the Corporation on the criteria for registering associations, and to advise on particular associations whose applications were referred to the committee. Its first key decision – how many associations should be registered – chose not to follow the advice of the Cohen Committee that there were too many associations (Cohen Committee, 1971: 75). Rather it was the housing association sector's view – that there should be no attempt to reduce the size of the sector – that prevailed. For it was known that the many thousands of voluntary committee members throughout the country had the political influence to effectively oppose such a move. The importance of continuing support for the *voluntary* donation of time and resources by well-meaning housing committee members weighed heavily against *rational* arguments of the efficient use of public resources (c.f. Titmuss, 1970).

The establishment of a register could have been used as a key tool for (re-)shaping the housing association sector. Instead, the sector shaped the regulator in what was termed 'a decision to register everyone except the obvious crooks' (Noble, 1979). Research into the operation of regulatory control through setting conditions for registration seems to have itself been shaped by the wide discretion operated by Corporation officers. So, while the Corporation adopted centralized criteria, officials in regional offices were given a wide discretion enabling them

> ... to exempt associations from the full force of the criteria with little or no justification by such a wide and unpublicised, unstructured discretion, many associations were registered although they breached one or more criteria; for example, the rule requiring proof of financial viability. (Noble, 1981: 175)

However, despite the establishment of a body intended to regulate the sector, the principal mechanisms for scrutinizing associations' activities continued to be minute technical scrutiny of scheme development. Despite the transfer of officials from the Department of the Environment to the Housing

Corporation, the Department appeared reluctant to relinquish its hold over the housing association territory – a territory it had worked to create. For some time, a system of double scrutiny by both the Department and the Corporation was in operation, which was the cause of much complaint by associations (Lewis and Harden, 1982). The regulatory strategy involved a combination of technical scrutiny by professionals concerned about housing standards and administering the rules of funding, with the *assurance* that assets would be kept in the public domain by rules requiring the Corporation's consent for any disposal of housing association assets. The technologies of regulation were still contained within a set of knowledges that had largely developed within the context of public sector control – the setting of rules, and the exercise of professional discretion. So while the rhetoric of professional administration would claim that the technologies of regulation are the *logical* outcome of rationalities, in practice the relationship is considerably more complex (O'Malley, 2004: 173). The tools of regulation arise from the understood knowledge of the regulatory space – a mixture of 'common sense' and professional expertises – and gives rise both to new technologies and new ways of thinking. 'Regulatory truths' are both rationalities and technologies of the regulatory sphere.

Techniques of regulation

With the benefit of hindsight, we can view the Housing Act 1974 Act as a critical event that made possible new and different forms of regulatory strategies and service delivery. An environment was created in which a sector, operating across the public/private binary, was working with and through an organ of the central state to create a regulatory space that had a (high) degree of autonomy arising from shared personnel, expertise and goals. As regulator and funder, the Corporation has been required to have its eye on government targets for expanding housing association provision, a regard that was said to influence both decisions on the allocation of resources and regulatory strategies (Day *et al*, 1993; Mullins, 1997). While it was, and still is, argued by the Corporation that the funding role compliments the regulatory role (Housing Corporation, 2000), the biggest stick to bring associations into line is the threat of withdrawal of funding. We have already argued that, particularly in times of rapid expansion of resources and expectations, regulatory decisions will be motivated by concerns to meet financial targets. In this regulatory space it becomes increasingly difficult to distinguish the regulator from the regulatees, as the regulator's rules are designed by the regulatees on the basis of what will work. Questions of 'why regulate?' and 'what values should regulation seek to protect/enhance?' become subsumed by pragmatic concerns to meet the programme and spending targets set by the central state.

During this development of a new regulatory community, municipal housing authorities' freedom to govern was being increasingly structured by central government, through the Housing Investment Programme (HIP) process and other financial controls (see Chapter 4). Working alongside this increasing structuring was the broader shift towards New Public Management (NPM). Social housing provision too came under the shaping influences of the rationalities and technologies of NPM. That reflected a shift in values towards economy and efficiency, the increasing privatization and contracting out of service delivery, as well as shifts in techniques of control and accountability towards performance indicators and audit (Harlow and Rawlings, 1997: 131–32; Hood, 1991).

Regulating through contract

Competition became a prominent feature of social housing provision, principally through three mechanisms. First, as the Conservative governments of the 1980s continually reduced authorities' powers to borrow through the HIP process, there was a simultaneous 'top-slicing' of funding into Supplementary Credit Approvals (SCAs), Single Regeneration Budgets (SRBs) and City Challenge. Access to these funds was through a competitive process. Local housing authorities were required to compete against each other in 'quasi-markets' (Vincent-Jones, 2001). There appears to be little research about the impact of this marketization on social housing, the notable exception being a case study of Bristol City Council's failure to 'win' City Challenge funding – twice (Malpass, 1994). This study demonstrated that authorities were required to conform to certain forms of policy-making processes and implementation arrangements set by central government in order to compete in these new quasi-markets. Bids had to be formulated in partnership with the private sector, voluntary and community organizations, and an implementation vehicle outside the local authority structure had to be created. The Council's experience in the first round bidding for City Challenge funding led them to downgrade the importance of housing in their second bid, as it became clear that Ministers considered the objective of *economic* regeneration more important than meeting local housing needs. The effect of these competitive environments was to reshape actors through a process of 'mid-way governance' (Cooper, 1998: 13). Local authorities, as the subjects of governance, clearly saw the rules that were being established – if not immediately, then through the experience of failure – and altered their strategies accordingly. They even chose to re-create their own image – two thirds of the local authorities that successfully bid for City Challenge set up separate companies to run the programmes, an acceptance of the attempt to temper the leading role of the municipal organization (Malpass, 1994: 377).

Second, particularly post-1988, competition also became a key factor in the allocation of funding to housing associations. Competitions between associations were set up by the Housing Corporation and those local authorities with land or capital receipts for housing development. While bidders were asked to supply a wide range of information concerning design, management, environmental features and other factors – such as the provision for training of local people in the construction process – it was the value for money as measured by the grant required (and later, the rent levels – see Chapter 4) that was to be the decisive factor. These competitive processes also reshaped the organizations involved. The sector's trade body, the National Housing Federation, blamed the associations' willingness to enter wholeheartedly into the process of grant-cutting, and alignment with the requirements of the funders, on the sector's apparent lack of independence from the central and local state (Tickell, 2002). Competition had shaped associations and was seen, perhaps perversely, to have brought them into closer alignment with the state. What was less visible to the associations was their increasing alignment with their private funders.

The third route through which competition became a significant feature was Compulsory Competitive Tendering (CCT), introduced by the Local Government Act 1988. Initially the services subject to CCT were limited to those run by manual workers, requiring authorities to put out to tender contracts for maintaining council housing, previously run by Direct Service Organisations. However, the Local Government Act 1992 extended CCT to the provision of professional services, and in 1994 CCT was extended to housing management. The central–local government relationship had become far removed from one of trust and discretion, as legislation now tightly defined those activities that were to be considered as 'housing management' (and therefore to be included in the tender document), leaving little to the discretion of local government (also see SI 1994/2297; Cowan, 1999: 156–9).

Through these mechanisms competition became a powerful technology, re-structuring relations in social housing. It shaped the actions of social housing providers by controlling the terms of entry into the sphere of competitive relations – in a very explicit way – by determining that new power relations should be set up that further diminished the role of local government, and make particular provision for new partners. It also led to a longer term re-structuring of housing associations as they aligned their practices and interests to those of their funders.

Competition, and competition law, became a route for introducing new values; those of the private sector, values which are, at best, in tension with public service values, at worst, incompatible (Prosser, 2005: 14). At the same time as competition has become a dominant feature of social housing, the parameters within which competition law operates have shifted. In the 1970s, competition law could accommodate public interest concerns (for example, Fair Trading Act 1977). However, Prosser (ibid: 27) notes that:

> ... UK competition law has now reached the end of a process of change from a regime in which the public interest is built into the basic test used by competition authorities ... to one in which the test is wholly competition-based subject to very limited exceptions for public interest considerations, and is applied by independent competition authorities.

The redirection of social housing away from public sector values occurred through a double movement: the increasing domination of the rules of competition, at the same time as competition law itself was moving away from any alignment with public interest values, to a focus almost entirely centred on efficiency, economy and effectiveness. However, for these local providers of social housing there was another twist. For, while central government sought to shape local providers through the rules of competition, associations and local authorities were not able to avail themselves of the certainty of the contractual relationship. The allocation of funding did not come through the negotiation of terms of a legally binding contract, but was still contingent on maintaining a good 'working' relationship with the regional office of the DoE or the Corporation. At the other extreme, the requirements of CCT meant specifying minutely a housing management service that had previously been provided through flexible, discretionary and professionalized service delivery mechanisms. The relational nature of contract (Macneil, 2001) appeared to provide local government in particular with all the disadvantages but none of the advantages of contract.

Regulating through performance: performance indicators and audit

We have seen that the 1970s and 1980s marked a fundamental shift in the values of the social housing sector. A regulatory/funding body had centralized what was to become a significant vehicle for social housing provision, and in the process had marginalized local authorities' role as strategic planner – and then provider. The process of privatizing provision had rapidly progressed, first through the right to buy and then through large-scale voluntary transfer. Private sector mechanisms of competition had been introduced into the planning/programming process, along with a change in competition law values from public interest protection to economy and efficiency. 'Managerialism' had become a feature of most levels of public services, as a product of competition, NPM and private finance initiatives (Walker, 1998). This standardization of practices across institutions on the model of the market (Fairclough, 1995: 231) blurred the boundary between the public and private provision of goods and services as the activities of the former were redefined in the image of the latter (Marston, 2004: 11).

Given this fundamental shift in values, we might look to regulatory strategies to attempt to reinstate the centrality of values. However, in the United Kingdom, regulatory strategies frequently separate off economic regulation from social regulation. The former is considered to be the role of the regulator, the latter to be left to government with its democratic mandate (Foster, 1992; discussed by Prosser, 1997: ch 1). Regulatory tools themselves have also become the subject of managerialism, as the private sector technologies of *audit* have gained purchase within the public sector. Indeed, Harlow and Rawlings (1997: 133) described audit as the Conservative government's 'transmission-belt' for importing NPM values into public services.

For many, financial audit, and more recently, performance audit, is considered a central element of accountability within the UK. 'In the British constitution, the 'power of the purse' is central to the ability to call government to account' (White and Hollingsworth, 1999: 1), and this principle also applies at all levels of government. It is the Audit Commission, set up by the Local Government and Finance Act 1982, that has the primary role for auditing local authorities, and more recently, for inspecting housing associations. The Commission's mission statement (see its website at http://www.audit-commission.gov.uk/aboutus/index.asp) describes the organization as:

> ... an independent public body responsible for ensuring that public money is spent economically, efficiently, and effectively in the areas of local government, housing, health, criminal justice and fire and rescue services.

The Commission's roles have gradually increased. Under the Local Government Act 1992, it became responsible for the supervision of locally appointed auditors and for standard setting. It is now responsible for overseeing the development of performance indicators for local government as well as for preparing and publishing the Comprehensive Performance Assessment (CPA) league tables. In April 2003 the Commission's Housing Inspectorate took over the role of inspecting housing associations from the Housing Corporation.

Performance indicators are key tools in the process of audit. It is through these that audit:

> far from being passive, ... actively constructs the contexts in which it operates. The most influential dimension of the audit explosion is the process by which environments are made auditable, structured to conform to the need to be monitored ex-post. (Power, 1994: 13)

Performance Indicators are a classic demonstration of the inter-dependency of knowledge and regulation/power: '[g]overnance always involves knowledge .... Knowledge is used to select objects of governance and knowledge is used in the actual instances of governance' (Hunt and Wickham, 1994: 87). Key to this perspective is the understanding that the knowledge which they augment does not exist independently of the desire to govern – 'knowledge does not force the hand of governance. Rather, we assert that the reverse is the case' (ibid: 88). These indicators, and audit processes that assert their centrality, evolve from a desire to structure the actions of housing organizations. Along with subsidy controls, they have become key mechanisms for structuring the discretion of local authorities.

Audit, and self-audit, of an organization's performance against indicators, can be a highly critical formative tool through two principal attributes: audit's claims to neutrality through which it is able to import a set of normative demands into professional practices; and its facility to operate through mechanisms of self-control within organizations. As Power (1997: 7) put it:

> Auditing may be a collection of tests and an evidence gathering task, but it is also a system of values and goals which are inscribed on the official programmes that demand it. ... The idea of audit shapes public conceptions of the problems for which it is the solution; it is constitutive to a certain regulatory or control style which reflects deeply held commitments to checking and trust.

Performance indicators, normalization and professionalization

Research into the impact of performance indicators on housing management concluded that '[t]he reliance on [performance indicators] by the Audit Commission and the Housing Corporation has had a major impact on the organizational practices within housing agencies within recent years' (Jacobs and Manzi, 2000: 86). While they may appear neutral, the selection of particular tasks for the scrutiny of audit affords 'symbolic dignity' (Luhmann, 1985: 160) to the selected indicators, creating a normalizing effect. Jacobs and Manzi's research demonstrated that the overriding focus within housing organizations was on performance against a *small* number of measurable outputs, in particular the amount of unpaid rent recovered, and on the numbers of empty properties (p 96). The concern to minimize the time that properties stood empty, and were therefore not income generating, led to minimizing the work carried out on their repair, and requiring tenants to move prior to completion of work. As efficiency became the paramount – and measurable – goal, the professional, common sense knowledges of front-line staff, to achieve fairness in allocation and tenant satisfaction, lost its value as common sense. It was this propensity to enable the hierarchical imposition of management values that paradoxically appears as one of the outcomes of performance management, with Performance Indicators being seen as a management tool for restructuring and staff reductions (p 97) – paradoxical because the tools of NPM were meant to free the 'entrepreneurial self' in public sector managers (see Osborne and Gaebler, 1993).

It is in the use of league tables, star ratings and 'naming and shaming' that performance audit can be viewed as a tool for shaping public perceptions of what a service is about, as well as for hierarchical, disciplinary control. By contrast, Casey and Allen (2004: 396) point to the potential for performance management to be appropriated by front-line housing managers in a 'professional project of the self'

> ... by working on their attitude towards their work so as to present themselves as more professional and this substantiate[s] their claim to a professional status ... as well as for systemic ends ... by producing outputs compatible with the performance criteria 'imposed' on them and 'enforced' on them by consumers.

The 'best value' regime

League tables were initially a service-based tool, most prominent in their use in school performance. However, New Labour's 'best value' regime, introduced by the Local Government Act 1999, has elevated Comprehensive Performance Assessment tables to the status of a generalized and powerful tool for shaping public opinion *and* justifying central government intervention in local services.

The technologies of NPM – audit and contract – very explicitly sought to take public services into a different arena. In doing so, they created very real and high profile tensions between local and central government. Previously understood norms, of governing through local authorities' freedom to govern, had been severely eroded throughout the 1980s and early 1990s. Within this context, the best value regime can appear as a means of reducing the conflict between central and local government that had arisen during the 18 years of Conservative governments particularly through the imposition of CCT (Martin, 2000). Alternatively, it can be seen as a means for enhancing the power of performance management through self-regulation at the same time as continuing to enhance the importance of competition (Higgins *et al*, 2004; McAdam and Walker, 2003).

In New Labour's White paper, *Modern Local Government: in Touch with the People* (DETR, 1998: 5), local government appeared to have been put back into centre stage:

> Among all our public institutions councils have a special status and authority as local, directly elected bodies. They are uniquely placed to provide vision and leadership to their local communities.

Section 1 of the Local Government Act 1999 developed a new statutory duty on a 'best value authority' to 'secure continuous improvement in the way in which its functions are exercised, having regard to the combination of economy, efficiency and effectiveness' (3(1)).

Best value authorities include all local authorities (s 1(1)(a)), and although not directly named in the Act, housing associations have effectively come within its compass horizontally through the inspection and audit carried out by the Housing Corporation (also a best value authority), now the Housing Inspectorate. The content of best value is not specified in any further detail in the Act, although primacy is given over to measurement. For example, performance indicators are central to the definition of best value, being the 'factors by which a best value authority's performance in exercising functions can be measured' (s 4(1)(a)).

It has been argued that the best value regime demonstrated an intention to move away from the excessive emphasis on economy that characterized CCT, by requiring authorities to achieve continuous improvement and consider efficiency and effectiveness alongside economy (Vincent-Jones, 2000). The regime also appears to be a move away from the regulation by prescriptive legislation, an attempt to 'modernise' local public services through 'persuasion and exhortation' (Martin, 2000: 213). The detailed specification of what best value is was deliberately avoided as Ministers expected that local government would oppose this (Martin, 2000: 214–15); obscurity once again emerges as a more powerful technique of governance. Rather, by introducing best value in the pilot schemes, the framework appeared to be encouraging change and improvement from the bottom up: a partnership networks programme, benchmarking clubs and central government support for the creation of the Improvement and Development Agency (IDeA) in conjunction with the local government associations, have all been aimed at creating new norms within the sector, with the impression at least that the pace for best value is being set at the local level.

However, as the Local Government Act 1999 makes apparent, this bottom-up approach is to be carried out in the shadow of the law. It is the Secretary of

State who sets the performance indicators by which best value is judged; internal auditing of authorities requires auditors to comply with nationally set standards; and regular inspection by the Audit Commission is aimed at ensuring that best value is being achieved. The regulatory pyramid is topped by the powers of the Secretary of State to take enforcement action and put in personnel to run failing authorities. At the top of the pyramid, there is a reward strategy, through the award of 'Beacon' status. Local authorities achieving exemplary performance can apply to be Beacon councils, giving them 'recognition for delivering an excellent service' (ODPM, 2003a: 8), and conferring a greater freedom from statutory controls (though this part of the scheme has still to be put into place; Leigh, 2004: 312).

Best value appears then to be working through the freedom of the regulated bodies, through the encouragement to share best practice, and the incentives to achieve excellent performance. Indeed, professionals working in both housing associations and local government have taken the concept of self-improvement a step further: the Chartered Institute of Housing and the National Housing Federation have joined to establish *Housemark*. Its aim, according to its website (http://www.housemark.co.uk), is to help organizations achieve efficiency and value for money; compare service costs and quality with peers; identify and adopt better service processes; prepare members for inspection, stock transfer or Arms Length Management Organisations; and reduce costs through collective procurement. It claims that its 'benchmarking methodology is the recognised industry standard', and provides an 'unrivalled gateway to housing information, guidance and practice to help you find solutions to improving performance' through a team of 'Knowledge Managers'.

Vincent-Jones (2001: 255) argues that best value is in fact a centralizing agenda, contributing to the 'responsibilization' of local government by realigning the organizational thinking and strategic orientation of local authorities with central policy objectives. Best value appears to undermine attempts by both local government and the housing association sector to govern to their own agendas. 'Housemark' could be seen as a radiating effect of governing at a distance, the internalization of the performance/knowledge agenda, an acknowledgement that the freedom to govern requires the joint development of new mechanisms of control across the sectors. In effect, a transformation has taken place in which central government, local government and housing associations have all taken part. The power to achieve change is 'not with those who "hold" power in principle, but [with] those who practically define or redefine what "holds" everyone together' (Latour, 1986: 273). While it might be tempting to conclude that it has been the auditors who have been the agents of this transformation, that answer would be too simplistic. Managers and politicians, as well as the standard setters and the checkers, have all been party to the practical process of transformation, which then becomes ordered into a new rationality rather late on in the day.

Competition (again)

Significantly, research into the impact of best value suggests that the regime has entrenched the role of *competition* in the delivery of public services. The regime requires that the 'four Cs' must be considered by organizations in the carrying out a best value review:

- *challenge* why and how a service is being provided
- *compare* the service with performance of others that are achieving
- *consult* with local taxpayers, service users and the wider business community on how the service can be improved; and
- Embrace fair *competition* as a means of securing efficient and effective services. (DETR, 1998: 9)

McAdam and Walker (2003: 192) argue that 'due to CCT and the thrust of "Challenge" and "Compete", the potential for externalisation has become synonymous with best value'. Higgins *et al* (2004: 254) conclude from their findings that:

> It cannot be easily argued that BV reviews are, in contrast to CCT, serving to accord a straightforwardly lower priority to the involvement of the private sector in the provision of services. In fact ... the frequency with which outsourcing was reported is not that much lower than the proportion of cases where it occurred in education catering, leisure management and vehicle maintenance as a result of CCT.

In the housing association sector, research by Mullins (2002: 26) indicates that 'formal competition through outsourcing, tendering or market testing was the least commonly embraced of the "four Cs" '. However, he argues that this must be placed in context – the sector is already the main external contractor for the state for social housing, *and* they are organizations in which competitiveness has already been firmly embedded in their operations (also see Walker, 1998). In effect, competition has become a new 'common sense' within the housing association sector to the extent that its existence is no longer 'special' or subject to resistance.

Regulating through risk management

Regulatory technologies have moved a long way from technical supervision and monitoring the minutiae that was the norm for local authorities in the 1960s and the Housing Corporation and DoE in the 1970s. In particular, the rationale of audit has brought into regulation a new sophistication – there are now tools available to measure many variables at once, to take a 'holistic' view of the operation of social housing organizations and to enable a variety of public interest concerns to be targeted and altered – a response perhaps, in part, to the failures of technical regulation as experienced by the GLC. Dean (1999: 168) memorably refers to a 'swarming of ... technologies of performance'. Such has audit changed our image of the environment that the creation of the Housing Inspectorate has been discussed in terms of a 'coming of age' of the housing profession (Chilton, 1998). According to Bob Chilton of the Audit Commission, the

> ... government was determined that performance be enhanced, not only to ensure the efficiency and effectiveness with which money is spent, but crucially to focus on the sometimes unacceptable circumstances in which some tenants survive. (ibid: 28)

Audit and inspection has, however, come in for considerable criticism. Mark Lupton (1998), of the Chartered Institute of Housing, echoing Paul Hoggett's (1996) 'centralised decentralisation' theme, raised concerns that the Inspectorate was part of an agenda of 'centralising' and the erosion of the power of local authorities, once again under the 'watchful eye of central government' (Hetherington, 2003). And the policy of naming and shaming failing councils has been seen to be counterproductive: 'authorities in difficulties do not need to be told that [they] are failing – they usually know already. They need to know, in concrete and practical terms, how to go about improving' (Warburton, 1998).

Despite the broad public interest rationales put forward for widespread performance monitoring, there is a sense in which all the sophisticated new tools could be said to be directed towards one principal aim – the minimization of possible catastrophic and embarrassing financial failure in the social housing sector. In this section we turn to the role of the 'new' technology of regulation, risk management, and the ways in which this technology is reshaping regulatory strategies towards the narrow concern of financial failure.

'Risk' has become an all-embracing rationale and set of technologies that appears to have taken over at all levels of individual and corporate life (Power, 2004), characterized by Beck's use of the term 'risk society' (1992). One explanation for the rise of risk is that it is just yet another fashion or fad promoted by the professionals and think-tanks who have a self-interest in promoting its prominence. But, argues Power:

> The fashion-based explanation [of risk management] is inadequate. Fads succeed because they are able to appeal to deep-seated fears, aspirations and values. So the risk-management of everything has a deeper basis of explanation as a continuation of control and accountability ambitions begun by the audit explosion. (Power, 2004: 40)

Indeed, as O'Malley (2004: 30) points out, risk consciousness and risk management are direct consequences of the shifts that have taken place in the delivery of public services under neo-liberalism:

> '[M]arkets' and 'enterprise' were to reconfigure governments, communities, corporations and individuals in the image of risk-taking and competition. Self-fulfilment would replace 'Victorian' self-denial, and sophisticated risk-management would replace or at least modify conservative prudence.

'Risk' works on fears, it legitimizes, appearing to be able to order and control fears; it 'organises what cannot be organised, because individuals, corporations and governments have little choice but to do so' (Power, 2004: 10). As social housing has become increasingly reliant on private funding from 1988 onwards, the monitoring and auditing by the government's regulator, the

Housing Corporation, has become increasingly focused on the risk of financial failure. Day *et al* (1993: 6) asked 'should the regulatory system safeguard the collective reputation or should it guarantee the credit-worthiness of individual associations?'. In setting out the main aims of regulation by the Housing Corporation – ensuring probity, economy, efficiency and effectiveness in the management of housing association affairs, a high standard of service and implementation of national policy aims – Day *et al* were tempted to add a further aim: 'providing reassurance to private lenders'. This concern for safeguarding both private as well as public investment led to a skewing of monitoring resources towards the largest and the developing associations (ibid: 36). The demands of the regulatory system were, at the same time, encouraging the growth of larger associations with the appropriate managerial capacities, and threatening the viability of 'the less orthodox associations which, although often difficult to regulate, fill in some of the gaps in housing provision left by the mainstream organisations' (p 38).

Risk management became *the* means for ordering regulatory strategies, and at the same time the regulatory system internalized the needs of private lenders – in effect the 'capture' of the regulatory system not just by the regulatees but critically, by the external, private interests (Mullins, 1997). The tendency to focus on financial risk to weed out the unorthodox is demonstrated in a highly unusual case of judicial review of the activities of the Housing Corporation, *R (on the application of Clays Lane Housing Co-operative Limited) v The Housing Corporation* [2004] EWHC 1084 (Admin), CO/4578/2003. The case arose after a statutory inquiry by the Corporation into the affairs of Clays Lane HC (a housing co-operative based in the London Borough of Newham) found mismanagement of the Co-operative's affairs, complete lack of effectiveness in the work of the management committee, a lack of proper financial controls and a lack of proper day-to-day management and governance (para 4). The Corporation proposed to use its powers to direct the transfer of the co-operative's properties, not to another co-operative but to the Peabody Trust, a large, established charitable housing trust. But tenants of Peabody, while enjoying a higher degree of security of tenure in law, did not have the co-operative working practices of a direct relationship with the day-to-day running and direction of the organization by the occupiers. In order to protect their co-operative status, Clays Lane proposed a voluntary transfer of assets to Tenants First Housing Co-operative, registered as a social landlord in Scotland and regulated by Communities Scotland (the Scottish equivalent of the Housing Corporation). Tenants First was the largest fully mutual co-operative housing association in the United Kingdom. Despite the seeming compatibility of organizational values, the Housing Corporation's board rejected a transfer to Tenants First on the grounds that:

(a) Public funding would be more at risk in such a transfer because of the 'relative financial strengths' of Tenants First and Peabody,

(b) Peabody would be more likely than Tenants First to attract new public funding,

(c) tenants would have greater security as assured tenants of Peabody than as contractual tenants of a fully mutual co-operative (such as Tenants First) (para 13), and

(d) both the Corporation and Communities Scotland were concerned about creating 'a complex governance framework' and the impact on 'control, policy, planning, risk management' of cross-border regulation (para 14).

While the importance of the security provided to tenants by the assured tenancy regime should not be underestimated (see Carr *et al* (2001)), one cannot help but echo Day *et al*'s concern that unorthodox social landlords cannot survive under a regulatory regime dominated by concerns for financial security. This is despite the fact that it became public knowledge during the course of negotiations over the transfer that the Peabody Trust too was facing financial difficulties due to the need to bring its aging stock up to the 'decent homes standard' (Evans, 2004d). Despite apparent encouragement for entrepreneurial, not bureaucratic solutions, it appears that bureaucratic regulatory concerns about complexity have been allowed to prevail over normative concerns to retain the co-operative nature of some social housing. One conclusion might be that the regulators' desire to minimize their own risk was an overriding factor. Criteria of risk minimization becomes as much a shaping factor for regulatory strategies as performance indicators.

Corporate governance, risk and market

The creation of markets and quasi-markets, together with the ever-increasing reliance on private markets to fund new social housing (and the backlog of repairs to the existing stock), has created an environment in which the independent, entrepreneurial organization is now the primary unit for advancing policy programmes. The consequent perception of an increase in risk had to be matched with mechanisms that recognized the independence of these units, and which governed through the freedom of these organizations. The internalization of risk management, through mechanisms of internal control, has been the primary means of providing both public and private reassurance – the translations of risk into internal controls have been the 'necessary conditions of possibility for risk-based regulation' (Power, 2004: 24).

In the financial services sector, the Cadbury Code on Corporate Governance (1992) reconfigured the idea of corporate control from control by external markets to a matter of internal organizational structure and design (Power, 2004: 25). In 1994, the housing association sector too became focused on internal governance, partly as a response to the increased perception of risk faced by the sector arising from a system of mixed public–private funding (see Ashby, 1997). The sector also perceived there to be an increasingly unfavourable external representation of housing associations, combined with a general concern (among MPs and others) about the corporate governance and accountability of these organizations which had a significant impact on the 'public' domain (Malpass, 2000: 257). The NFHA established an 'independent inquiry comprising respected professionals from a range of disciplines' to 'overhaul the governance of the [housing association] sector' (NFHA 1995/6). It was chaired by an Executive Director of Hambros Bank who had previously held the post of Permanent Secretary at the Department of Education and Science. That choice was significant given the transformation of a significant proportion of the sector from voluntary organizations to private businesses. However, voices of concern were expressed during the Inquiry process that, for example, comparisons with the Cadbury Inquiry were 'not ... appropriate' because associations were not commercial organizations (evidence of the London Voluntary Committee Members Working Group; NFHA, 1995b).

Even so, that the sector had absorbed the language of markets and competition was clearly evident in the resultant report. The report's conclusion was that housing associations should be 'competent, accountable, independent and diverse ... building homes that work for a competitive price ... enjoying the confidence of tenants ... staying solvent ... discharging financial, statutory and regulatory obligations'. Independence, in the Inquiry's terms, meant being independent of party politics, pressure groups and Ministers (NFHA, 1995a: 5). The Institute of Housing criticized the report for being weak on the issue of accountability to tenants (Kearns, 1997: 63). Malpass (2000: 259) described it as 'rather bland', failing to take a decisive stand on the 'really big issues', and suggested that 'its main purpose was to demonstrate to government and financial institutions that the movement was taking seriously the need to strengthen its governance arrangements'.

In producing a 'Code of Governance' the Federation borrowed a mechanism of self-regulation from the financial services industry. Like the financial services industry it sought to avoid further statutory controls, 'preempting a review of housing associations by the Nolan Committee' (NFHA, 1995a: 9), a strategy that appears to have been largely successful as the Nolan Committee (1996) 'overwhelmingly endorsed the code's principles' (ibid).

The Housing Corporation's regulatory mechanisms have adopted the strategy of transferring responsibility for meeting regulatory requirements onto the governing bodies – or boards – of housing associations. The 'streamlining' of the regulatory system required associations to 'take primary responsibility for monitoring compliance with the [Regulatory] Code', requiring the association's board to give an annual statement of compliance (Housing Corporation, 2002: para 3.2). That focus on internal mechanisms of governance elevates 'the internal control function from its lowly historical position to the top of a risk management process ... responding to crisis by creating new risk accountability structures supporting chains of public and private reassurance ... the risk management of everything seems little different in principle from the audit explosion' (Power, 2004: 26–7). And like audit, risk management too has the potential to shape organizations in the liking of those who are most able to articulate their risk concerns. The first responsibility of all housing association boards is to the financial viability of the organization. Reading the Corporation's Regulatory Code one is reminded of Mullins phrase 'public probity, private comfort' (1997: 470) – a board's first duty is to ensure that the association operates as a viable business, 'with adequate recourse to financial resources to meet ... current and future business and financial commitments' and fulfil 'loan-agreement covenants' (Housing Corporation, 2002: para 1.1). The responsibilization of the board, coupled with an ever-increasing focus on the risk of private lending, is leading to greater professionalization of boards and the potential marginalization of other voices – such as tenants.

Regulation by private agents

The discussion above has focused on the role of private funders in shaping regulatory processes. Perhaps unsurprisingly, this 'privatisation' of regulation has been extended beyond the capture of the state regulator – private regulators are also directly seeking to regulate the housing association sphere. Statutory powers of regulation are to be 'contracted out' to the private regulators because of their (alleged) expertise that is not possessed by the state regulator.

Colin Scott has already noted 'the emergence of private regulatory power' in controlling what we would classify as public activities (2002: 73). In the RSL sector the exercise of this private power is most clearly seen in the influence of the private lending sector, through their use of the credit ratings agencies to provide a measure of financial strength of an organization in terms that are intelligible to them (see for example, Baron, 1996; Kerwer, 2002). These agencies do more than simply provide a statement of financial health. In order to maintain a 'triple A' rating, an association must provide regular monitoring reports of rental income, void levels and spending on maintenance to show that they are keeping their stock to a standard acceptable to the lenders and ensuring a steady income stream – operating what Scott (2002: 58) terms autonomous 'complete' regimes of regulation. Their role is increasingly to 'govern at a distance', as housing associations internalize the understandings and rationales of 'credit-worthiness' developed by these agencies. For example, on the basis of advice from ratings agencies, housing associations previously based solely in low value areas such as Liverpool have become regional, even trans-regional players (McDermont, 2005: ch 6) – a decision that has a significant impact on such matters as management policies and tenant participation. Financial interests structure the freedom of action of associations.

Private regulatory power is also likely to be the Housing Corporation's chosen route for controlling the controversial social housing grant to developers contained in the Housing Act 2004. Having admitted that it needed to sharpen its financial expertise in order to match the more 'innovative' financing routes adopted by associations (Evans, 2004a), the Corporation announced that it was planning to 'outsource' the accreditation of management of the homes that will be built by those developers (Evans, 2004b).

Conclusion

In this chapter we have shown how ways of thinking about, and acting upon, the regulation of housing providers is intimately linked to the identity of those who are concerned about regulation – to their professional knowledges, as well as the tools with which they work. So at times when professional interest in control came from medical officers, surveyors and those concerned with the minutiae of funding rules, regulation was the detailed supervision of these tasks – large-scale mapping of only a limited area of the terrain. However, with the increased importance of private – often global – capital in housing provision, new regulatory tools have become available, and so too have new ways of thinking. It is both the tools and the rationalities of NPM – the creation of quasi-markets, performance monitoring and risk management – that have significantly shaped the social housing sector through a mix of direct, mid-way and governing at a distance. State policy-makers and housing providers appear to be internalizing the demands and normative values of this transformed perspective – to the degree that resistance appears to be dissipated. Government believes the present system to be working, but needs improving. Interestingly, it is the Treasury and ODPM that has raised the concern that regulation has a 'greater focus on accountability to central government rather than to local people' (ODPM/HM Treasury, 2005: para 1.12). But as the case of Clays Lane Housing Co-op demonstrates, it is the norms of the regulation system, promoted by the ODPM and Treasury themselves, that leads to regulatory decisions that prioritize the minimizing of financial and bureaucratic risk at the expense of issues of the social.

However, the discussions in this and the previous chapter point to a concern that the system allows one particular set of norms – those of the private lenders – to dominate. This points to the central thrust of our thesis in this chapter – the 'meaning' that becomes attached to regulation, and the types of technologies employed, depends on who is asking the questions. If it is the technocrats – medical officers, architects or surveyors – they will look for the minute detail; if it is the 'programmers' (in the sense used by Rose and Miller) then what they would want are the overview and the technologies of accountants, auditors and risk managers. This operates as an extension of Michael Power's argument that the perspective of auditors shapes the organizations they audit.

Chapter 6:
The 'Social' Contract

In this chapter, we consider three ways in which occupiers of social housing are treated differently from those in the private sector through the particular medium of the contract. Despite its late appearance in this sector, contract law is now routinely used in a variety of ways as it offers a particularly potent incitement to self-government both through the self and by reference to the other. As Collins (1999: 20) offers, the contractual metaphor is used to create 'both a new legitimacy for government based upon its respect for the individual, and new type of bureaucratic control that appears a much tougher instrument for the purpose of disciplining and punishing errant citizens'. And, contract ties in to prevailing notions of the individual's responsibility; but here responsibility has a social 'feel' because contract is being used to generate community responsibility in rather different ways. Contract offers a way to responsibilize occupiers. Thus, although we are talking in part of this chapter about enforceable contracts, enforceability is not our primary concern. The three ways considered in this chapter are, first, contracting for enterprise; second, contracting for behaviour; and third, contracting for debt. In each of these, our research question is really rather simple: why treat social housing differently?

Underpinning each of our foci is a different vision of the relationship between landlord and occupier, as well as a vision of the role of manager and occupier. As Flint (2004b: 169) suggests, this 'realignment of governance is complex and at times contradictory'. Undoubtedly, they have been made possible by the entrepreneurialization of housing management, and the shift to market-based understandings of public management. At the same time, the discourses of social exclusion combined with understandings of the 'underclass' are being worked upon in different ways in each part of the discussion (Haworth and Manzi, 1999). At heart, the underpinning problematization is about stigma and unpopularity of social housing compared to other tenures, and the need to remoralize its population. The resort to market understandings, as with the allocation of social housing, is understood as *the* way of resolving these issues.

Contracting for enterprise

In this section, we consider the roles implied by the participation of social tenants in the management of their housing. Tenant participation has a long, somewhat inglorious history – for example, Octavia Hill used it as a management technique and there are also stories of resistance to the process (such as in an episode of the comedy *Only Fools and Horses*). For example, the co-operative housing movement employed the technique as did many Registered Social Landlords (RSLs) in the early twentieth century. Its use in the 1980s by the Thatcher governments was, in part, designed to highlight the inadequacies of municipal landlordism – it being assumed that, if tenants were given a say about their housing management (except about their rent levels), they would use it as a means of voicing their opposition to it – and as a means of responsibilizing and entrepreneurializing tenants so as to engage the '... independence and self-motivation of communities'. (DoE, 1987: para 1.10). Cairncross *et al* (1997), however, noted that tenants could view housing managers' use of participation as a cynical exercise (p 121) and managers viewed the tenants who engaged in the process as self-interested (p 73). McCulloch (1997) also noted how tenants negatively viewed those others who did engage in participation, as well as how gender became an issue in the process.

At heart, the epistemological claims made for tenant participation are significant and challenging. The argument is that tenants themselves – and, in some arguments, *only* the tenants – have sufficient expertise to manage their properties because they know about their experience/s. Tenant participation in housing management offers the opportunity to harness this knowledge for the good of the community through their active involvement. The process constructs the tenant as an entrepreneur, who can envision new and better methods of managing whole estates. It is a trite observation within the academic literature that there is no core understanding of tenant participation (for example, Goodlad, 2001: 190–1), but this misses the point in a way – that entrepreneurialism in this context is organic, and requires localized development. Expertise has no core.

Expertise can also be harnessed in diverse ways – through 'tenant management organisations', 'tenant participation compacts', 'tenant fora' – each of which play with the role and relations of the tenant occupier, and each of which owes its genesis to different visions of the social. One example of this capillary of tenant participation is the role of tenants as members of RSL boards of governance. In itself, this initiative had a number of different underlying rationales. First, it operated as a response to concerns about the accountability of the voluntary sector which emerged in the 1980s and 1990s as RSLs began to gain ground in the provision of housing. These concerns were voiced in various high-profile, official publications at around that time concerning 'governance' – from the Nolan Inquiry (1996) to the Cadbury Report (1992) to the sector-specific Governance Inquiry Panel (NFHA, 1995a). Second, there was the expectation that one-third of the membership of large-scale voluntary transfer (LSVT) landlord boards should be tenants (in part as a sop to the concerns of tenants that they were being 'sold out' by their landlords). However, the central rationale is that which underlies all approaches to tenant participation – tenants know best. There is, nevertheless, an empirical question underlying this observation, which is how the tenant board member understands their own position as tenant and, as Davina Cooper (1998) puts it, concepts of 'public principles'. Once enrolled as a decision-maker within the board structure, there will be diverse forces operating on them particularly through education and training programmes discussed below. One particular force is the shift to marketization and professionalization of boards of governance themselves – a quite marked shift in RSLs from the 'old boy network' which used to operate (see Cowan, 1999: ch 4) – which leads to concerns about divisions within expertise itself, and about the role of non-professional expertise.

Tenant participation works in tandem with the current vogue, offered voice by a certain academic audience (see, for example, Coleman, 1986; Power, 1987), to retraditionalize housing management through a return to small-scale units instead of large bureaucracies. The assumption is that management closer to the occupiers, in which the occupiers can engage, is better management. The product of this closer engagement between the tenant and their neighbourhood is a more 'sustainable community' which simultaneously is supposed to tip estates into becoming more popular and better places to live in. Despite this strong lobby, it is based upon the presentation of 'artificial dichotomies' – assumptions that 'big is bad, small is good' (see Murie, 1997a: 453). Further, a 'focus upon housing management at an estate level does not address the underlying factors leading to the concentration of deprived households on estates and contributing to the downward spiral within these estates' (Murie, 1997b: 33).

Why then does tenant participation occupy such a prominent role in the imagination of social housing today? We would not wish to argue that tenants' groups are sector selective – private sector housing offers a variety of different residents' associations and organizations. Yet, there is something distinctive about the council/RSL sector because what is being required, or envisioned, is a particular type of involvement in housing management itself. And the subject of this, the 'tenant', is an important device because it demonstrates a kind of empowerment of the disempowered. The use of the word tenant is not neutral but implies a juxtaposition within the landlord–tenant, power–powerless, dyad.

We suggest that there are a number of reasons for this sector-specific approach, which are not altogether consistent nor coherent, but which are powerful. First, the increasing entrepreneurialization of housing management as a result of the processes of compulsory competitive tendering (CCT) and best value required a new vision of the managed. The vision of the managed on which that entrepreneurialization seems to hinge is of a simultaneous entrepreneurialization of the occupier. If one follows this line, then it is no surprise that when New Labour first touted its best value techniques, it tied them into its 'Tenant Participation Compacts'. The shift from the pre-1980s view of occupiers as 'passive recipients of landlord bounty' (Gilroy, 1998) to active managers can then be seen in the context of the new managerialist imperatives. More than this, tenants have active roles in developing managerialism and holding it to account:

> Tenants have shown they can have an important role in monitoring and setting housing service standards and targets and, where they want to, take on direct management responsibilities. The growing emphasis on consumer accountability and statutory tenant consultation has ensured that landlords routinely provide information to tenants and seek feedback on services, and that tenants and landlords regularly share information and ideas. In many cases, tenants influence and share decision-making with their landlord. (DETR, 1999a: para 1.2)

> A true measure of quality will only be achieved if tenants and residents are consulted effectively about housing services. The direction of future service changes and improvements will also have a clearer focus and increased validity if they reflect tenants' and residents' needs and aspirations. (DETR, 1999b: para 3.8)

Although some policy publications accept that some tenants will not wish to participate (see Riseborough, 1998, for such a study), or at different levels, it is clear from this that they need to participate to make the accountability of providers and the delivery of services possible. The system is premised on activity. There is no legal requirement for such activity – indeed, legislative requirements remain distinctly underwhelming – but, as John Flint (2004a: 904) observes, 'such a development [ie tenant participation] is not divorced from ethical assessments of individual behaviour'. The use of contract (or, 'compact' in New Labour terminology) here is as a device to engage and legitimate the role of tenants, and offers a vision of that role which matches the shift in understanding of housing management under CCT and best value.

Second, although the rhetoric is of power-transfer, of involving tenants, harnessing their strengths, the reality is often one of controlling their freedom. This can be sensed from the discussion of the inculcation of tenants into housing management versions of truth through education and training (Furbey *et al*, 1996). Equally, evaluations of tenant participation have demonstrated the way in which tenants are controlled through the process, or have no interest in it anyway. Thus, Helen Carr and colleagues' evaluation (2001: 172) of Holly Street argued that:

> ... [it] was a top-down approach, imposed by the council and modelled on the council's own bureaucracy. It was established for pragmatic purposes rather than to change the power structures or challenge the entrenched inequalities experienced by the Holly Street tenants.

They contrast tenant participation with the right to buy to draw an illuminating conclusion about the collective/individualist balance: 'tenant participation as a method of empowering tenants cannot be separated from the contemporaneous reduction in political, economic and legal accountability' (p 174). It would be fair to say that these findings are known and reflected in policy publications – indeed, they were partly the background to the TPC programme itself.

Third, tenant participation was linked into the various reports by the Social Exclusion Unit's Policy Action Teams. These seemed to accept the importance of tenant participation as a process of actively engaging the marginalized in the regeneration of their estates. The report on housing management, for example, uncritically accepted the need for tenant participation:

> Social landlords must promote the best possible working relationship with their tenants if they are to turn around deprived estates. (PAT 5, 1999: para 13; see also PAT 7, 1999)

Tenant participation, therefore, links into the psyche of solutions to unpopularity, of turning around estates, and dealing with the social exclusion of the residents. It offers a way out and a strategy for inclusion through active involvement in community (DETR, 1999c). Thus, as Flint (2004b: 156) observes, tenant participation hooks in to the notion of 'stakeholding, in which the perceived arbitrary, temporary and anonymous nature of social housing provision is transformed through creating individualised times of incentives and responsibility between tenants, their homes and their communities'.

Fourth, by the 1990s, there was already a well-defined, state-funded organization and role for expertise in relation to tenant participation. The Tenant Participation Advisory Service, the National Tenants Resource Centre, and the Priority Estates Project offer expert advice and training packages; and the National Housing Federation offers support for tenants who become members of their (RSL) landlord's voluntary committee.

The role of training, mentoring and other strategies adopted by RSLs in turning someone into a board member is to shape these understandings into its own fashion. And one of the difficulties for tenant board members is that there is no counterweight to this official view of the role of board members. This is combined with the formal division between tenant as occupier and governor as manager, each holding very different interests. Some training approaches, for example, that offered by the Priority Estates Project, provide a positive account of the role of tenant board members, but do not account for the role of tenants as representatives of other tenants. They provide neutral guidance, without taking account of the difference between tenant board members and others (professional persons and local authority nominees) who are often more experienced in committee work and bureaucratic structures.

Furbey et al's (1996) study of tenant participation training is important here. Central funding to tenant training organizations seeks to work on the active entrepreneurial role of tenants. They note (p 259) that the training is devised 'to increase the choices for the "citizen-as-consumer" and to encourage the qualities of initiative, independence, autonomy and risk-taking characteristic of the "enterprise culture" '. It is 'informed by notions of "dependence" and "enterprise" and finances the entry of consumer-citizens into a limited marketplace of options' (ibid: 262).

Contracting behaviour

In this section, we concentrate on the way in which contract has been used more formally as a device to control individual occupier's behaviour and those of third party visitors. The focus is on the issue of anti-social behaviour (ASB), which is currently the motor behind most debates about social housing in

England. Ultimately, practically all the innovative managerial techniques discussed in this book have involved rooting out ASB as one of their primary objectives. This leads on to our research question: why is it that, in responding to 'ASB', most effort and attention has been given over to social housing? Is it that social housing is inherently criminogenic? Although ASB is now discussed tenure neutrally, if it is related to tenure at all, most of the interventions in the early 1990s were targeted on social housing. Even after the introduction of tenure neutral interventions, such as the ASB order in the Crime and Disorder Act 1998, the evidence is that they are used primarily against social housing occupants, or for commercial purposes (Campbell, 2002; Coleman *et al*, 2002; Nixon *et al*, 2003). An important part of the discourse of ASB, though, is that it is also mobilized to *protect* social housing occupiers from problematic behaviour, and proactive policing is something which occupiers request.

Although ASB may be utterly shallow, the space in which it exists is also one in which the circles of control have become much closer together. This is, we suspect, partly because of the ragbag of ideologies, understandings and concepts which have invested power upon the term. In particular, the space of ASB has been shaped by understandings about risk which, in turn, have related ASB to housing tenure; specifically social housing. That location of ASB has also been shaped, we suggest, by two further factors. First, historically, ASB taps into a series of ethical values about poverty and pauperization which have existed in this tenure since the heyday of private philanthropy and the development of the charitable instinct in housing (Cowan and Marsh, 2005). Second, and related to this point, social housing is fundamentally *managed* housing and thus provides the conditions through which the control of the marginal becomes possible. We suggest that a combination of rather diverse, unconnected disciplinary and governance techniques, combined with a synoptic focus on the management of the poor and marginalized, have provided the architecture for these strategies of control.

Management implies a certain set of power/knowledge relations, more so when we now talk of the imported concept of 'zero tolerance' housing management (see, for example, the commentary on schemes in New York and Middlesbrough in Johnston and Shearing, 2003: ch 6). Although our attention is taken by the more coercive, disciplinary schemes prescribed by law, management implies a set of techniques which operate at a different level, but which are also underpinned in this context by reference to legal obligation (see Crawford, 2003: 488).

Our analysis is split into the following sections – first, we discuss the potency of the ASB label; second, we draw attention to some of the ways in which social housing has been used as a form of social and moral control; and third, we discuss the association between entrepreneurialism and ASB.

Labelling

The Government is placing increasingly high emphasis on the level of [ASB] and methods to tackle it through the formation of the Home Office Anti-Social Behaviour Unit, publication of the White Paper, Respect and Responsibility – Taking a stand against Anti-Social Behaviour, and the Anti-Social Behaviour Act (2003). The Home Office's Research, Development and Statistics Directorate (RDS) is now developing a programme of research on ASB to fill important knowledge gaps.

(Home Office web site accessed 29/04/04, www.homeoffice.gov.uk/rds/antisocial1.html)

It is a rather glib observation to say that, despite all of the attention given over to it, there is no definition yet of ASB (Papps, 1998; Scott and Parkey, 1998). The government's Social Exclusion Unit argued that there could be no single definition as it covers such a 'wide range of behaviour from litter to serious harassment' (PAT 8, 2000: 14). As Hunter (2001: 223) has pointed out, 'problems of definition clearly lead to problems of solution; if the nature of the problem has not been defined then defining a solution seems impossible'. At the heart of the discourse about ASB lies a paradox – we don't know what it is, although it is sometimes said in response, we all know it when we see or experience it. This paradox is about knowledge and measurement. As Whitehead et al (2003: 6) have noted in a report to the Home Office, 'measurement of ASB is difficult because it is not clear what should be measured' and it is also problematic because the range of behaviours falling within any particular definition are covered by a wide range of agencies operating under different definitions.

This seems an important gap in our knowledge and, in one sense, a kind of break in the relationship between power and (statistical) knowledge. There has been an assertion of sovereign power on the basis of apparently no evidence – beyond 'what everyone knows'. It is perhaps not surprising then that, using what can only be described as questionable statistical techniques,[1] the Home Office produced an audit of ASB through a 'one day count of incidences. It discovered that 66,107 reports were made to participating agencies:

This equates to more than one report every 2 seconds or around 16.5 million reports every year. Anti-social behaviour recorded on the day of the count cost agencies in England and Wales at least £13.5m; this equates to around £3.4bn a year. (Home Office, 2003a)

This problem of knowledge provides an opportunity to observe a certain mentality of government, borrowing Valverde's discussion of 'knowledge formats' (2003a; 2003b). There are two objects of interest – the lengthy lists of what constitutes ASB, and the appeal to common sense.

First, the sometimes lengthy lists in various government, and government-funded, publications concerning ASB are important techniques in highlighting the core concerns about low level deviance. What is remarkable is the range of behaviours regarded in these documents as 'anti-social', and placed in such lists. In Table 6.1 below, we juxtapose three such lists from respectively, the Social Exclusion Unit's report on ASB (PAT8, 2000: para 1.4), the Home Office White Paper on ASB (2003b: para 1.6), and the Home Office's own one day count of ASB on 10 September 2003.

The range of behaviours placed together in each column seem random, with little replication at the margins. The Home Office and one day count lists

Table 6.1 Lists of anti-social behaviour

Social exclusion unit	Home Office White Paper	One day count
Noise	Harassment and intimidating behaviour	Litter/rubbish
Conflicts, including harassment, domestic violence and racist incidents	Behaviour that creates alarm or fear	Criminal damage/vandalism
	Noisy neighbours	Vehicle related nuisance
Litter and rubbish dumping	Drunken and abusive behaviour	Nuisance behaviour
Graffiti and vandalism	Vandalism, graffiti and other deliberate damage to property	Intimidation/harassment
Uncontrolled pets		Noise
Using and selling drugs	Dumping rubbish or litter	Rowdy behaviour
Nuisance from vehicles, including parking and abandonment		Abandoned vehicles
		Street drinking and begging
Unkempt gardens		Drug/substance misuse and drug dealing
		Animal related problems
		Hoax calls
		Prostitution, kerb-crawling, sexual acts

do not include behaviours which have been regarded as anti-social in some documents (such as racism, domestic violence or homophobic attacks – PAT 8, 2000: paras 1.11–1.19) but include low-level incidents (litter, unkempt gardens, rubbish). Nevertheless, the use of such lists is somehow persuasive. As Valverde (2003a: 162) argues:

> ... it is a police powers, commonsense argument that persuades readers by listing a variety of objects that have a certain family resemblance to one another and that combine to form a general impression of disorder, without any quantitative or theoretical proof being given of these connections.

These lists also have an important quantification function. It is not for want of trying that government was unable to quantify ASB until the 'dodgy' one day count. Attempts were made to do so (for example, PAT 8, 2000: paras 1.8–1.10), but it was the translation of the list into hard cash which talks to us, and which becomes the headline figure. We now know that ASB costs £3.4bn per annum. Carr and Cowan (forthcoming) demonstrate how this simple quantification is translated into everyday life through reference to one of the multitude of different posters and street information which enjoin us in the process of ASB/crime control through education:

> However part of the power of the discourse of ASB is the coincidence of vernacular and technical language. Often professional language is used to defeat common sense, and

local and particular knowledge. Here, in a vivid and direct manner, the poster fuses professional and common sense understandings of a social 'problem'. The poster thus exemplifies the circularity of the discourse of anti-social behaviour and the way in which that discourse both constructs the problem of the anti-social and the solution. For the poster is in Bakhtin's terms dialogic. It simultaneously constructs *us* – the social – and the '*other*' – the anti-social.

The second point is about the creation of problem spaces: the importance of 'common-sense knowledge of specific, untheorized problem places and things' (Valverde, 2003b: 248).

> [I]n a world in which there has been a huge explosion of technical knowledges that render risks 'calculable', there are still spaces ... in which other knowledges manage to govern without much contestation. (ibid)

The link between common sense and space is both powerful and important in our analysis. What has been interesting is the ever-expanding circles of tenure which the state tells us is affected by ASB. In 1995, the Conservative government issued a rushed Consultation Paper entitled 'Anti-social behaviour on *council estates*'. That document began with the assertion:

> Anti-social behaviour by a small minority of tenants and others is a growing problem on council estates. Every tenant has a right to quiet enjoyment of their home. ... Whole estates can be stigmatised by the anti-social behaviour of a few.

That stigmatization, however, is clearly reflected in the then government's proposed solution – 'probationary tenancies': 'even the colloquial name itself, coined by the government, suggested that these tenancies were part of the system of crime control' (Cowan, 1999: 490).

The debate was subsequently broadened to include housing associations (Housing Corporation, 1997), and, more recently, broadened again to include parts of the private rented sector (DETR, 2000) and owner-occupied sector (Home Office, 2003b). One reason for these circles may relate to the influence central government has on each particular tenure – it explicitly exercises oversight on local housing authority accommodation, implicitly over housing association accommodation, has certain levers over parts of the private rented sector but little influence over the owner-occupied.

However, a more persuasive analysis is provided by John Flint (2004a), who argues that the normalization of home ownership in the United Kingdom creates a presumption that the social sector is occupied by the other, the 'marginalised "flawed consumers" '. To précis the discussion in Chapter 8 below, the normalization of owner-occupation in English life exercises a particular disciplinary hold on policy-makers and population (Gurney, 1999a). As Murie (1997a: 27) suggests, there has been a 'clear sorting of the population into different tenures much more closely related to their affluence and employment'. Thus, hopes of social housing providing sites of social inclusion have given way to the realization that the occupants of social housing are economically marginalized and that the stock has become residualized (see Forrest and Murie, 1991: 65–85). Broadly, social housing provides safety-net accommodation for those in the poorest income groups and has done so for some considerable time (Murie, 1997b). In particular, the role of social housing is partly as provider to those deinstitutionalized persons, single mothers, asylum seekers, and others whom society considers to be dangerous either to morals, public funds or the body.

Social housing, in this sense, is also reproductive – as Murray (1990) argued in his essay on the UK underclass, describing such persons as 'the new rabble', there is no way out for such persons. It is this division from the norm which justifies a racism and a killing, in the sense in which Foucault used those terms. A focus on ASB in social housing is part of a process inherent in the normalization of owner-occupation; social housing occupiers offer a threat to owners. And, 'the death of the other, the death of the bad race, of the inferior race (or the degenerate, or the abnormal) is something that will make life in general healthier: healthier and purer' (Foucault, 2003: 255).

Legislative responses

Over the past ten (or so) years, there have been a number of quite dramatic responses to the problem of ASB at the level of sovereign state. A key force in this process was the formation of a local authority pressure group – the Social Landlords Crime and Nuisance Group – which has had a similar impact on the centre of government as other (blue-coated) police pressure groups. Yet, these legislative responses to crime control have, however, also provided important structures for the devolution of crime control in two ways.

First, these approaches have sought to 'join up' the local approach to crime control, implying the 'collective deliver[y of] their services from coterminous locations developing common practices of information collection, collation, processing, management, and exchange in the process of so doing' (Johnston and Shearing, 2003: 108). So, for example, although much is (rightly) made of the ASB orders contained in s 1 of the Crime and Disorder Act 1998, s 5 also required a multi-agency 'crime and disorder plan' to be promoted and published. Section 17 requires local authorities to exercise their powers and duties with reference to crime and disorder:

> Without prejudice to any other obligation imposed on it, it shall be the duty of each authority to which this section applies to exercise its various functions with due regard to the likely effect of the exercise of those functions on, and the need to do all that it reasonably can to prevent, crime and disorder in its area.

Second, they also work through the regulatory and self-regulatory capacities of the individual. Although the recent history of legislative intervention has been to increase the powers of landlords, these presuppose and work on the role of the tenant. As with all these powers, it is not their use but their appearance and translation into everyday life which has power. Their form is both legislative and contractual – they are additions or alterations to the landlord–tenant contract. Social housing providers can now grant introductory (or probationary) tenancies up to 12 months; they can take out injunctions against *anyone* where two conditions are satisfied:

(3) The first condition is that the person against whom the injunction is sought is engaging, has engaged or threatens to engage in conduct [which is capable of causing nuisance or annoyance to any person, and which directly or indirectly relates to or affects the housing management functions of a relevant landlord].

(4) The second condition is that the conduct is capable of causing nuisance or annoyance to any of the following –

(a) a person with a right (of whatever description) to reside in or occupy housing accommodation owned or managed by the relevant landlord;

(b) a person with a right (of whatever description) to reside in or occupy other housing accommodation in the neighbourhood of housing accommodation mentioned in paragraph (a);

(c) a person engaged in lawful activity in or in the neighbourhood of housing accommodation mentioned in paragraph (a);

(d) a person employed (whether or not by the relevant landlord) in connection with the exercise of the relevant landlord's housing management functions.

This wording from s 13, Anti-Social Behaviour Act 2003 (which was designed to solve the technical problems of earlier similar powers in the Housing Act 1996), means that anyone can be the subject of such an injunction when their conduct *is capable of* causing nuisance or annoyance to any person as well as indirectly affecting housing management.

Then, there are expanded grounds of evicting a household on the basis of anti-social behaviour. Under s 144 of the Housing Act 1996, new eviction powers were given on this basis, where:

The tenant or a person residing in or visiting the dwelling-house –

(a) has been guilty of conduct causing or likely to cause a nuisance or annoyance to a person residing, visiting or otherwise engaging in a lawful activity in the locality, or

(b) has been convicted of

(i) using the dwelling-house or allowing it to be used for immoral or illegal purposes, or

(ii) an arrestable offence committed in, or in the locality of, the dwelling house

In *Kensington RLBC v Simmonds* (1996) 29 HLR 507, it was made clear that the tenant him/herself does not have to be personally responsible for the actions of the perpetrator. Merely allowing it to happen is sufficient. As Hunter and Nixon point out, these powers have been particularly used in dealing with non-conforming households, such as single parents: 'The language used by judges to describe single mothers reflects a view of single parents, which suggests that in the absence of a husband, they are "inadequate parents" ' (2001: 404).

Eviction is only possible where it would also be 'reasonable' to evict. Concerns over the failure of judges to give effect to this newly expanded ground of eviction lead to Parliament seeking to structure the court's discretion. So, in the Anti-Social Behaviour Act 2003, it was said that in any action under this ground for possession:

The court must consider, in particular –

(a) the effect that the nuisance or annoyance has had on persons other than the person against whom the order is sought;

(b)   any continuing effect the nuisance or annoyance is likely to have on such persons;

(c)   the effect that the nuisance or annoyance would be likely to have on such persons if the conduct is repeated.

Although the occupier must be a social housing tenant, it should be noted that the range of persons covered here is, essentially, any person other than that tenant. Yet, in the *Simmonds* case, the courts had pretty much already reached this position. The Court of Appeal indicated a balance in such cases (p 511):

> As to the justice of the position, it must be remembered that not only are the interests of the tenant and her family here at stake; so too are the interests of their neighbours. It would in my judgment be quite intolerable if they were to be held necessarily deprived of all possibility of relief in these cases, merely because some ineffectual tenant next door was incapable of controlling his or her household.

Judicial ventriloquism

In interpreting these new powers, what has been interesting has been the epistemological basis of judicial knowledge. For example, in *Manchester City Council v Lee* [2004] HLR 11 161, 170, Pill L.J. observed that 'The court is conscious of the social problems which exist on many housing estates and that Parliament has intended in the 1996 Act and elsewhere to increase the power of local authorities to deal with them'. And in *Clingham v Kensington and Chelsea RLBC* [2003] HLR 17, in which the implementation of an ASB order was challenged as being contrary to the Human Rights Act 1998, Lord Steyn described what he termed 'the social problem':

> It is well known that in some urban areas, notably urban housing estates and deprived inner city areas, young persons, and groups of young persons, cause fear, distress and misery to law-abiding and innocent people by outrageous anti-social behaviour. It takes many forms. It includes behaviour which is criminal such as assaults and threats, particularly against old people and children, criminal damage to individual property and amenities of the community, burglary, theft, and so forth. Sometimes the conduct falls short of cognisable criminal offences. The culprits are mostly, but not exclusively, male. Usually they are relatively young, ranging particularly from about 10 to 18 years of age. Often people in the neighbourhood are in fear of such young culprits. In many cases, and probably in most, people will only report matters to the police anonymously or on the strict understanding that they will not directly or indirectly be identified. In recent years this phenomenon became a serious social problem. There appeared to be a gap in the law. The criminal law offered insufficient protection to communities. Public confidence in the rule of law was undermined by a not unreasonable view in some communities that the law failed them. This was the social problem which section 1 was designed to address. (para 16)

Where this knowledge comes from is unknown, beyond what is common sense. There is a clear mapping of the spaces of deviance, and agents of deviance, as well as the security fears of other residents. To draw on Valverde again (2003a: 47), the courts are 'ventriloquiz[ing] the "national" community'. This expression of empathy and identification of the age and location of the 'culprits' as well as the 'outrageousness' of their anti-social behaviour. It constructs the need for protection and justifies the introduction of new, more extreme sets of controls. Carr also tells a different narrative story of the complex decision-making process by the landlord against a backdrop of empathy with the lives of the Clinghams:

> Other stories too are silenced. We hear nothing about Clingham's personal tragedy, of his mother dying of cancer when he was 13, or of his father's subsequent suicide, Clingham's trauma made worse by the fact that he found his father's body. His sister, barely an adult herself, succeeded to the secure tenancy, but was understandably unable to provide for the adolescent's needs. Thus there is no space for therapeutic or other responses to Clingham's circumstances. Nor do we hear of the difficulty that the local housing trust faced in making a decision which reconciled the needs of the other residents, the needs of the sister and the young man's needs. In this version of events seeking an ASB order becomes a complex balancing act which is justified managerially as preferable to evicting the sister. The story told by the House of Lords renders such complexity invisible and marginal and means solutions can be achieved by the straightforward application of common sense.

Managing anti-social behaviour

Despite the discourses of marginalization and deviance discussed above, intervention is premised on the occupier as *consumer* of the service provided by the housing agency. The consumer–manager relation, as with tenant participation, plays an important role in locating ASB and also in explaining in part its recent appeal. It is this apparent contradiction between, on the one hand, the occupier as marginal, as socially excluded, and, on the other hand, as sovereign consumer which is particularly distinctive in the debate. This reflects the reach of consumerism – even the marginalized have the right to act as consumers but, more so, have the obligation to act as responsible subjects. As Flint (2004a: 151) has argued, 'the specification of the subject of social housing as consumer is closely linked to the responsibilized agent of social control, acting within a dominant discourse of ethical conduct based upon prescribed aesthetics of consumption and moral codes of behaviour'.

However, anti-social behaviour also works through the notion of consumerism in a different way. For, while the occupier has been recast as consumer, there has been increasing focus on the other, the anti-consumer. In the name of *social* housing, the *anti-social* have been excluded and segregated. Probably at no time since the foundation of social housing has more effort been put into dividing the anti-social from the social.[2] These anti-consumers are just too costly for housing management, in terms of supervisory and disciplinary interventions and the households' negative impact upon the communities that housing management aspires to create for its estates.

The anti-social are, in some cases, divided off from the population in new therapeutic communities such as that pioneered in Dundee. There is the battery of measures – injunction, eviction – described above. There are therapeutic strategies for the anti-social, and there is the possibility of redemption held out for them on their moral reform; at the same time there is a show of sovereign force through the eviction process and intensive disciplinary techniques, such as demotion of tenancy status. New teams have been set up by housing providers to develop expertise in specifically dealing with the problem of anti-social behaviour. Risk communications are now the stuff of everyday housing management, as housing officers engage in regular cross-disciplinary dialogues with other social agencies about individuals they perceive as risky. This notion of housing management is in the name of the community – indeed, often it is something which the community wants.

Focusing on housing management enables Alison Brown (2004: 210) to make a crucial point about locating ASB:

> Anti-social behaviour is 'found' largely in social housing areas because the physical presence of 'investigatory' people and technology ensure that it will be found. Anti-social behaviour is thus partly a *product* of social housing management.

Social housing is *managed* housing in ways beyond what is possible in private housing. The pinpointing of social housing as dangerous and productive of ASB thus creates a self-fulfilling prophecy – if you go looking for it, you will usually find it (particularly when you're not sure what it is); and if you intensively go looking for it, you will find it in greater abundance (see also Hunt and Wickham, 1994: 87 *et seq*).

These management techniques are historically situated. They provide an illustration of the link between moral cleansing of the poor, their self-regulation and training (see Chapter 2 for discussion, especially about the role of Octavia Hill). The connection between the social and the moral was a key feature of housing management throughout the twentieth century. Throughout their reports, for example, the CHAC continually sought to grapple with this overlap. Damer (2000: 2010) notes the early linkage between housing management and the Public Health department's interest in housing as a social practice seeking 'to systematise the surveillance, control and moralisation of the burgeoning working class'. These techniques took on a new role in the debates over whether to re-house slum-dwellers. When they were re-housed, it was in 'schemes' which appeared as 'open prisons' (p 2017). Each of the estates had a resident rent collector/manager as well as a 'supervising nurse inspector' and a 'lady sanitary inspector': '[Their employment] duties reflect the continuous obsession of the social hygienists with the physical – and moral – dirtiness of slum tenants' (p 2017). The problematization of slum dwellers also required a new, more intensified management, as the Ministry of Health (1934: 161) recognized:

> It is probable that, as the slum clearance campaign proceeds and local authorities find themselves confronted with the problem of housing a number of tenants who have hitherto lived under extremely bad conditions and a proportion of whom may present special difficulty, the need for skilled management will become more widely recognised.

Thus, it can be argued that housing management itself made this focus on ASB in social housing possible. What is different now is the intensified gaze on the occupiers, through the use of closed circuit TVs, concierges, single issue teams and the like.

The occupier-manager as entrepreneur

One of the consequences of the fascinating outbreak of entrepreneurialism at the level of management are the ways in which the targeting of ASB involves working on the self. Ultimately, the concern of the managers is the creation of stable, or sustainable, communities as this will impact on the economics of managing estates and, at the same time, create positive living environments. Underlying many of these developments is a shift in rationality from rights towards responsibility and an explicit communitarian ethos (see Flint, 2002, 2003, 2004b).

An outbreak of localized practices have been developed which reflect this ethos. There are informal mechanisms of social/moral regulation. So, for example, Saugeres (2000: 595), in an interesting note on neatness and tidiness suggests:

> The landlord is supposed to 'investigate' why tenants do not look after their gardens and either educate them to culturally acceptable standards or punish them through the enforcement of tenancy conditions or referral to other agencies of social control. Gardens can also be a way of rewarding well-behaved tenants. Indeed, in some organisations, it has become common practice to organise garden competitions for their tenants to enter, giving a prize to the tenant with the best garden.

And Irwell Valley Housing Association has pioneered a form of 'good customer' scheme through which certain customers are given a 'gold service'. This housing association had issues of low demand and high turnover of stock. It had focused its housing management on ASB and related issues: 'it was apparent that 80% of the association's efforts were being focused on 20% of customers, who presented problems to the association' (Lupton *et al*, 2003: 7). Members of the gold service obtain a variety of benefits, from a quicker response to repair issues to one-off benefits such as free flower seeds. These responses not only incentivize tenants but also work through housing management staff to 'go the extra mile' (ibid). This management scheme has been replicated in other areas, 'reflecting a growing recognition of the image and branding of social housing in relation to the owner-occupied tenure' (Flint, 2004a: 164).

A particular part of the toolbox of the social landlord is the tenancy or occupation contract. This device enables landlords to govern and responsibilize tenants, setting out norms of behaviour. Although local authorities have always set out the obligations of tenancy, in the past they were criticized for doing so (see, for example, Saunders, 1990). Actual tenancy or occupation *contracts* have only become a formal requirement since the Housing Act 1980. This formalization of the rights of occupiers of social landlords was something for which consumer groups and others campaigned (see Loveland, 1992). Setting out an occupier's rights is a positive development, but it has also created the conditions through which occupiers' behaviour can be more closely controlled. Ultimately, in setting out rights, one also sets out obligations, including the threat of eviction in their breach.

Contracts offer a vision of the role and responsibility of the occupier, as well as seek to engage and invoke their entrepreneurial juices. First, contracts are now extremely long in many areas, and are also often written in 'plain English'. They contain detailed rules on what behaviour is permissible and what is not. Scottish tenants have an 80-page agreement; others have agreements which are lengthy. As Crawford (2003: 481) suggests, 'these contracts have a decidedly behavioural characteristic in that they seek to govern *individual* conduct and secure a defined *sense of order*'. Yet, at the same time, 'the classical contract assumes a utilitarian understanding of human calculation and expresses virtues of freedom, autonomy and choice' (ibid: 488). It is this tension between freedom and constraint which makes the contract a potent technique. In defining what is acceptable, they leave open the occupier's freedom to act either in accordance with those norms or not. Failure to do so implies a tacit acceptance of eviction or therapeutic intervention.

Second, contracts, in the entrepreneurial world have meaning in their own right. One way in which that meaning can be put over to the occupier is by making the signing of the contract into an event. Contract signing ceremonies have become a recent invention in social housing. These seek to engender respect for the contract and its terms, make the occupier appreciate the significance of the contract, and make them responsible for their conduct in relation to it.

Third, although these ceremonies are not commonplace in the United Kingdom, what has become increasingly the case is *enforcement* of the contract, and an incitement to enforce it against the anti-social from all levels (centrally and locally, from officials and occupiers). The narrative of enforcement exercises a powerful control on the behaviour not only of the anti-consumers, but also the occupiers more generally. In other words, although enforcement is patchy – different landlords have different practices – it is the possibility of enforcement which is important in generating the will to self-governance. Those unable to work within this construct are liable either to re-training, injunctions, ASB orders or eviction. So, for example, parents with problematic children might be invited to multi-agency meetings, the purpose of which is 'to identify new strategies for these parents to be able to regulate the behaviour of their children within expected norms of behaviour, without the need for future housing agency intervention' (Flint, 2002: 630).

But self-governance has a broader relation in that it is not only the occupier that is controlled, it is also their visitors for their deviance can have negative consequences. Just as the pub landlord is made responsible for the behaviour of their customers, so in social housing the control of deviance is sub-contracted by making the occupier responsible for the behaviour of their visitors. As Mele (2005: 129) notes in discussing similar provisions in the United States, such 'affirmative obligations' compel the responsibilization process as 'tenants are contractually obligated to control and monitor the sets of social relationships they and their guests engage in and to assume the risks associated with those relationships' to achieve the desired goal of security.

The final point to make is that those who are made the subject of ASB sanctions are generally found to be those who are not able to act as entrepreneurs. They have extreme vulnerability arising from their marginal position (Hunter *et al*, 2000). This is not a particularly surprising finding of research studies, for these are the households who are perhaps less likely to be able to accept the freedom of contract, and are more likely to be highly controlled in the community. The 'new' label of ASB combined with the increasing resources given over to its control means that there has been a shift from reliance on social work as a rehabilitative tool in favour of mesh-thinning social control. This is the important point made by Alison Brown (2004: 209) who argues:

> In other words, the situations were generally not neighbour disputes, but problems in themselves, which the system (the penal–welfare complex) had failed to manage before and was now, in response to demands from neighbours, attempting to control by the anti-social behaviour route.

Contracting debt

Occupiers of social housing have a contractual duty to pay rent. If they do not pay their rent, they are in breach of contract and liable to be evicted. Since 1989, the distribution of subsidy to local authorities has made an assumption that a certain proportion of rent has been collected. This was set at 95 per cent. Rent collection and arrears are key performance indicators in the new regime, but were regarded as indicators of performance well before that. The need to service loans, combined with Housing Corporation performance regulation and performance indicators, have also acted to ensure that the emphasis on rent collection is as important within housing associations. There are now considerable incentives on landlords to evict tenants for non-payment, in terms of writing off debt for audit purposes, or in persuading a regulator that their performance is excellent (and, thus, qualifying for some benefit).[3] And, anecdotally, some landlords now describe officers responsible for rent collection as 'income maximisation officers'.

Given all of this, it is not particularly surprising that court actions for rent arrears increased sharply during the 1990s. In this section, we focus on the discursive hold of the 'social' in these court actions by drawing on interviews conducted with 26 District Judges (DJs) in three geographical locations during 2004 (Hunter *et al*, 2005). The purpose of the project, in which one of us was engaged, was to find out the factors which impact on judicial decision-making in rent arrears possession cases. Generally, social landlords are entitled to an order for possession where there are arrears *and* it would be reasonable to grant possession. Despite the gravity of the cases – the occupier can lose their home as a result – the hearings themselves are often over very quickly, within a few minutes. They are, in fact, often rather mundane – observations of the proceedings themselves found that they are often akin to an administrative process. Nevertheless, mentalities of government often arise out of the mundane and the 'gut feeling'.

The study found different practices and outcomes between the courts, and sought to explain these by reference to a number of different factors. Our discussion here, however, is partial in that we focus on the particular aspects of this study in which the judges constructed 'social housing' and its occupants.

The social

The researchers did not ask explicitly whether the nature of the landlord impacted on the decision in rent possession cases. However, there was evidence from our interviews that this did have an impact on decision-making. Social housing cases are treated differently from private landlords. In most courts, the practice is to list these cases separately, so that private sector cases were not heard at the same time.

There were three more general reasons given for treating social landlord cases differently – first, there was a balance between entitlement to rent and social landlordism; second, there was the relationship between the current occupier and others on the waiting list in housing need; and third, there was the problem of rehousing occupiers.

First, DJs expressed a dichotomy between social landlordism, on the one hand, and the contractual duty to pay rent or the duty to council tax payers more generally, on the other hand. This tension was expressed by different DJs in the following ways:

> It's social housing, it is a contract. It cuts both ways. The tenant has got to realise he's probably got an easy landlord. He's got to do something to help I mean at the end of the day, even social landlords, we're all paying for that as it were. The money doesn't come from nowhere.

Different elements within this dichotomy might be emphasized at different times. For example, two interviewees drew upon the contractual duty to pay rent when feeding back to the tenant, as part of a tactic to scare the tenant into paying their rent. Thus, for example, one interviewee said:

> I would suspend. I would scare her ... before I suspended. ... 'Why should all the other local authority tenants have to pay rent, increase rents because you can't be bothered to get your act together, Miss Jones, it's just not good enough. There's no reason why I should suspend this, is there? You've been warned once.' At this point they burst into tears. And then I suspend it. It may sound cruel, that's the way I happen to feel that I can get people to realize ... and this is why I would say it, I would write 'last chance'.

The nature of the landlord became an important factor to balance against the occupiers' rights:

> Local authorities and a lot of the housing associations really can't fulfil their obligations as they would like to, because they simply haven't got the means to do it [...] If they didn't have various people owing them quite a lot of money, there would be more to do the repairs.

Second, our interviewees expressed concern about the rights of the occupier who had not been paying their rent against the needs of others on the waiting list. For one DJ, this was a 'subsidiary consideration' and 'it's just my slight concern that perhaps I should be more bullish ... particularly with the more persistent defaulters'. On the other hand, another would ask of some occupiers: "look, if you've chosen not to pay it then why do you expect the court to help you now?" If there's a lot of people screaming out for accommodation, willing to pay for it, why should I give priority to people who are not prepared to do so. Not are unable to do so, but not prepared to.'

Again, this factor could be deployed at different parts of the process. For example, one interviewee used this in discussion of one of the scenarios as a scare tactic:

> Look, £4.50 a week, it's not a king's ransom, and you're working. You've got to pay it otherwise you've got to go. And then, if the landlord's there I invariably ask, 'How many people on the housing list?' A scare tactic to, not to frighten her, but to make her realise that if she wants to stay she's being housed for £4.50, you know, 60p a day is not a lot to ask.

This factor could, however, be used to swing the other way, in favour of the tenant. At least, the social obligation implied in the role of 'social landlord' would not outweigh the duties to the occupier. Thus, for example, it was said that if you evict a mother and her children, you are creating more problems in society at large 'than you are trying to deal with the particular problem of them not paying the rent, and other people who would be good tenants being in the waiting list'.

Finally, it was said that, where tenants of social landlords were evicted, the problem was that the social landlord – or, rather, the local authority – would be required to re-house the tenant at some considerable cost. Although some interviewees recognized the likelihood of a finding of intentional homelessness, others raised concerns over the costs of rehousing, using this as a technique to deny possession to a social landlord:

> But the local authority is really the end of the line in terms of housing. And they're gonna be the ones that pick up the pieces when somebody presents with a priority need. So I think that's why, I suppose, I take a slightly different, you know, I say, 'Look, hang on, you know, where's this family going to go? You're gonna have to pick up the pieces anyway.'

Mandatory possession

Housing associations give occupiers a contract which is the same as private sector occupiers, but which is also the subject of Housing Corporation regulation and good practice guidance. Because of the security of tenure regime within which they operate, they are entitled strictly to use a mandatory ground for possession on rent arrears where the arrears are more than two months or eight weeks in arrears (known as 'Ground 8'). Mandatory means that there is no requirement to prove reasonableness; provided that the arrears have been shown at the date of the hearing, the District Judge must grant possession.

The study found that District Judges generally were not in sympathy with the use of Ground 8 by RSLs. There was a tension, however, between this mandatory law and a notion of the social which underpinned their approach. So, for example, one interviewee commented, 'I personally believe that housing association who have a social duty should not be using Ground 8.' For another interviewee, there was a contrast between social and private landlords arguing that it would be 'more obviously justifiable' for a private landlord to use the Ground as opposed to social landlords ('I'm talking about social landlords here ... ').

The occupier

A number of studies have found, as did Hunter *et al*, that attendance by the occupier at court has a considerable (generally positive) impact on the outcome of the hearing (Genn and Genn, 1989). Where the occupier attends, it is rare that an outright possession order will be made, although a suspended possession order is possible. One reason for this is sentiment – District Judges are rarely willing to evict somebody to their face. A further reason, though, ties in with the ethical responsibility of the occupier to face up to their situation and actively seek to resolve it:

> They're clearly taking the proceedings seriously and they're concerned about their position and they want to do something to resolve the problem. I'm always reasonably happy to try to help people who are prepared to help themselves.

Ultimately, the question framed by some interviewees was 'can't pay, won't pay?', a kind of modern poverty/pauperization division. The study found evidence that District Judges might size up the tenant, looking at various factors such as dress and attitude to the court.

> DJ: I'm particularly concerned about a tenant's motivation to do something about their predicament. Mmm.
> Q: And how would you gauge that?
> DJ: (Pause) Probably differently in every, every single individual case. It's very difficult this … cos everyone's different. You have to be aware of stereotyping them … some people have very great difficulty in, in saying, something across the desk to a strange judge, you know, and you have to … dig it out of them. And it doesn't necessarily mean they're not interested in sorting themselves out. Other people can be a bit too glib about it … but in the end you just have to use your experience of people and common sense to assess them.

Conclusion

We have covered rather diverse ground in this chapter, seeking to link different understandings of contract into the government of occupiers of social housing. Our discussion has followed a route from the relatively informal – tenant participation – through to a more mixed jurisdiction – ASB – to the formal – court-based eviction processes. In each, there has been a role for contract, but it has been a different role. As regards tenant participation, contract was drawn on loosely and used as a way of harnessing individual occupier's entrepreneurial spirit, to take advantage of their expertise in self-government. As regards ASB, the use of contract is more formal. It defines the freedom of occupiers, setting out the constraints on that freedom (and, by implication, what is acceptable conduct), and the requirement to act in accordance with the norms of housing management. Finally, as regards housing debt, we have noted the way in which the relationship between the contract and social is manoeuvred, working on both management and occupiers, by studying the formal processes of enforcement of the contractual nexus.

We set out in our introduction a rather basic research question for this chapter – why treat social housing differently? – and, in truth, there seem to be a number of different reasons. Chief among these are the different ways in which the social is being employed in each. Understandings of the social exclusion/inclusion dichotomy permeate tenant participation with the assumption that directing the occupier's entrepreneurial activity will both benefit the estate as well as result in them escaping the circuit of exclusion. On the other hand, when dealing with ASB, the social is constructed as defining dangerous spaces, places and persons (often in traditional terms); in this sense, the problematization is how to control these persons and create more 'sustainable communities' in the process. The justification for the resort to sovereign power lies in the need to control the anti-social and, thereby, constructing the social itself. Finally, as regards housing debt, the social is deployed as a counter-discourse to the discourse of contract as a method (or justification) of resistance to ordering eviction. This came across particularly clearly when considering the almost emblematic role of Ground 8. While judges approached this differently, at heart, they were unhappy about its use by social landlords as opposed to private landlords. This is not particularly about social housing as an arena from profit-making, but about social housing adopting appropriate management techniques for ensuring that their occupiers pay the rent.

Anti-social behaviour is perhaps the apotheosis of governance through obscurity – we illustrated the diverse range of behaviours included within its ambit by different official documents. And, indeed, it has created the space for an increasingly intrusive surveillance of behaviour, made possible by the existence of relatively co-ordinated and responsive management. Obscurity also permeates our discussion of tenant participation. The 'what is it?' question underpins the variety of projects under its label, as well as providing a space for responsive governance. Less obviously, obscurity is also prevalent in possession proceedings, through the different understandings of 'reasonableness' – which simultaneously also highlight constructions of the social and moral occupier.

Chapter 7:
Private Renting

Private renting and profit-making landlords hardly seem the stuff of 'social housing'. Yet, this is a sector which provides accommodation for a large number of households in need. As the housing Green Paper in 2000 pointed out, 'in some areas social rented housing is in short supply and many low-income households are forced into renting privately' (DETR/DSS, 2000: para 5.5). Indeed, until recently local authorities could draw on it as a resource to fulfil their obligations under the homelessness law (and did so before this was formal law). Although the sector may be 'profit-making', as opposed to 'surplus-making', the cost of at least part of the sector is heavily controlled by the state through what it is willing to pay out through a personal subsidy, housing benefit. And, it is also a sector in which other housing providers intervene in recognition of the support needs of some occupiers.

The sector has been the subject of diverse regulation or control really from the early nineteenth century. The primary line that has been drawn is between regulation (or control) on the one hand, and freedom, on the other. The discourse of freedom has been deployed particularly powerfully, because it has been combined with a deregulatory ethic – that is, deregulation equals freedom, which also equals growth; regulation equals control, which also equals decline. These simplistic associations form the heart of the problematization which has dominated discussion about the private rented sector, but also generated new problematizations as a result.

Indeed, thinking about the private rented sector occurs often through 'common sense' knowledge, rather than statistical or other forms of knowledge. Its residual nature in policy for much of the twentieth century is reflected in the fact that the official statistics treat private renting as a 'catch-all category that is defined simply on the basis of the housing being neither owner occupied or socially rented' (Ball, 2004: 15). This means that 'the privately rented sector when treated as a whole is as much an artefact of statistical convenience as an expression of reality' (ibid: 17). The important point is that the label 'private rented *sector*' obscures a high degree of fragmentation and segmentation.

In the first section, we discuss the relationship between freedom and regulation as it has been conceived in the policy of security. We also consider how this relationship has been framed in the policy discourse since the crucial interventions in the Housing Act 1988. Control or regulation have only been grudgingly accepted because of the particular temporary problems created by wartime, and immediate post-war emergency. If only we can loosen the controls, the argument goes, the sector can rebuild and continue with its historic mission of providing housing for the population. One consequence of that problematization, almost by chance, was the creation of a new version of landlord deviance and a new set of emergencies which required to be dealt with. The re-emergence of the vital role of the sector from the mid-1980s – pretty much by chance as a result of a lack of other options more than desire – has given rise to a new set of divisions premised on binary oppositions between good/bad, scrupulous/unscrupulous.

In the second section, we trace how that problematization of landlord deviance – regarding harassment and unlawful eviction – was played out against a backdrop in which the sector was re-envisioned as both desirable and essential. Landlords, in this conception, are not regarded as deviant but as partners with consequences on the construction of crime. Yet, there is a continuing discourse of the 'bad' which is also linked in with concerns about some occupiers. While the deregulatory instinct has been particularly strong, the Housing Act 2004 engineers what we term a 'panoply of control' by returning to the nineteenth century vision of healthy housing. Nevertheless, what is so interesting about this set of controls is their apparent incoherence, each building different versions of regulation and drawing upon different understandings of the sector; although, underlying each, we suggest are neo-liberal mentalities of government, of partnership, risk/trust/insurance and technology.

In the final section, we discuss the way in which housing benefit has been reformed to coincide with new understandings of the social. Without housing benefit propping up market rents in part of the sector, the Thatcher reforms of the mid-1980s would not have been possible. Yet, housing benefit has also proved theoretically problematic against a number of models of government – economic, psychological and citizenship. Its reform then speaks of a new version of the social as it affects and works through the occupiers of this sector.

Regulating freedom

When the private rented sector is discussed today, the prime consideration generally is that it is a necessary, desirable feature of the housing system which is required to expand. Expansion is required because the sector provides accommodation for a diverse array of households – students, the economically mobile, those excluded from council and RSL accommodation, those unable to afford ownership and the like. The mantra goes on to say that expansion is only possible if the private rental market is deregulated and landlords entitled to a market rent. Both Conservative and New Labour governments have clearly stated this proposition. In their housing Green Paper, the New Labour government sought to assuage the concerns of landlords that they would re-introduce greater security of tenure (through which occupiers cannot be evicted without a court order granted on one of a limited number of grounds):

> In England, only one in ten households live in private rented housing. That is
> exceptionally low by comparison with most other developed countries. We therefore
> want the sector to grow and prosper. That means building on its strengths as much as

tackling its weaknesses. Landlords can be assured that we intend no change in the present structure of assured and assured shorthold tenancies, which is working well. Nor is there any question of our re-introducing rent controls in the deregulated market. Our many good landlords deserve support and encouragement – to help them improve their position in the market-place and to help them deal with tenants who misbehave or refuse to pay the rent. (DETR/DSS, 2000: para 5.2)

This set of understandings builds on the foundations of concern over state involvement in the unfurnished private rented sector in 1915 by introducing rent control and security of tenure. Rent control meant rents set centrally, pegged at 1914 levels. On some accounts, this state intervention in private housing was a result of rent strikes by munitions workers because rents were being raised as a result of increasing demand for the accommodation. Intervention only occurred after considerable inactivity, the government being more concerned with legislating to control munitions output (Damer, 1980; see Watchman, 1980;).

The inter-war period

The 1915 legislation was due to expire six months after the end of the war. What then occurred were a series of official reports, chaired by the 'great men', ostensibly concerned with an enquiry and report on the workings of the law. However, these reports were designed to determine whether and when the state could withdraw rent controls and security of tenure from the private rented sector. In the inter-war period, there were five such reports (Ministry of Reconstruction, 1918 ('the Hunter report'); Ministry of Health, 1920 ('the Salisbury report'), 1923 ('the Onslow report'), 1931b ('the Marley report'), 1937 ('the Ridley Report')).

At stake in these reports was the cause of the housing problem – was it a temporary result of the war or that there were fundamental concerns over the capacity of the private sector to provide appropriate quality housing (Bowley, 1945: 15). What is apparent in these reports is that the private sector should be made free as soon as possible and, when it is, it was thought that it should be able to cater for the population. The evident belief was that the free market would provide decent quality housing at an affordable rent, if it was given the chance. It was a belief in the value of enterprise, conceived as providing a 'social service'.

The narrow problem for the official committees was concisely stated by the Hunter report:

The problem upon which our advice is sought is an exceedingly difficult one. The policy adopted may determine whether housing is to continue on an economic basis, or whether it is to be permanently subsidised; and thus, in effect, to become a state enterprise. (para 4)

It was clear where the sympathies of the report's authors lay: '... the aim should be to return to economic conditions as soon as possible' (para 30), a claim repeated in more urgent terms subsequently in the report (para 32). To the claim by tenants' organizations that there should be collective ownership, in place of private ownership, they argued that if tenants are able and willing to pay a fair rent, then landlords would be able to provide better quality housing (para 32). Thus, their concern was that occupiers be paid a sufficient wage (para 61). Indeed, while the majority of this committee recommended that rent control and security of tenure should remain, they argued that there should be a summary remedy for non-payment of rent 'having regard to the privileges enjoyed by tenants at present' (para 57; regarded as 'astonishing' in the minority report).

Two immediate issues exercised the minds of the 1918 and 1920 committees – first, there was the 'house famine' (the Salisbury report: para 5) and, relatedly, the economic problem that landlords in such conditions would be able to charge 'scarcity rents' were rent control to be removed. Both reports, however, recommended significant increases in rents to give landlords an incentive to conduct repairs. Each report recommended that the Acts be renewed for a further limited period until the 'emergency' had passed. By the time of the Onslow report in 1923, it was suggested that the Acts should be renewed for a further two years only and that, in the meantime, certain houses should be decontrolled. Their argument was that the reason why private investors had not rejoined the market was probably not related to the controlled rents but to the 'psychological factor ... the property owner dislikes the prospect of increasing interference by the state in relations between himself and the tenant' (p 7). Indeed, the Acts themselves were said to have 'helped to prolong the shortage of accommodation that rendered them necessary' (p 8). In Holmans' withering critique of this report, those observations were regarded as 'no more than wishful thinking unsupported by analysis or calculation of any kind' (1987: 394).

The two subsequent reports are most notable, in some respects, for their minority reports. In these, the authors seek to construct the underlying reasoning of the majority (which is not always apparent on its face) and then provide arguments against it. The Marley report is interesting in this respect. By this time, there were a large number of houses which had become decontrolled, as well as those (such as furnished accommodation) which had never been subject to control. The report categorized houses into three groups depending on their rateable value. In the highest rateable value, the houses were to be decontrolled immediately (if they were not already); in the middle group, they were to be decontrolled when the current tenant moved on; in the lowest rateable value group, the houses were to be controlled. On the question whether the then decontrolled houses in the lowest rateable value group should be brought within the ambit of the Act, the majority concluded that they should not:

> [W]e fear that the psychological effect of the proposal, if adopted, would be to shake the confidence of private capital and private enterprise in the building industry; and so, on a long view, would do more damage, in our opinion, to the good housing of the working classes ... The proposal, moreover, ... might also have the effect of closing the door finally on the hope that private enterprise may presently return to the building of working-class houses. (para 56)

The minority report of Duncan Graham, however, took the alternative view arguing that the concern of the majority was that 'private enterprise should be induced to come in as quickly as possible to meet the housing needs of the country' (p 58), a view which he could not accept. The Ridley report recommended further decontrol on an area basis where there was sufficient accommodation, evidenced through statistics on overcrowding which had just started to be produced. The minority report, however, did 'not accept the implication that control is, of itself, an evil the ending of which should be a sort of ideal of all right-thinking people. Frankly, we consider that control of some kind is desirable as a permanent feature of the housing service' (para 6).

The 1957 Rent Act

The 'evil' of control and the stifling of private enterprise which was said to ensue were revisited by the Conservative government in the 1950s against a backdrop of neglect of houses, to which the Conservative White Paper of 1953 attributed the 'more serious cause' to rent control (and, otherwise, the previous high costs in the building industry) (MHLG, 1953: para 23–4). The Ridley committee recommendations had not been brought into effect as the advent of the Second World War had led to regulations re-controlling all rented housing. The original purpose of the Rent Act 1957 was the decontrol of the private rented sector in order to seek to provide some curb on the costs to the state of providing new housing. Furthermore,

> [A] discourse for reform grew from officials within the Ministry of Housing and the Treasury, as well as a caucus of Conservative opinion both in and outside the party, which viewed rented housing as too cheap. Controls discriminated against landlords, created shortages, and produced enormous anomalies in the market. (Simmonds, 2002: 848)

Decontrol, then, was *the* solution – freedom would lead to rent rises, efficiency in pricing and investment in the sector (Kemp, 1997). Against this argument was a belief that the sector itself was a failed and failing institution. Indeed, the post-First World War oppositions seem to have been repeated at this time, but in a more instinctive way (there being no developed statistical knowledge of the extent of control – Simmonds, ibid: 855).

It was the failure of the 1957 Act to stimulate the sector which led to a consensus that the sector could not respond to 'market incentives because of the past history of controls, the financial unworldliness of so many small landlords and the economic and social attractions of owner-occupation' (Milner Holland, 1965: ch 3; Nelken, 1983: 33). Indeed, by this time, a new problematization of the sector – landlord deviance – had overtaken the regulation/freedom binary. The Rachman story is well known, if shrouded in mystery. Briefly, in the late 1950s and the early 1960s, Rachman took advantage of the lack of statutory control on furnished properties. In London in 1954, he began his operation cheaply buying property let unfurnished (this could be done because controlled rents were low and capital values were low because he was able to buy the short end of long leases). Initially, he offered money to the tenants to move out and their vacated properties were sub-divided and turned into furnished dwellings.

Tenants of furnished dwellings had fewer rights and hardly any control over their rents. The scarcity of property meant that Rachman could charge considerable sums for it. Furthermore, 'at best, he was "not particular" about whom he accepted as tenants': prostitutes and others for whom alternative accommodation was difficult to find (Nelken, 1983: 4). Subsequently, rather than paying people to leave (a practice known as 'winkling'), Rachman began to harass indirectly those tenants of unfurnished parts into leaving the accommodation: 'what perhaps began naturally Rachman began to exploit, seeing, perhaps, no point in paying controlled tenants to go if they could be persuaded to do so by other means' (Milner Holland, 1965: 252). The properties went unrepaired ('One ex-employee was reported as saying: "One way or another we reckoned we could keep a defective drain going for four or five months without the legal penalties becoming uneconomic" ': Nelken, 1983: 4). Despite the circulation of stories concerning Rachman in the late 1950s and early 1960s, his property management only became the subject of controversy after it was linked to the Profumo affair (call girls with whom Profumo, the War Minister, had associated lived in Rachman-run properties). For two weeks in 1963, after Rachman's death, considerable political debate about the private rented sector dominated all discussion. Nevertheless, what is interesting about this problematization is how it was linked to the decontrol agenda of the Conservative party; whereas Rachman's property management straddled two different regimes, one based on control, the other based upon market principles (at least in part). Neither hindered his progress because he was able to avoid the regulatory structures anyway.

The private landlord as deviant was a particularly powerful political issue, one which apparently necessitated 'emergency' legislation. This identification of the private landlord symbolized the *image problem* of the sector and operated as a disincentive against institutions becoming or remaining involved in the sector. The subsequent reordering of the sector in the Rent Act 1965 – from rent control to rent regulation, combined with security of tenure – was an attempt not at consensus, but 'as a technocratic response to one prominent example of the "rediscovery of poverty" in the 1960s' (Nelken, 1983: 34). The idea was to offer a balance between the interests of landlord and tenant, to offer fairness to both. The technocracy was a panel of rent officers to whom occupiers or landlords could refer their rent for a determination as to its fairness (although few, in fact, did so: Partington, 1980).

This image problem was aligned with a new truth about the sector – that it was dead. Richard Crossman, who introduced the Rent Act 1965, believed that the choice for the future was between ownership and the public sector; certainly, there were also attempts to stimulate cost-rent housing societies under the Housing Act 1964 and the promotion function of the Housing Corporation. Although the Francis committee on the Rent Acts in 1971 did not agree that the role of the private landlord 'is finished' (Francis, 1971: 203), there were plenty of experts who viewed the sector as in terminal decline – as Berry (1974: 123) put it, 'the private landlord seems destined to perish sooner or later'.

'Motherhood and apple pie'[1]

Despite the view of the sector as being in terminal decline, the 1980s offered a rebirthing experience. The Conservative government's antipathy towards municipal landlordism combined with a recognition that owner-occupation was reaching its limits, signalled a rethinking of tenure structures. By the mid-1980s, private renting was regarded as in tune with the voguish ideals of mobility and contractualism. Indeed, John Patten, the housing minister at the time, referred to the role of institutions as private landlords as being as natural as 'motherhood and apple pie' (see Kemp, 1993). A 'bewildering display of projects and acronyms' were set up to revive the sector (Carter and Ginsburg, 1994: 100) and the gradual removal of subsidies from ownership created a less harsh fiscal environment. The 1987 White Paper, while co-locating private renting and housing associations within the label 'the independent rented sector', was careful to offer a balance between a reasonable return for landlords and reasonable security for tenants 'in their own homes' (DoE, 1987: para 3.16). Nevertheless, what was apparent about the presentation of this policy was the return to prominence of the old view about the stifling effect of rent control and security of tenure (paras 1.3 and 1.8).

The creation in the subsequent Housing Act 1988 of the now prevalent 'assured shorthold tenancy' – which combines a market rent with minimum period of security of tenure of six months – was the subject of political controversy at the time. However, what is apparent now is the degree of political stability which exists in relation to this sector – indeed, Cowan and Marsh (2001a: 275) refer to the privilege extended to the sector in policy today as opposed to other parts of the social rented sector. The shift from Labour to *New* Labour was significant in this respect; it is also significant in heralding a degree of apparent consensus on the supposed stifling effect of regulation.

The 2000 housing Green Paper is therefore a momentous document in signalling a series of discursive strategies which seek to encapsulate the shift in political rationality undergone by New Labour, specifically as it concerns private renting. The first strategy deployed in the Green Paper is to signal a departure from the historical association of the Labour Party with rent control and the extension of security of tenure in favour of a broad endorsement of the value of private landlords, again in contrast to the party's historic position:

> Landlords can be assured that we intend no change in the present structure of assured and assured shorthold tenancies, which is working well. Nor is there any question of our re-introducing rent controls in the deregulated market. Our many good landlords deserve support and encouragement – to help them improve their position in the market-place and to help them deal with tenants who misbehave or refuse to pay the rent. (DETR/DSS, 2000: para 5.2)

The previous government's deregulation strategies are effectively deployed to delimit the 'regulatory space' of the contemporary private rented sector (PRS).

However, while the Government has taken a broadly non-interventionist stance, it is unable to ignore apparent problems afflicting the sector, to which some form of regulatory response would seem appropriate. In order to manage this tension, the housing Green Paper then divides landlords between the 'many good and well-intentioned landlords' and 'a small minority of private landlords [who] set out to exploit their tenants and the community at large in flagrant disregard of the law' (para 5.4). The dividing strategy has both moral and ethical overtones. The regulatory strategies proposed for each group diverge sharply. For the former, the hallmarks of ethopolitics – responsible self-government, community regulation and self-policing (voluntary licensing, accreditation, kitemarks) – are appropriate. For the latter, an array of more intrusive, disciplinary regulation is prescribed – licensing, housing benefit restrictions, risk-based regulation of property quality.

As Blandy (2001: 79) argues, this discursive 'technique is used to justify intervention in a sector which in general the government is concerned not to over-regulate'. It involves an identification of, and link between, dangerous persons – the 'anti-social', the 'bad', and the 'exploitative' – and dangerous places – 'low demand'. In this dividing process, the Government exploits the established *image* of the private rented sector as rachmanite, while at the same time maintaining both that problems are not widespread – 'a small minority of landlords' – and are overstated: 'All of this earns for the sector as a whole a far worse image than it deserves' (para 5.5).

The broad-brush distinction offered by the Green Paper would seem to require that we can categorize landlords as good or bad. Yet, such categories are unlikely to be stable over time and landlords may be both 'good' and 'bad' at the same time. Indeed, those members of industry-based regulatory organizations such as local landlord associations – often held up as the model of good practice – may not be good at all times and 'good' landlords may act 'badly' towards tenants for what they see as the greater good (Marsh et al, 2000). The Green Paper does not see the categories 'good and well-intentioned' and 'bad' as separating the law-abiding from those acting unlawfully. It argues that many good and well-intentioned landlords face a 'great mass of legislation' and 'fall foul of the law ... more often than not ... through inadvertence' (para 5.10). Hence, the identification of these categories becomes decidedly problematic and turns on the identification of those who are 'well-intentioned'. At the same time, it seeks to challenge the label 'crime' applied to these activities of the good landlord, downgrading them to 'inadvertence' as opposed to intentional. Yet, we lack robust data on even basic issues (such as the number of unlawful evictions or the incidence of harassment) that might assist in sustaining this division (for example, Marsh et al, 2000: ch 3); the various arts of government – statistics, population – seem irrelevant to the problematization. This lack of empirical evidence is implicit in the Green Paper: 'We *believe* that most private landlords are basically well-intentioned and anxious to do a good and responsible job' (para 5.8, emphasis added). In contrast, what it is claimed is known is that:

> Areas of low housing demand face severe and complex problems ... This often attracts unscrupulous, even criminal, landlords and anti-social tenants, who may have been evicted from social housing. Together they may force out law-abiding tenants and owner-occupiers. (DTLR, 2001: para 3)

> In such areas unscrupulous landlords can operate on a large scale and to the detriment of the community as a whole (not least responsible landlords and tenants). (para 13)

In the Consultation Document from which these quotes are drawn (on selective licensing of landlords), it subsequently becomes clear what 'unscrupulous' landlords do – they 'take no interest in their tenants or the neighbourhood. Some may even encourage anti-social behaviour in order to intimidate owner-occupiers into accepting low offers for their properties' (para 15). This knowledge is not supplemented with information about the scale of the problem; rather the concern is to establish that landlords should take responsibility not only for their own behaviour but that of their tenants.

The Green Paper therefore styles the core of the regulatory space of the PRS to be standards – of properties, management and behaviour. And having constructed the issue in terms of good/well-intentioned and bad landlords, it addresses directly the key proposal of those keen to guarantee minimum standards are achieved:

> Some commentators have suggested that we should extend ... compulsory licensing proposals to take in the whole of the private rented sector. We do not think that this would be the best way to try to raise standards ... Licensing the whole sector – over 10% of our entire housing stock – would be a massive undertaking which would risk collapsing under its own weight, not least as a great many homes enter and leave the private rented sector each year. The extra red tape involved would also be likely to encourage some perfectly respectable landlords to leave the business altogether and to dissuade others from joining it. (para 5.31)

This statement is clearly rooted in the regulation-as-burden argument. However, unless the content of 'licensing' is specified more clearly, statements about 'extra red tape' and 'massive undertaking' are difficult to evaluate. While the dissuasion of landlords is undoubtedly a possibility, at what level the regulatory burden would have a significant negative impact is not clear. To some degree, as a general argument this relies for its force on the audience accepting that landlords will behave in particular ways – and this appeals to established, rather negative, images of amateurism and profiteering. Without being active in the policy process, landlords *en masse* exercise considerable power over policy through the reaction anticipated by government. This power has been enhanced because the government now needs private landlords as 'partners' to mitigate on-going local shortages of social housing (Cowan and Marsh, 2001b). In this context, anything that might reduce supply 'unnecessarily' is to be avoided.

The nature of deviance and the re-envisioning of the sector

Re-envisioning the landlord

The re-discovery of the 'good' and 'bad' landlord (see, earlier, Milner Holland, 1965: 178), as opposed to general suspicion or outright hostility, has tempered the deregulatory instinct of New Labour. This understanding of a simple binary good/bad is made to work hard for its creation. Assumptions of deviance among a small minority of landlords make assumptions about a certain fixity in the nature of landlord deviance itself. However, as Nelken (1983) reminds us in his study of landlord practice, such assumptions are dependent upon broader understandings of deviance and establishing boundaries for the legitimacy of property rights.

One of the important historical legacies is that responsibility for regulating private renting exists beyond the landlord and tenant relationship. Deviance is also policed by the local authority. This was the foundation of their 'enabling' role in the nineteenth century, and has continued as well as being strengthened over time (see Goodlad, 1993: ch 1). Identification of landlord deviance is made by the local authority. The reasons for them having this role, rather than police forces, have been said to be due to the complexity of the civil law, and the problems in making judgments about civil rights which might be encountered by the 'constable on the spot' (Francis, 1971, 106; Milner Holland, 1965: 175). One consequence of this division of responsibility is that landlord deviance is a regulatory crime and somehow different from *ordinary* crime. Nelken's study made clear that the crimes of harassment and unlawful eviction, framed against the backdrop of Rachman/ism, were largely committed by resident landlords living in close proximity to their tenants.

The re-envisioning of the enabling role by the Conservative government in the 1987 White Paper – 'ensur[ing] that everyone in their area is adequately housed; but not necessarily by them' (para 1.16) – combined with the prominence in housing policy given over to reviving private renting and the shift to assured shorthold tenancies to alter the local authority role in 'policing' the sector. Despite a weakening in the evidential requirements of the offence of harassment and unlawful eviction – to offer 'protection against the minority of landlords' (DoE, 1987: para 3.17) – few prosecutions are, in fact, brought (let alone successfully brought). Cowan and Marsh (2001b) demonstrate that the shifts in thinking about the PRS have altered local authority officer perceptions about the value of prosecution. Beyond this, though, the marketization of local authorities, the desire to regard clients as consumers, affect the kind of information provided to occupiers so that the occupier-consumer can make an informed choice. For example, information might be provided about the length of time it might take to prosecute, as opposed to the easy access nature of the sector.

Also significant in this re-envisioning process was a recognition that landlords were not there to be prosecuted, or treated with suspicion. Rather, landlords could be active 'partners in meeting housing need'. Local authority engagement with private renting was a *sine qua non* of the receipt of extra funding from central government – for example, urban regeneration schemes required extensive use of the sector (see Malpass, 1994). Even before they were required to use the sector to house homeless households, local authorities across the political spectrum were making use of it (University of Birmingham, 1998). Cowan and Marsh note

> The significance of this was that the authorities' oppositional stance towards housing tenures were breaking down into a more co-operative strategy. ... Most authorities in our

study had some form of strategy to work with the sector – whether this was through simply providing advice and information to landlords, through the development of a landlord forum (almost ubiquitous throughout our study areas), or through an accreditation scheme. The essence of all these schemes was to provide some level of encouragement to landlords, whilst at the same time informing landlords about required standards, housing benefit, and other related matters. (2001b: 847)

This role has been emphasized by best value Performance Indicator 64 concerning, in part, the advice given by the local authority which leads to the re-letting of private rented properties. Local authorities seek to work with landlords; they recognize that, when landlords break the law and engage in harassment or unlawful eviction, they do so because they are amateurs. And prosecution is counter-productive to the broader mission of ensuring that they meet housing need (as the landlord might exit the market-place and the property would be lost). Rather than eviction without due process, local authorities emphasize eviction with it: ' "once landlords are aware that it's a fairly straightforward procedure and it's not costly, there's going to be more chance of a lawful eviction than a non-lawful eviction" ' (2001b: 851).

What this discussion emphasizes is that the simple binary of good/bad tends to break down either by reference to historical practice, or by reference to broader contextual factors affecting the sector. Resort to this binary is more a common sense division of inherent good/bad, a kind of instinctive sorting process. If regulation and its enforcement are techniques of government, as we suggest in Chapter 1, which reflect its mentality, the identification of landlords as partners in meeting housing need is important in constructing a particular understanding of social housing. Its by-product – compliance work with landlords – works through the freedom of landlords, and by emphasizing the limited rights of occupiers.

Re-envisioning the occupier

In contrast to the ways in which the state conceptualizes, and consequently regulates, landlords, the state's conceptualization of the tenant has shifted from the protective embrace of much of the nineteenth century towards a more responsibilized conception. In this conception, the tenants are required to exercise their own self-regulation and to conform to the norms of civil society. There is a twin meaning here of responsibility – it relates, at once, to the necessity for the tenants to conform to the contractual relationship with their landlord; but it also relates to a broader (non-legal) contractual relationship with their community or neighbourhood. The state has become concerned with *how* the tenants should exercise their responsibility *qua* tenant.

Given the short-termism inherent in the sector and the consequential lack of organization among tenants, the principal problem for the state has been how to envision the regulation of tenants. There is considerable trust in the self-regulatory capacity of the individual, particularly those at the upper end of the market. There has been a shift in thinking towards viewing occupiers as consumers, rather than as tenants, to whom the force of consumer protection is to be applied (Law Commission, 2002). The implication of this shift is not about 'who is on top?' or about the state and condition of the property, but about a return to contract; a requirement that the contract governs the relationship. The consumer obtains information and a 'plain English' statement of the terms of their agreement, but little protection. Their protection effectively comes through an improved, more efficient contract (O'Malley, 2004: 49).

What has been innovative in the Labour government agenda has been the attempt to exercise its sovereign power over the responsibility of tenants to behave in conformity with broader norms. So, for example, although much has been made of the legislative and policy focus on *social* tenants' behaviour, there has been increasing consideration of the use of ASB Orders against private tenants. Government commissioned research specifically targeted 'mixed tenure' areas (Nixon *et al*, 2003); and the output discusses strategies to responsibilize tenants to publicize the types of anti-social behaviours to which they have been subjected. For all this, though, it is significant that the recent extensions of powers of social landlords with regard to their tenants have not been extended to the behaviour of tenants in the PRS.

Further, the 2000 Green Paper drew a parallel with the use of financial mechanisms to discipline landlords when it floated the possibility of using the Housing Benefit system as means of enforcing conformity to desirable norms: those tenants exhibiting anti-social behaviour would have their benefit entitlement restricted. This would represent a significant regulatory stick – a more malevolent big gun. The rights/responsibilities dichotomy has explicitly been proffered as the rationale for making the payment of housing benefit condition on the tenant's behaviour (DWP, 2003: para 1). The essential question posed by this document is why the state should offer financial support to people 'who behave without regard to their neighbours' (para 9). The Consultation Paper was keen to point out that there should be little impact on landlords (para 14; Annex B):

> Neither of the [proposed] options involves placing new duties on landlords or regulating the landlord/tenant relationship. The contractual relationship between the tenant and the landlord remains the same: it remains the duty of the tenant to pay the rent. The tenant may however have more difficulty in paying the rent from his/her reduced income; but that is the penalty for his/her behaviour. (Annex B, p 5)

These proposals have not to date been clothed in legislative form. We should not however regard them as rhetoric or symbolic. The whole focus of debate has been on more intrusive, disciplinary techniques of government to enforce community responsibility norms and the proposals are fully in accord with the thrust of policy more broadly. Once a workable mechanism with which to implement them has been identified, and the responsibilization agenda more fully established, it is probable that policy will continue in its current direction.

The Housing Act 2004 – A panoply of control[2]

Seemingly against the grain of governing through freedom are the panoply of controls contained in the 2004 Housing Act. This Act contains a potent mixture of governance techniques – licensing, regulation, codes of practice, and the creation of standards. It offers partly a targeted form of control (houses in multiple occupation and selective licensing), and partly general (tenancy deposits and housing conditions).

It seeks to respond to the current direction of housing policy as it affects the PRS – a shift away from rights to the construction of a 'healthy' sector (Blandy, 2001), one in which abuses can be minimized or controlled. The focus on health signals a return to the concerns of the nineteenth-century interventions in the housing market. This is partly moralistic and partly ethical; it also signals the re-envisioning of expertise regarding the sector around understandings of risk and uncertainty.

Helen Carr (2005b) has memorably encapsulated the question facing New Labour as how to govern the ungovernable. The ungovernability of the sector 'is stressed in explanations ... which highlight its fragmentation, its incoherence, its polarisation, its very unknowability'. It forms a policy arena in which common sense knowledge about landlords and the sector becomes crucially combined with certain statistical knowledges about risk and dangerousness – for example, we are told that there is uncertainty in the category of 'houses in multiple occupation' but, nevertheless, these are the most dangerous, unhealthy parts of the sector (see DETR, 1999d). We are told that unscrupulous landlords are attracted to areas of low demand and work in tandem with anti-social tenants (DTLR, 2001), but there is no statistical evidence which demonstrates such attraction nor any attempt to identify the meaning of 'unscrupulous' or 'problem' landlords (see Valverde, 2003b: 239, for discussion of the link between licensing and area, something perhaps less apparent as regards the HMO sector).

Licensing is the solution for both – compulsory licensing for HMOs and (area) selective for the unscrupulous. It is important in this process that:

> ... landlord licensing should not be seen as a one way relationship. The Government would like to see as a starting point a local compact between local authorities, RSLs, landlords, police and other agencies. This would be based on an understanding that local authorities and others would provide guidance and practical support, with police back up where necessary, while landlords would meet their side of the bargain by abiding by licence conditions. (DTLR, 2001: para 25)

Licensing as a governance technique is, then, a multi-faceted enterprise. At one and the same time, it enables the different organizations offering/bringing their own disciplinary expertise together, it imposes a set of ethical values on the sector (licensees are 'fit and proper' people who work within certain codes) as well as filling a knowledge void. In this process, the technology of the licence enables constant surveillance. It is the fuzziness of the knowledge about this sector and 'unscrupulousness', as with ASB, which enables these significant techniques of control without overt rule to be imposed. By contrast, however, they are designed to generate information about the sector; this is the important point made by Valverde (2003b: 238): '... licensing and its attendant techniques for privately governing public order risks is not just a matter of allocating powers to use force and otherwise maintain security: it is also – and crucially – a matter of epistemological duties, duties to know and to manage risks'.

Risks are explicitly dealt with through the innovative 'Housing Health and Safety Rating System' (HHSRS). This is a system of clinical risk assessment and management which has been productive of expertise. Local authority environmental health officers are to assess the risks, or hazards, of properties against certain broad requirements: physiological, psychological, protection against infection and against accidents. There is a mass of guidance produced to amplify these requirements (discussed in Carr *et al*, 2005), but the emphasis is on their reflexive use and their adaptation to the particular household concerned. Indeed, it is this which creates the area of uncertainty which calls for professional judgement. The HHSRS in other words is a classic example of the 'variable array of assemblages of risk and uncertain elements' to which O'Malley (2004) refers. This assemblage is made possible by the development of sophisticated computer programmes, transferable onto PDAs, which 'standard[ize] the risks of all hazards on the basis of equivalent annual risk of death creat[ing] an objective measure of risk and allow[ing] comparisons across hazards' (DETR, 2001: para 3.3). As Cowan and Marsh (2005b) have put it:

> [I]t is clear that the perceived benefit of this development is the production of knowledge about housing conditions upon which various strategies and programmes will be able to work. In these senses, the proposals exemplify a governmentalization of property quality by experts 'using professional judgment' (DETR, 2001: para 3.1). And this professional judgment is to be used to provide advice and control uncertainty in their prediction of the future 'hazard of death'

And professionalization is cemented within the discretionary judgements required of the assessing officer. The new system requires interdisciplinarity in judgement and is dependent on distinguishing between risks to occupiers and risks to the most vulnerable occupiers. Although the output of the HHSRS is a neutral score, the inputs are value-laden.

What does not necessarily fit within this schema is the new system designed to deal with tenancy deposits. This system requires landlords of assured shorthold tenancies to pay the deposit received from tenants into one of two types of compulsory scheme (custodial or insurance). Such schemes can be maintained by professional organizations. They are, in this sense, an example of enforced or co-regulation. One might well ask whether this was a necessary response to the much publicized issue of landlords withholding some or all of the deposit at the end of the occupation (see NACAB, 1998; and http://www.citizensadvice.org.uk/winnn6/index/campaigns /social_policy/ parliamentary_briefings/pb_housing/cr_tenancy_deposit_scheme). The ODPM's own research suggested that the problem was probably not significant enough to require a legislative scheme (Rugg and Bevan, 2002) and any intervention was decried by the landlord lobby. On one level, this might be perceived as a success of the 'anti-landlord culture' (Rugg and Rhodes, 2003: 943–4), but Carr's sensitive analysis suggests a rather different, more complex story in which the anti-landlord message is wrapped up in a campaign to regenerate the image of the sector. It 'is focused on addressing expressed concerns and the creation of trust' but at the same time 'allows space for the reassertion of neo-liberal rationalities simultaneously with the protection of tenancy deposits'. Thus, private landlord agency organizations might apply to run such a scheme – indeed, some already do so on a voluntary basis (see Carr *et al*, 2005: para 10.22).

Housing benefit

> Housing Benefit is now centre-stage in the Government's welfare reform programme. The reforms promote choice and responsibility for Housing Benefit customers as well as making the scheme much more transparent. (http://www.dwp.gov.uk/housingbenefit/ reform-agenda/index.asp, accessed 13/04/05)

A key part of the 1988 reforms to the private rented sector was the opening up of rents to market processes. In doing so, it altered the nature of the subsidy from state regulation of rents to market system with a personal subsidy, housing benefit, 'to provide help to those who need it' (DoE, 1987: para 3.18). Housing benefit is an unusual subsidy in that it pays up to 100 per cent of the 'eligible' rent charged by private landlords and thus offers protection against the market for certain persons. Marsh (2004: 192) summarizes the critique of this subsidy:

> Almost from its inception in 1983 the system has attracted criticism because it provides tenants with limited incentives to optimize their housing consumption and, given that they are effectively insulated from rent increases, the system is seen in principle as embodying incentives toward 'up-marketing' and over-consumption. In the private sector a complex system of supplementary regulations was felt necessary to ensure that HB was not abused.

Furthermore, there have been repeated concerns about housing benefit fraud and abuse of the system by both landlords and tenants (see Kemp, 2000: 268–71; particularly the anti-social (DWP, 2003)). Much effort has been given over to curbing fraud – variously costed at up to £8 bn per annum – which has led to lengthy, complex application forms (the current form is 39 pages long) and a complex verification process. Concern was expressed about the process of paying rent directly to the landlord, by-passing the tenant, who therefore had no effective responsibility for the rent. Rents were assessed by the Rent Service which determined the 'eligible rent' and, apparently restricted the eligible housing benefit in 70 per cent of cases, averaging around £20 below the rent actually charged by the landlord (DWP, 2004: para 84). Finally, the administration of housing benefit has generally been poor and is well known to operate with a considerable backlog of claims leading to early eviction (see Audit Commission, 2004; Hunter *et al*, 2005) – problematic administration is, in part, a result of the fairly regular modifications to the system which has produced complexity.

Both Conservative and New Labour governments sought to reform housing benefit because of the apparent lack of independence and responsibility inherent in the system. However, it was not until the early to mid-2000s that New Labour have tentatively begun the reform process under the heading 'building choice and responsibility' (DWP, 2003). The aim of this reform is:

> To restructure the benefit support for people on low-incomes, to create a simpler, fairer system which gives them more power to make decisions about the home they live in and how they spend their money, and which reduces barriers to work. (para 1.2)

Using a 'pathfinder approach', the department of work and pensions (DWP) has set in train ten pilot local authorities to trail a 'standard local housing allowance' under which claimants receive a fixed amount depending on factors such as household size. The benefits of this new system are said to be fairness, choice, transparency, personal responsibility, increased work incentives and simplicity (DWP, 2004).

Housing benefit reform, although important in its own right, also fits into the New Labour canon of citizenship – activity, responsibility and workfare. The presupposition in this is of the housing benefit applicant as a rational economic actor, an 'active manager' (Walters, 2000: 139) responding to market incentives – although, undoubtedly, the flat rate will also shape the particular sub-sector of the market (c.f. Marsh, 2004) just as its predecessor did. In this reconstruction of the applicant, the expertise of the rent service bureaucracy has become nullified; it is the applicant-consumer who has the active expertise to negotiate the housing market and with their prospective landlord; to adopt Dean's phrase, 'the structures and values of the market are folded back onto' (1999: 172) the housing benefit claimant who is given the freedom to act entrepreneurially under licence from the housing benefit authority. And if they fail, then that speaks to their inability to act with the requisite responsibility of the consumer (although there are insurantial safeguards 'in recognition of the risk that some tenants may struggle with this responsibility' (DWP, 2004: para 42). What is particularly interesting about these set of reforms is that they focus on the occupier, rather than on the landlord; the assumption must be that the landlord will be disciplined by the market mechanism into charging rents which fit with the standard local housing allowance (or that they will exit the sector completely).

Conclusions

We began this chapter with an assertion that to exclude private renting from the make-up of social housing is to exclude an important outlet of housing supported by the state. In this way, we sought to draw upon our primary question about the 'social' in social housing. Our argument spoke to a reality in which private renting is used to support and supplant the state's provision of housing. The growth of council housing in the post-First World War period was at least in part a response to the failure of the PRS. However and by contrast to that truth, we have drawn attention to a series of official narratives throughout that period, in which there is an assumption that controls placed on the PRS should be regarded as a temporary blip. Afterwards, so the assumption goes, ordinary market processes will enable the sector to resume its previous 'great' mission of providing the social service of housing the citizenry. The diagnosis in these reports was that failure lay elsewhere – a failure to pay adequate wages to enable the landlord to charge a rent sufficient to provide suitable accommodation. That view of landlordism suffered a crushing blow in the 1950s with the rhetoric and reality of Rachmanism (although this built upon previous experience of landlordism and their willingness to exploit the free market – anti-landlordism runs deep). Even so, the assumption that freedom from control or regulation would renew the market is one that has continued unabated since the First World War. Boundaries have clearly shifted over time, as have constructions of the social.

The simplistic assumption that rent control (with or without security of tenure) was responsible for the demise of the sector, which was the premise of the reforms in the 1950s and the 1980s as well as some of the reports in the inter-war period, has been the governing problematization. The deregulatory instinct has therefore been strong in this sector. On one level, that is precisely what has occurred through the creation of the assured shorthold tenancy and market rents which fit neatly into that neo-liberal canon of market-subjection. It has been the subject of what Marsh (2004: 202) has termed the 'deregulatory dismissal' – that 'if the policy hasn't worked so far then it's because it hasn't gone far enough'.[3] Furthermore, the market is maintained and enhanced further by housing benefit and its reforms, which have engaged the active, entrepreneurial subject, licensing the claimant to engage in the happy market pursuit of choice and negotiation.

On the other hand, we might observe the paradox of private renting – that the sector has never been more regulated or controlled. The apotheosis of this regulation/control is the Housing Act 2004, which returns housing policy to its nineteenth-century roots of focusing on 'healthy' housing and a 'healthy private rented sector'. To observe the current state of the government of the PRS is to observe a welter of Consultation Papers, concerns and formal/informal mechanisms of control. Partnership, as the relationship between private renting and the state is now conceived, comes at the price of a loss of freedom.

Further, these reforms are designed to weed out the 'bad' landlord, and to protect the reputation of the 'good'. This process of division has been a wonderfully simplistic device through which a new regulatory dimension has been produced. Such a dimension harnesses the moral capacity of landlords and occupiers.

Our discussion of this legislation, however, suggests that these assertions of sovereignty are rather more nuanced than first appears. Although by no means representing a coherent single mentality of government, the reforms adopt and adapt different forms and relationships. Compulsory and selective licensing, controls on the use or holding of tenancy deposits, and the HHSRS all utilize different techniques of government and, to an extent, are premised on different understandings of the role of government as well as different forms of knowledge (one might also say that *the* government exhibited differing levels of commitment to each set of reforms). As Rose (1999) reminds us, these apparent incoherence and inconsistencies are hardly surprising – government is a polyvocal activity. This reflects the fact that there is no single regime of truth about the PRS, just as there is no single PRS. Rather, these truths are rooted in a diverse set of historical problematizations, which are continually in action.

Chapter 8:
Owner-Occupation

The story of social housing is contingent – it certainly was not inevitable that councils would be chosen for the historic mission of building 'homes fit for heroes' in the post-First World War period, nor, indeed, that they would build for letting. Indeed, the earliest council housebuilding was specifically earmarked for sale. Although owner-occupation has currently taken on a hegemonic form, it is equally possible that its evolution during the twentieth century might have occurred earlier, during the nineteenth century when the building societies, rather than terminate, became permanent.

In this chapter, we begin with a section which examines the literature about desire for ownership. Our argument, broadly, is that ownership operates at the interface between neo-liberal and neo-conservative desires. It is used discursively to emphasize the freedom of the occupier, the ability to make choices, and, most importantly, constructs the renter as unable to exercise that freedom. It is used as part of a strategy of 'government through the calculated administration of shame' (Rose, 1999: 73) – that is, shame not to be a home owner, shame to be within the 'social' system. We then consider three examples which demonstrate how this desire works as a control – building societies, the right to buy, and the scandal caused by the mis-selling of council property by Westminster City Council.

In each of these examples, the desire for ownership is used as a discursive technique of governing, successfully, unsuccessfully and unlawfully. Government is a constant process of trial and error. This chapter, then, concerns the contingent construction of the social in social housing over time, demonstrating the pivotal role of ownership in those constructions. We emphasize the moral regulatory role played in the discourse of ownership and its translation into central and local policy.

The desire for ownership

Over 70 per cent of households currently own their accommodation, and polls regularly put the demand for ownership at around 90 per cent (although questions are designed to elicit such a response) (see, for example, ODPM, 2005: para 1.1). Housing and urban studies have sought to provide explanations for this (r)evolution in the way in which households hold land. In doing so, they have at times fetishized the home ownership tenure, imbuing it with particular assets and attributes. They follow a long line of the great and the good who have sought to promote the tenure.

One set of arguments has proceeded to demonstrate how the tenure has been promoted in policy discourse. Ownership has been constructed over time as *home* ownership; and as a normal, rational human desire. This is its most regular presentation in policy documents presented by different political parties in the post-Second World War phase of housing policy. It is conveyed in the title of the publication by the ODPM's Home Ownership Task Force (2003), *A Home of My Own*; indeed, it is conveyed in the setting up of such a task force. Gurney's linguistic analysis (1999a: 172–3) of the 1995 housing White Paper (DoE, 1995) makes the point that:

> ... 'home' is used not only more frequently but more evocatively and more emotionally in relation to home ownership than to private and social renting. ... 'Home' as a normalising discourse is expressed ... through ideas of love, warmth, comfort, pride, independence, and self-respect. The chapter concerning home ownership is dripping with these ideas. This is normalisation through repetition and association.

Gurney notes that this White Paper, as opposed to earlier housing policy statements, combines home and ownership, a linguistic strategy also evident in the New Labour Green Paper (DETR/DSS, 2000). However, this is not a tectonic shift from what went before. In the 1977 Green Paper (DoE, 1977: 50), it was suggested that the reason behind the 'secular trend towards home ownership is the sense of greater personal independence that it brings. For most people owning one's home is a basic and natural desire.' One can go further back, but the basic point has been made (see further, for example, Gray, 1982: 268–70; Murie, 1998: 84–8). Some academics, most prominently Peter Saunders in his important (but flawed) book, *A Nation of Home Owners* (1990), have argued that alongside this naturalness of the tenure runs the 'ontological security' that comes with being a home owner.

This normalizing discourse has been part and parcel of a certain tenure prejudice, most clearly expressed in the aphorisms and metaphors used on a daily basis about ownership as opposed to renting. The work of Craig Gurney (1999a; 1999b) on these points has cleared much of the conceptual ground for us in this book. Home ownership, and the values associated with it, has come to be regarded as truth. Home owners, Gurney (1999a: 177) suggests, are constructed as 'better citizens, better parents and better caretakers', whereas tenants are 'a stigmatised stereotyped outgroup'. These kind of values are conveyed in certain metaphors about renting – 'money down the drain' 'dead money' – which Gurney (1999b: 1715) analyses as an 'idea that money has an anthropomorphic quality and that a tenant, in paying rent, is responsible for its death'. The 'murder' of money is 'the antithesis of the positive images of "husbandry" and "stewardship" associated with home ownership' (ibid).

Much of this discourse of home ownership can similarly be found in the self-help literature of the nineteenth century, especially that which associated itself with the values of building societies. Here, one finds a link between thrift, on the one hand, and ownership (specifically of land), on the other. For example, Samuel Smiles' book, *Self-Help* (1859), extols the virtues of economy:

> Economy may be styled the daughter of Prudence, the sister of Temperance, and the mother of Liberty. It is evidently conservative – conservative of character, of domestic

happiness, and social well-being. It is, in short, the exhibition of self-help in one of its best forms.

And Price (1958: 139–40) quotes a lecture given by Smiles in 1864 in which the virtues of thrift are explicitly linked with those of ownership:

> The accumulation of property has the effect which it always has upon thrifty men; it makes them steady, sober and diligent. It weans them from revolutionary notions, and makes them conservative. When workmen, by their industry and frugality, have secured their own independence, they will cease to regard the sight of others' well-being as a wrong inflicted on themselves; and it will no longer be possible to make political capital out of their imaginary woes.

These links between economy, property and conservatism (as opposed to the pauperized revolutionary) became part and parcel of the social identity of home ownership during the twentieth century. Harold Bellman, manager of the Abbey Road Building Society and Chairman of the Building Societies Association (BSA) (as well as being a paid-up member of the Conservative party, assisting that party during its 1935 election campaign (Craig, 1986: 91), for example, noted (1927: 54) that:

> Home ownership is a civic and national asset. The sense of citizenship is more keenly felt and appreciated, and personal independence opens up many an avenue of wider responsibility and usefulness. ... The benefits of home ownership are not only material, but ethical and moral as well. The man who has something to protect and improve – a stake of some sort in the country – naturally turns his thoughts in the direction of sane, ordered and perforce economical, government. The thrifty man is seldom or never an extremist agitator.

Bellman goes on to note the comment that ownership provided a 'bulwark against Bolshevism and all that Bolshevism stands for'. Similarly, it prefaces the post-Second World War campaign for a 'property owning democracy'.

Property ownership, thus, provides a key method of governing individuals, working through their freedom. It prevented the descent to pauperism, as well as providing stability, responsibility, thrift, health, wealth and an example to others. It offers an incentive to self-government, without the imposition of external forms of rule. It links tenure with the project of creating the healthy city, the private form of ownership with the public good. It is for this reason that enabling home ownership has often been talked of as a 'social service'. Indeed, James Taylor, a manager of a large (albeit unknown) number of building societies in Birmingham, argued before the Royal Commission on Friendly and Benefit Building Societies in 1871 that the building societies were 'the greatest social reformers of the day' (Royal Commission, 1871: para 3745). These assets carried it not only into the twentieth century but also into the twenty-first century.

This desire for home ownership was bolstered (or constructed) around a set of taxation and other advantages, which have until recently consistently favoured owners and their lenders (generally, until the mid-1980s, building societies). Although the property legislation of 1925 was primarily designed to facilitate the growth of ownership, it is often forgotten that the 1925 Acts built upon and consolidated the legislation, particularly from 1881, which had that aim. During part of the nineteenth century, building societies had the benefit of not being liable for stamp duty. And, during the latter part of the twentieth century, the tenure market was distorted by different taxation interventions which favoured ownership. So, for example, although we rightly talk about the importance of housing provided by the local state, it should not be forgotten that ownership was at times the subject of greater financial privilege (Hills, 1990: 27–8). As Forrest and Murie (1991: 123) suggest, 'tenure preferences are not formed in a vacuum but are heavily influenced by the pattern of subsidy, general housing policies and the individual judgements regarding financial expectations and changes in family circumstances'.

The building society movement

In this section, our purpose is to bring building societies back within the firmament of social housing. Over the past couple of centuries, they have been looked on with some favour as organizations which have encouraged thrift, forward planning and activity on the part of a certain class. Although it is probably true that the middle classes obtained most benefit from them during the nineteenth century and they had little impact on property ownership beyond landlordism, as we discuss below, building societies have proved adept at self-publicity, self-formation, and producing a set of truths about their role in the social. Property ownership made citizens, but it was the building society which facilitated that transition into the self-responsibilities of citizenship.

Building societies, thrift and property

While the rise of council housing in the post-First World War period has proved contentious among housing studies scholars, the rise of property ownership during the same period has been less so. What is clear is that property ownership gained during this period, probably at a greater rate than state provided housing, as a result of the widespread investment by building societies in the ownership market combined with investment through state subsidy and cosy relationships with builders. The seeds of this movement, as well as the considerable levels of political support offered to building societies (in generating, developing and retaining the market), lie in the nineteenth century. Indeed, although their foundations were in the better-off artisan class and amateurism (probably) at the end of the eighteenth century, by the latter part of the nineteenth century they were a political force in their own right. There were, it is true, certain counter-discourses which railed against the lack of expertise and unfulfillable promises made in prospectuses. Despite this, there appears to have been no stopping the development of new societies.

However, by the mid-nineteenth century, they had taken on a professional ethic, their practice was underpinned by 'a sound mathematical reasoning' and expertise, and they had formed themselves into a strong pressure group which clearly had irked successive governments (see below). A key figure, almost totally neglected in housing studies, was Arthur Scratchley who was largely responsible in the 1840s for developing actuarial practices and tables to govern building societies, and who was probably responsible for developing permanent building societies (see Price, 1958: 118).

While the original building societies were terminating (that is, they terminated once all their members had been housed) and were founded on personal relationships formed in local inns, by the 1840s it seems they had become taken over by the 'great men' of the day. Permanent building societies (which didn't build) had begun, and, rather than meeting in the pub, their association with the temperance movement led to them meeting in more professional places (particularly like the mechanics institutes). The Leeds Permanent Building Society, for example, began as a society for working men but, by the 1870s, was dominated by lending to middle classes and the wealthy; indeed, the evidence suggested that by this stage, most of its lending was to petty landlords (evidence of Thomas Fatkin to the Royal Commission, 1885b: paras 10,865–9). Gauldie (1974: 206–7) notes that there was resistance to this embourgeoisiement but also offers an explanation as to the interest of the middle classes in building societies:

> [T]here was willingness to allow money to be used towards that end, with of course the assurance that the money would not be diminished but increased in the process. The building society idea too did not challenge any of the tenets dear to that society. It did not hand out charity, it encouraged self-help. It provided no haven for the undeserving, it encouraged those who worked to be respectable. And it showed the outward and visible signs of grace because it made money safely for its supporters. (p 200)

As important, though, was the encouragement of thrift and order which was an explicit part of the ideology of the building society and related to property. As James Taylor made clear in his evidence to the Royal Commission in 1871:

> The effect of our operations was given before a committee of the House of Commons some time ago by the Chief Superintendent of Police in Birmingham, namely, the effect upon crime; he then distinctly stated (and I believe it to be so now), that we have less policemen in Birmingham than we had 20 years ago, although we have 70 miles more streets and 60,000 more inhabitants, and he directly attributed it to the habits of temperance and frugality engendered and increased by these societies.

> You mean that such habits are increased by the possession by persons in that class of life of their own houses? – Yes; they save their money, and instead of spending it in public houses, they spend it upon property. They go home at night and cultivate their gardens, or read the newspaper to their wives, instead of being in public-houses. We are the greatest social reformers of the day. (Royal Commission, 1871: paras 3745–6)

The Royal Commission itself accepted the need for facilitative regulation but, for its rationale, could come up with no better than that the societies 'must have had great influence in training [the working] class to business habits'.

Despite the public face of building societies' support for ownership, in the latter part of the nineteenth century they tended to concentrate their loans on landlords: 'owner-occupation played a larger part in building society ideology than in most societies' mortgage portfolios until well into the twentieth century' (Craig, 1986: 89). Nevertheless, as Craig points out, the ideals and purposes of the movement chimed with the political settlement after the second Reform Act.

The Building Societies Association

In the mid-nineteenth century, many societies began to work collaboratively largely to procure a beneficial, facilitative statutory environment for their business. A long-running Gazette served the emerging movement from 1869 (although there were forerunners). Such was their success in promoting their business that, despite (or because of) several high-profile scandals and failures as well as some less than scrupulous dealings under the category of the Starr-Bowkett societies[1] (see Cleary, 1965: chs 6, 8–9), they retained their profile and importance. It was those failures which enabled the well-organized movement to declare that those organizations were more like banks than building societies; and they were thus able to separate themselves off and immunize themselves from the negative publicity. Indeed, this was the point made by the Building Societies Protection Association, which developed in the mid-nineteenth century to protect the association's beneficial position on stamp duty, and which subsequently became the BSA. It was this association, which enabled both the defence of the movement as well as developing a facilitative legislative environment during the nineteenth and twentieth centuries. Its president (William McCullagh Torrens, who had also been responsible for public health legislation) and many of its members were senior members of Parliament, taken from all sides. Indeed, during this period, building societies had a gilded existence.

It was this association, created out of its own community, which was designed to govern not only that community but also the external environment such as legislative change. Thus, the Building Societies Act 1874 was partly driven by the association and its concerns about more restrictive legislation previously put before Parliament. It was also designed to paper over the cracks which had emerged over the legality of their operations. Similarly, as Craig's work demonstrates, the Building Societies Act 1939, designed to protect the societies in the face of possibly unlawful operations, came about eventually as a product of a change of heart by the Treasury. What lay behind that change 'seems to have been an appreciation of the building societies' importance in the small savings market, and a recognition that the only alternative to the building society system was an expansion of public housing with a consequent increase in state subsidies' (Craig, 1986: 100). The Building Societies Act 1986 was designed to remove some limits on their operation and enable them to compete with the emergence of banks in the deposit/lending game. Boddy (1989: 102) demonstrated how the BSA was intimately involved at every stage in the progression of that legislation which 'represented much more than even "strong lobbying" in the pressure group sense'. These episodes not only demonstrate the contingent nature of the governance capacity of the movement, but also how the relationship between the different tenures was imagined and governed.

Between 1939 and 1983, the BSA set the interest rates for both deposits in societies and mortgages paid out by them. From 1973, societies protected their market monopoly by operating a cartel under which the largest societies accepted those rates (although smaller societies oscillated within and around them: Boddy and Lambert, 1988). The basis for setting the rates appears to have reflected 'the requirements of the housing market, the general level of interest rates, the conflicting interests of investors and borrowers and the societies need to maintain adequate operating margins and liquid assets' (Boddy, 1980: 87, although it was often inaccurate; Boddy and Lambert, 1988). A significant factor was the involvement of central government, particularly when market interest rates rose rapidly in the 1970s. During the early 1970s, governments paid bridging loans to societies in order to keep mortgage interest rates at acceptable levels (which contrasts with the exhortatory tactics used in the 1950s and 1960s) (Holmans, 1987: 278–82). This government involvement made for cheaper, but fewer, mortgages (see, for example, Stewart, 1996: 69).

High interest rates in the 1970s effectively ended the cosy monopoly enjoyed by the building societies, as the beneficial advantages of the taxation environment were gradually eroded (and withdrawn in 1982); and the banks began to compete more effectively for mortgage and savings business as restrictions on their doing so were gradually whittled away. Higher interest yielding accounts became a major new source of deposit but this led to 'a squeeze on margins and evidence of a reduced rate of growth' (Boddy, 1989: 94). At the same time, the increased competition between societies spelt the demise of the cartel, particularly given that the broader financial marketplace was rapidly being deregulated. The knock-on effect of the competition for investors, through increasing interest paid on deposits, was higher mortgage rates to offset those increased costs (Ball, 1983: 36) which therefore provided an incentive to other organizations to join the mortgage market. Finally, when interest rates began to fall, the money markets became more competitive and provided an alternative, higher yielding outlet for personal savings.

Mutuality

One of the governing principles of building societies is mutuality – when there is talk of demutualisation (for example, take-overs by banks, or simply taking corporate status), mutuality is talked of as a hallowed principle and one of the hallmark benefits of the organization, even if it is one which stems the flow of the entrepreneurial juices. Indeed, one of the first acts of the first president of the BSA was the protection of the principle of mutuality against the suggestion that societies should take the corporate form. At a National Conference in 1872, Torrens was quoted as saying:

Joint Stock Companies were formed, in a spirit of speculation, to enable me to enter into speculation with a view to profit. They savoured far more in their nature of the principle of gambling than of that self-helping, self-restraining principle of Building Societies, which was antagonistic to the idea of speculation. (Price, 1958: 224)

As mutual societies, they were supposed to have 'an equitable balance' between the interests of their members – borrowers and depositors – even though that balance was difficult to maintain (Holmans, 1987: 219). However, this discursive truth was less part of the make-up of the societies from the time when they became permanent and the link between investors and borrowers was broken (see Barnes, 1984: 10), and the relationship between members and directors became distant (ibid: ch 11). Indeed, they tended to 'be closed oligarchies subject to little control by the membership ... , so [their] objectives became closely linked to the importance for senior management of high salaries, status, perks and power: all of which are associated with increasing size in terms of turnover, branches, etc' (Ball, 1983: 296). This partly explains the declining number of societies during the twentieth century, in turn holding a greater proportion of the movement's assets.

The search for 'surplus' effectively contradicted their mutuality. In seeking new markets in the 1980s, it was natural that they called into question their mutual status. The BSA itself attempted to resolve this issue by eventually focusing on expanding their role in the housing market in a series of inward-looking reports in the early 1980s:

> In emphasising a distinctive role for the societies in housing [the 1984 report] also attempted to head off concerns that diversification into the realm of financial services, combined with common fiscal treatment for all financial institutions, called into question the societies' mutual status and different and separate system of regulation. (Boddy, 1989: 97)

However, one can argue that throughout the twentieth century societies were more concerned about their collective and individual market share than about the principles of mutuality. While their concerns during the 1970s about keeping mortgage rates at affordable levels might have partly reflected their mutual background (although no doubt was heavily influenced by government policy during the same period), these concerns were not replicated during the bust cycle in the late 1980s and 1990s at which point societies were rather more concerned with efficient collection of arrears and repossessions. Indeed, during the nineteenth century, a system of fines existed for those unable to pay their dues for whatever reason. Market share was equally important to societies during the lending boom in the 1930s when the 'builders' pool' arrangements effectively protected their surpluses and signalled a decline in the quality of building standards.

Buying social housing

Nowhere is the story of social housing more contingent than in its relationship with ownership. The twentieth century's apparent tenure dichotomy – ownership or council – was, in other words, not necessarily dichotomous. We have already noted (in Chapter 1) Malpass' reading that social housing in the immediate post-Second World War period was regarded as a temporary stopgap – for two years – until 'it would be both possible and desirable to revert to the pre-war pattern of provision' (2004: 215).

However, the relationship between ownership and council housing has rarely been dichotomous. Tenure has represented a relatively rational (if blunt) technique of government, and reflected different perspectives about the most appropriate or effective way of governing people through the way in which they 'hold' their property. In the late nineteenth century, the legislation made clear that the accommodation built by councils was for sale within 10 years of its completion. Indeed, since councils began building accommodation, there has always been either a power or a duty to sell it which some councils were more willing than others to exercise (Murie *et al*, 1976).

The relationship between ownership and the social is a key aspect of this oscillation. Ownership is imagined as social housing, and, indeed, is a method of creating wealth. In the 1980s, in some accounts, ownership was presented as having effected a 'consumption sector cleavage' because of the profits associated with property ownership over time (see Saunders, 1990). Ownership was presented as a choice and a dream, a means of making capital gain. Yet, on the other hand, the experience of ownership, and the reason for accessing this tenure in the first place, is differentiated and fragmented (Forrest *et al*, 1990). For some, ownership is a 'squalid trap', associated with capital losses and being 'forced to stay in a deteriorating asset which will be in a deteriorating condition' (Karn *et al*, 1985: 109). Hence, for some, this 'choice' or 'freedom' is illusory. Even so, it is the aspiration to ownership which is the desire through which government is made possible.

It was this aspiration which was manufactured through a body of sweeteners and incentives, and sold to occupiers of council housing in the late 1970s. The advent of the right of council and registered social landlords (RSLs) occupiers to buy their homes was a significant watershed in the 'history' of social housing, but only in the sense that it again brought to the fore the political choice for individual ownership over collective provision. It was the central part of a series of mechanisms for engineering what was referred to as 'low-cost home ownership' (Forrest *et al*, 1984).

Low-cost home ownership has been the label around which a quite impressive number of innovations have been developed. All of these are designed to fulfil the apparent desire for ownership for different groups. Council tenants were served by the right to buy, some RSL tenants by the right to acquire; then there are various 'exit schemes' which provide a cash incentive to buy a property (and thus vacate a unit of council or RSL property for another household – a modern filtering down approach) and 'shared ownership' schemes (broadly where the occupier pays part-rent and part-mortgage). The process of innovation now also includes 'Homebuy', which has been developed on the back of the Home Ownership Task Force's work. Homebuy is designed to 'offer a simpler, fairer range of home ownership products' (ODPM, 2005: para 1.3). Homebuy is particularly focused on the first-time buyer, and more especially on those key workers who are priced out of the market as well as those on the housing register (para 5.1). of all schemes, Homebuy is perhaps the most innovative, building on and expanding the range of possible options.

Occupiers of council housing bought their properties in large numbers under the right to buy, not necessarily because ownership was better, but because it represented a better deal. As Cole and Furbey (1994: 172) point out:

> ... it is not clear that this exodus [of council tenants to home owners] is to be viewed as an historical inevitability produced by ineluctable deficiencies in public housing. Faced with an exceptional deal, the relatively affluent households which form the majority exerting the Right to Buy have certainly voted with their feet, but their votes have been cast against an already strongly residualised, increasingly centralised, unmodernised tenure which was not resourced or managed to meet their changing aspirations.

This was also not necessarily a willing choice on the part of the landlords. In essence, the legislation forced councils to sell. Calling it 'the right to buy' was, in the words of Lord Rodger, 'Parliament's equivalent of a soundbite' which 'emphasised that under the Act the rights are on the side of the tenants and the obligations on the side of the landlords. ... Despite this, of course, politicians and the media have consistently spoken of "council house sales" ' (*R (O'Byrne) v Sec of State for the Environment, Transport and the Regions* [2003] 1 All ER 15: para 69).

If councils sought to avoid their obligation to sell, the then Department of Environment had power to intervene and take over the operation of the right to buy in that locality (see *Norwich CC v Secretary of State for the Environment* [1982] 1 All ER 737). This was command and control legislation, with the purpose of increasing property ownership (although other parts of the legislation had no similar enforcement powers, nor, indeed, were they brought into operation expeditiously: see Kay *et al*, undated). Indeed, the occupiers could, once they started on the process, force local authorities to sell in most cases by applying for an 'injunction'. This process became contentious when councils sought to avoid selling the property to occupiers, after the latter had started the process.

In the high profile cases, councils sought to avoid sales because of allegations against the occupiers (racial harassment, drug dealing) which would ordinarily have led to a reasonable prospect of success at obtaining a possession order. In these circumstances, could the council call a halt to the sale? The technical answer given by the House of Lords was that, where a court had an application from an occupier for an injunction to force the sale as well as an application from a council for possession, it was up to the court which it heard first. If the court heard the occupier's application first, then it seemed that the possession proceedings fell. What was interesting about this line of cases was not necessarily this result, but the way in which the courts accepted the coercive nature of the powers:

> [The history of the right to buy is that] it was introduced for the first time in 1980 at a time when a number of local authorities strongly resisted parting with the ownership of publicly owned accommodation to those who then lived in it, and it seems to me that we should be doing great violence to the obvious intention of Parliament if we did not recognise that it was Parliament's intention to block to the maximum the opportunities open to reluctant landlords to obstruct the acquisition of title by their tenants. (*Taylor v Newham LBC* (1993) 25 HLR 290, 298)

The right to buy was an act of sovereign law, meant to discipline local authorities and the occupiers. It was remarkably successful in so doing (although this success was geographically differentiated), in part because central government took an active role in its implementation; occupiers chose ownership because housing was a weak link in the social, and susceptible to attack (Cole and Furbey, 1994).

Although much is made in the literature of the effect the right to buy had on central–local relations; what is also clear is the way it redrew the map of tenure and created a new set of unquestioned/unquestionable truths. First, the right to buy posed a new set of housing problems (what follows is taken from Forrest and Murie, 1991). Not unforeseeably, the purchasers of property under the right have tended to be the better-off occupiers (although many had at one time or another been 'problem tenants' in terms of rent arrears and the like), of a certain age (between 30 and 50), in certain areas where the purchasers also bought the better quality stock. What this left behind in the council sector was a group of increasingly marginalized households occupying the less good quality stock in an increasingly residualized tenure. Hence, the right to buy effectively created the conditions in which the new problematizations about behaviour/dangerousness, unpopularity, social exclusion and the 'underclass' could flourish.

Second, despite that concern about the effects of the right, as Goodlad and Atkinson (2004: 457) point out, 'the principle of the right to buy [i]s sacrosanct' in a society in which ownership is still heavily promoted. This was not only the view of government but also the expectation, it was said, of tenants. Indeed, although the Housing Act 2004 and other quasi-legislative interventions have limited the right to buy, this has been primarily in response to concerns about its exploitation. Exploitation, in this context, is an expansive concept, covering the activities of private companies offering to assist occupiers with their negotiations with the council, or offering finance in return for a sale-leaseback agreement. The 2004 Act also includes a requirement on landlords to provide information 'on the responsibilities and consequences of being a home owner' (col 1348, per Lord Rooker). The concern was expressed that occupiers were insufficiently experienced as consumers to appreciate the costs of ownership, both initial and ongoing costs (as a result of the experience of some flat owners who have been faced with large service charges). Such information clearly prefaces the change of status from tenant to consumer, the latter having certain, different information rights. Even so, the rushed Consultation Paper produced by the ODPM maintains that the government is committed to the principle of the right to buy, and that the duty to provide information will be satisfied by provision of a simple fact sheet (ODPM, 2004).

Indeed, the principle of the right has remained unquestioned to the extent that there was apparently a tussle over the New Labour manifesto for the 2005 election. Alan Milburn, it is said, wanted the right to buy to be extended to all housing association tenants and 'has used a series of speeches in recent weeks to praise the Tory policy, arguing that property ownership is the route to greater social mobility, personal opportunity and equality' (Baldwin and Sherman, 2004). Both Tory and New Labour manifestoes promise to extend the right in this way; both, interestingly for our purposes, do so within a section of their manifesto concerned with health.

Third, over time, the right to buy has subsequently become associated with such ideas as 'sustainable communities', 'stable communities' and the policy preference for 'mixed tenure communities'. Tunstall (2003: 156), for example, drawing on Estate Action literature suggests that the policy preference for mixed tenure estates is partly a cost-saving device ('presumably through effects on behaviour and reduced maintenance and monitoring costs'); combating social exclusion; 'tenure mixing in areas dominated by social housing may change behaviour by allowing upwardly mobile residents – potential role models and sources of social capital – to buy without moving'; and changing the image of an area. These versions show how economy, behaviour and peer-learning elide together as justifications, as well as demonstrating the power of sale – that owners are, somehow, better households, households from which others can learn (and not the other way round). Nevertheless, the concept of stable communities remains unworked out, suggesting a flux in the governance relationship. So, reforms in the 2004 Housing Act increase the length of time that occupiers have to reside in the tenure before they are entitled to exercise the right, on the basis that this 'will encourage tenants to make a longer-term commitment to the community before they can buy' (HL Debates, vol 664, col 1328, per Lord Bassam). In this new framework, it is not necessarily ownership which demonstrates commitment to community formation.

Mapping policy onto the local – the case of Westminster

The construction of *home* ownership within policy and everyday discourse can also be mapped onto political events, choices and prejudices. Such was the case in Westminster City Council where, in the late 1980s, there were allegations about gerrymandering, or, as it was framed in the media, 'selling homes for votes'. This created a scandal which engulfed the Tory party at key times over the next decade. Broadly, the concern was that the council had sold off part of its housing stock for political gain (a policy similar to the nineteenth-century Land Societies, which built housing of a certain rateable value to sell to voters of particular parties, with spectacular lack of success: Cleary, 1968). In 2001, following an investigation and report by the District Auditor, John Magill, the sales policy was declared by the House of Lords to have been developed and used for an improper motive, to benefit the then ruling Conservative party. The leader of the council, Dame Shirley Porter, and the Deputy leader, John Weeks, were held liable to pay £26.5m to the council for their 'wilful misconduct' in selling the properties.

The story

In May 1986, the local elections reduced the Conservative majority on Westminster council to four. Porter set up 'The Chairmen's Group' – a group of Conservative committee chairs – to advise the party on matters of policy and political tactics. The group set about preparing a four-year strategy. A key part of this strategy was the initial development of ward profiles. A meeting of the Chairmen's Group on 2 September 1986 made clear that 'homelessness/gentrification' was regarded as one of the key issues to electoral success in the 1990 elections (Magill, 1996b: para 46 – unless otherwise noted, subsequent references are to this volume). The meeting suggested that homeless families should either be decanted to other areas or placed in Labour wards; gentrification was related explicitly to home ownership (para 51). At a subsequent seminar, attended by Conservative councillors and senior officers, one paper on homelessness/gentrification made the following observation:

> 5. What is gentrification? In short, it is ensuring that the right people live in the right areas. The areas are relatively easy to define: target wards identified on the basis of electoral trends and results. Defining 'people' is much more difficult and is not strictly council business. (para 57)

Homeless households were described in the documents as 'the tinted person in the woodpile' (para 60) and policies were subsequently said to require officers to 'be mean and nasty – implication – social services' (para 79). These assertions and concerns were continuously repeated in ruling party documents. One paper made it clear that:

> the problem [for the 1990 election] can be simply stated. If it is accepted that owner occupiers are more inclined to vote Conservative then we approach the City Council elections in 1990 with an enormous handicap ... The short term objective must be to target the marginal wards and, as a matter of utmost urgency, redress the imbalance by encouraging a pattern of tenure which is more likely to translate into Conservative votes. (para. 131, original emphasis)

Consultants were employed to conduct ward-level research on housing and the local economy. The subtext of this research was made clear to the researchers at a meeting between themselves and Porter and colleagues on 15 September 1986: '[Porter] told the [consultants] "we want the right answers" ' (para 66). As it happened, despite considerable political pressure on the researchers, their report did not justify the subsequent targeting of the marginal wards. Nevertheless, a members' subgroup was set up to take forward proposals to extend a designated sales programme under general powers in eight key marginal wards.

On 10 March 1987, a Chairmen's Group meeting used the term 'Building Stable Communities' to describe the sales policies. It was agreed at a Chairmen's Group on 14 March 1987 to have about 249 sales per annum in the eight key wards. That meeting appears to have been crucial in setting the parameters of the policy and the roles of councillors and officers. On 17 March 1987, the Director of Housing wrote to the Managing Director suggesting that the council's solicitor should be consulted about the reasonableness of designating up to 490 properties which would 'no longer be available for renting' (para 185). Subsequent discussion among members included the types of properties to be designated for sale, which were mostly blocks of flats. The Director of Housing (Private Sector) wrote a memorandum to the Chairmen's Group for 5 May suggesting that the target of 250 sales per annum also include right to buy sales and reinforcing the need for legal advice (para 229).

He was told that counsel's advice should be sought that day and a revised paper brought to the Group at its 6.00 pm meeting. Counsel advised that designating property for sale on the basis of electoral advantage would be unlawful, and that any designation of properties would need to be across all wards. He was, however, *misinformed* by the officers as to the content of the consultants' report which was described by them as justifying the designation policy (para 239). The officers were advised by counsel that provided they set out a balanced report with all the pros and cons and without reference to irrelevant considerations, the report would be 'completely judge-proof'.

A report was then prepared for the meeting of the Housing Committee on 8 July 1987. This report went through a number of drafts. The fourth draft was commented upon by counsel. In these drafts, there were two options for the Committee. Subsequent drafts, however, included a third option: designating up to 500 properties for sale city-wide. The report made clear that this option would cause the council's 'ability to meet homeless needs [to be] substantially reduced ... ability to house Category A medical needs drastically reduced ... most other priority housing categories closed ...' (para 376). About 9,360 dwellings were designated for sale, 40 per cent of the council's stock (Magill, 1996a: para 276). The committee divided on party lines and the option to increase designated sales by 500 properties was carried by seven votes to five.

From this time onwards, all further activities of the Chairmen's Group as well as various requirements made of officers were related to measuring the success of the policy. Over 200 pages of the District Auditor's report is given over to describing the extent of these monitoring activities. During this period, officers were forced to respond in detail to numerous allegations of impropriety made by the opposition party.

Home ownership, local politics and homelessness

What is perhaps most surprising about the various political machinations is not so much that they occurred, but that ordinarily intelligent people could buy into so many myths about owner-occupation. What occurred here was the normalization of a central political discourse within the outer reaches of the Conservative Party; it was the reproduction of discourses about *home* ownership that guided Westminster's housing policy during this period.

Here there is a disparity between the more formal council documents and those for internal party consumption. Even then, that disparity is not always uniform. The key document presented to the Housing Committee, the 'Review of Home Ownership' (reproduced at Magill, 1996b: Appendix 4), throughout its various drafts, prioritizes concepts of 'home' ownership. So, for example, it makes the point that 'the council has always been acutely aware of the need to promote particularly low-cost home ownership and to redress the balance between the various sectors'. At one point, the document counterposes 'the need to promote home ownership' (pt 5) against 'the need for social housing' (pt 7). Yet, pt 8 of the review refers to the 'conflict between the *demand* for social housing and the *need* to promote home ownership'. The counterposition of demand and need in this way (quite against policy pronouncements which focused then as now on housing need) provides an incidental inscription of values of the majority party.

There was an explicit assumption that owners were more likely to vote Conservative. That was the purpose behind the scheme. A reading of the District Auditor's recitation of the 'facts' demonstrates how both myths were so ingrained into the Conservative councillors' understanding of an election strategy. As was said in the Court of Appeal:

> By June 5 [1987], Mrs Kirwan, at [Porter's] request, had produced a note 'covering the possibilities of balancing the social mix in Westminster', analyzing voters 'who are not our natural supporters' and suggesting options which included increasing the number of designated blocks and decanting tenants. ([1998] 30 HLR 997, 1013, *per* Rose L.J.)

Local understandings of concepts such as 'gentrification' were driven by these myths. The targeting of marginal wards – 'battlezone wards' as Porter referred to them – was conducted on the basis that tenure was everything: 'as a matter of utmost urgency, [we must] redress the imbalance by encouraging a pattern of tenure which is more likely to translate into Conservative votes'. The homeless – the 'tinted person in the woodpile' – were regarded as *so* undesirable that they needed to be exported out of the borough. Where other councils were using accommodation in Westminster in partial fulfilment of their homelessness obligations, it became council policy to implement stringent 'enforcement' policies (under a 'quality of life' banner) to stop this process occurring.

In seeking to tame (political) chance in this way, the ruling party were buying into a further myth about *home* ownership: that home owners vote Conservative. On one set of understandings, the evidence at the time might have been interpreted sympathetically to this position (see Saunders, 1990: 227–39 for discussion). However, the bivariate analysis – tenure to voting pattern – is far too simplistic, as indeed even Saunders accepted. The equation of the Conservative Party with ownership represents a faith in numbers, rather than in the context of those numbers (Forrest *et al*, 1990: 167–70).

Nevertheless, the catchy description of the policy in the media as 'homes for votes' captured the underlying divisions and assumptions. It is unclear when the 'homes for votes' label became attached to the policies in Westminster (it was, for example, used in a secondary description in *The Times* in reporting on Magill's interim announcement in 1994, but without any reference point: Elliott *et al*, 1994); but the important point is that by December 2001, the label was so completely and successfully attached to those policies that all reports of the House of Lords' judgment drew upon it as the description of those policies. In setting out what Porter was guilty of, the phrase appears ubiquitously in the opening paragraphs, if not the title of the article (Eaglesham, 2001; Gibb, 2001; Rozenburg, 2001). By this time, this label was the reference point – it was assumed that the readership *knew* what this meant. These three words summarize the facts. They suggest that the strategy was a simple and unproblematic connection between the sale of 'homes' and the translation into Conservative votes. The assumption, of course, remains unchallenged (that is not the role of the media when they construct the 'facts'), but the point is similar to that made in relation to the courts. The translation of the story into these three words transmits a particular set of facts and assumptions.

There is a further set of assumptions conveyed by the label, particularly by the suggestive use of the word 'homes'. The suggestion is that somehow purchasers' votes were bought by the majority party when they bought the property. In other words, so grateful were the purchasers to the ruling party that they would thereafter vote for them. The designation of the word 'homes' in this context is used to suggest not only permanence but also belonging – it buys into the notion of stable communities. The word 'home' describes an intimate, private sphere; 'house' the external, depersonalized bricks and mortar (See Darke, 1994; Saunders, 1990: 290–303; Watson, 1999). However, this description did not reflect the reality. Most properties sold were flats which could not be bought outright (Blandy and Robinson, 2001) and purchasers were often subsequently hit with large service charges. So, although both of these assumptions were highly questionable, the label stuck; and it stuck precisely because it conveyed the whiff of notoriety, political antagonism and saga that was used to destroy the second Major government.

What is also interesting and important about the Westminster saga is the way the home is counterposed with homelessness. While home ownership was to be encouraged, homelessness was to be discouraged. Westminster used the discretionary underpinnings of the homelessness legislation to implement policies which were 'mean and nasty – implication – social services'. In practice this meant adopting strategies of *denial* of the status of homeless and *deterrence* from making an application in the first place (Carlen, 1994). At the Chairmen's Group on 23 September 1986, it was agreed that 'there should be a reduction in the intake of cases. Officers should adopt a tougher policy without reference to committee' – handwritten notes by the Director of Housing next to this minute include the observation 'take hard line lose in court to embarrass Government' (Magill, 1996a: para 74). So, they also used the law to test their decisions and were willing to enter into protracted legal proceedings. At the Chairmen's Group meeting on 2 September 1986, the minutes record that '[i]t was agreed that the interpretation of the law should continue to be tested at every available opportunity' (ibid, 1996a: para 48).

Deterrence occurred partly through the 'mean and nasty' approach and partly also because of the policy to export households out of the area: '[o]ur policy is to buy properties outside the City boundaries wherever possible' (Chairmen's Group, 7 April 1987; Magill, 1996b: para 214); 'targets ... to stop housing Westminster homeless in Westminster with immediate effect.

To move all homeless out of Westminster, starting with key wards by end 1988' (para 475). It also placed homeless households in tower blocks 'which [the council] knew were riddled with asbestos, some of it in a most virulent and dangerous form' (Hencke, 1995). The conclusions of an independent inquiry were said to be that the decision to place households in this accommodation 'was taken by chairmen, influenced by considerations of party advantage' (Hencke, 1996), and a report sent to the Health and Safety Executive. The flexible construction of homelessness law, both in statute and cases, enabled the council to engage in these processes of denial and deterrence in order to reduce the numbers of homeless households accepted by the council and housed in the borough. Despite the apparent harshness, these policies were *not* found to be unlawful themselves. Indeed, subsequent practice has confirmed the need and general lawfulness of London boroughs to place households outside the local boundaries. Individual applications of those policies might have fallen foul in judicial review proceedings but this would require applicants to challenge decisions – a rarity (Cowan *et al*, 2003).

Conclusions

It is appropriate to end as we began, if you'll forgive the cliché. In Chapter 1, we faced up squarely to the question, what is social housing, and went further by asking what is social about social housing. We argued that understandings of social housing must take account ownership because ownership has been promoted by social housing providers (which have rarely constructed themselves as narrowly as academics might wish). In the current 'mixed economy' of provision of housing, ownership is an increasingly important part of the social housing product. The Barker review, the promotion of 'affordable' and key worker housing, as well as new housing developments such as the Thames Gateway, are all constructed in terms of facilitating ownership (sometimes as 'low cost' ownership). Ownership is about meeting housing need, promoting choice and the values of consumption.

Although this all seems very 'New Labour', and old Toryism, what we have sought to do in this chapter is relate this desire to a certain set of political rationalities of ownership, promoted during the nineteenth century, becoming politically determinative in the twentieth century, and which provided linkages between liberal and conservative understandings of property. Indeed, the creation of docile bodies through mortgaged ownership is a key method of regulating, or governing, not only them but through them (Harvey, 1978: 15–16). Paying the mortgage, like paying the rent, implies a form of obeisance, and substitutes one type of financial control (landlordism) for another (finance capital). One of the key points in this chapter is about the contingent nature of the social provision of housing – collective provision of housing or individualized consumption can equally be conceptualized as social. This was precisely the point we sought to make in Chapter 1 when considering the contingent nature of the relationship between the provision of housing, welfarism and the welfare state.

Tenure, then, is a political choice and divides off populations – indeed, neighbours – from each other. Political choices also determine household tenure choices in this context, because tenures are differentially treated in the tax and consumptive systems. Council and RSL provision operates in a residual position, with increasing rents and uncertain futures; ownership offers the way to control one's future while at the same time potentially making a profit albeit from a risky situation. And, if one follows the argument through, ownership offers a social service in this way.

Ownership fits. It encourages – indeed, activates – the entrepreneurial juices and provides a privatized method of consumption as well as calculated, risky profit-making. Although a(nta)gonistic in the early 1980s, the right to buy fits as well. Exercising the right to buy somehow changes the identity of the occupier, not just from tenant to owner, but also from state-supported to self-supporting, and the discourse of *home* ownership clearly supports that shift. And it tells us something about the ideology of housing, through the assertion of self and the (further) creation of the other. The simple act of changed tenure also changes your political identity and marks you off from your (tenant) neighbour. It does not change either the location or the quality of your accommodation, but exercising the choice to purchase ensures security and well-being. In this conception, the other is a risky terrain containing dangerous, managed spaces and marginalized populations of non-consumers.

Chapter 9:
Conclusion

At times while writing this book, we have agonized over whether we have offered something different. Although we have supported each other through these crises, we now need to explain what we think is 'new' about our book. By seeking to do so in this chapter, we return to the themes identified briefly in our introduction, and expand on them.

1. *Seeking the 'social' in social housing* Although we instinctively 'know' what social housing is, only a slight scratching of the surface reveals that the term is highly contested – as indeed is the idea of 'the social'. In some respects, this book has offered an exploration of the variety of images through which 'social housing' has been (re-)viewed, as part of our exploration of this question about the social.

This question has been a frequent source of debate in the five years of our professional relationship. Underlying it, we think, are some of the most pressing issues that form part of the current problematization of housing, the new 'housing question'. This is a debate which has, to our knowledge anyway, only recently begun – despite the prevalence of the term 'social housing' in academic circles for some time without questioning its underpinnings. At the time of writing, a dialogue is being conducted in the pages of the specialist housing academic newsletter of the Housing Studies Association. Yet, one of the interesting things is that the conjunction of the term 'social' with 'housing' is a relatively recent one, and brings with it a particular intellectual, and practical baggage.

Our understanding of the term, as we have demonstrated, is expansive. No doubt, it is also controversial. In the pages of the newsletter, social housing has been constructed, by some, as purely not-for-profit housing; by others as including certain parts of the profit-making sector. What we have sought to demonstrate is that all housing tenures – whether for a profit or not – form part of the understanding of social housing at the level of political rationality; they cannot be understood without reference to each other. Social housing is a contingent term which tells us much about regulation, government and control.

However, part of our concern – anxiety perhaps – is that current pragmatic responses to the 'housing question' appear to be abandoning the 'social' altogether. The rapidity of the commodification of publicly funded housing continues unabated. Although the Housing Act 2004 did offer some opportunity for reflection and moderation, one result of the 2005 election was that the right to buy would be expanded to others originally excluded from its ambit – an outcome that would have arisen even if the Tories had won. That onward march needs to be coupled with a new understanding about 'housing need', which is tied in with the needs of first-time buyers and other owners. When government talks about housing need, they are often using this hallowed term as shorthand for the need for more ownership units. The social is, in other words, once again in a process of mutation.

2. Regulation and governing These two words could be said to be at the heart of our book. Coming at this project from a Foucauldian perspective, we are affected by Foucault's formulation of government as the structuring of the possible field of actions of others – and ourselves. We have sought to knit this perspective with the work of those who define 'regulation' in a broad sense, to encompass a wide range of forms of social control or influence. We have also been particularly influenced in our approach by the decentrists within the regulation literature.

In co-locating regulation and governance, we see the possibility for much creative thinking and work on the nature of regulation/governing (for the two terms almost come to be part and parcel of each other, if not identical). We think that it can throw some light on the interaction and interrelationship between the way we think about governing – its rationalities – and the mechanisms that are deployed as acts of governing – the *techne* or technologies. And so, while many would still view the history of housing policy as the formulation and imposition of one set of hierarchical regulatory techniques after another, our perspective has been different. We see the central state not as an all-powerful ruler, but more in the sense used by Alan Hunt, as a site at which power condenses. Of course, our analysis could not ignore the central role played by the state in shaping and regulating social housing. However, in recognizing its importance, we also seek to understand how a myriad of interests have seen the technologies of the state as a means of structuring the possible field of action of others, through problematizing particular modes of governing and creating new ways of thinking about the government of others. One particular example of this productive elision between regulation and government can be found in the seeming mish-mash of provisions in the Housing Act 2004. What is so interesting about this Act is the way it seeks to work through us and our communities. This does not necessarily happen explicitly on the face of the Act, but in the minutiae, the detail which appears in Statutory Instruments, Guidance and the like, as well as through the pronouncements of Ministers.

3. Social housing as a site of 'moral regulation' The moral agenda has been a frequently recurring organizing concept for regulating social housing. Nineteenth century social reformers and philanthropists were obsessed by the idea of the 'moral evils' arising from the slums and poor housing; early twentieth century housing managers became concerned, maybe obsessed, with the characteristics of their occupiers in the 1930s and they way they occupied their properties; and twenty-first century politicians frequently make statements that almost make anti-social behaviour synonymous with social housing.

Indeed it has been the image of the *anti*-social that has frequently been invoked in order to turn social housing into a site for regulation and government. Such schemes of 'moral regulation' problematize the values and practices of 'the poor' and 'the vulnerable'. They devise regulating practices that seek to alter the occupiers' conduct. The provision of housing has been seen as a particularly useful tool in such schemes because it has enabled 'philanthropists' and 'reformers' access to the homes and the intimate lives of those they seek to reform. Classically, Octavia Hill and the 'system' she developed involved such intrusions. And while modern-day housing managers are less likely to make visits to the homes of their tenants – primarily because tight budgets constrain such actions – they have at their disposal other techniques of regulation, from the modern (closed circuit TV, Introductory Tenancies and Anti-Social Behaviour Orders) to the traditional (the contract). It has been the rebirth and innovations around the contract, particularly new understandings about that contract, which have been a galvanizing influence on the new housing managers.

However, a central theme of governmentality studies and this book is the potential for *self*-governing. Another route explored in this book, then, has been those mechanisms by which the occupants of social housing have themselves been responsibilized, and whose conduct is to be altered through the government of the self. A particularly potent illustration of this has been the various technological innovations around the allocation of social housing through the inculcation of choice into the system. This system presumed passivity on the part of the housing applicant, and seeks to work through the newly envisioned 'homeseeker', inciting them to activity in their search.

4. On obscurity as a governance technique Social housing is governed through obscurity. There are a series of meaningless mantras which are now trotted out as its purpose – social housing is about meeting housing 'need', social housing is about providing 'affordable' housing, and social housing is about housing the social and controlling the anti-social. When we ask, what is social about social housing, we are seeking the root of the governance structures, and what we find often enough is obscurity. Obscurity enables power and resistance to feed from each other in a productive relationship, which can perhaps best be seen through responses to the obscure term 'anti-social behaviour'. Of particular importance here are the various lists of behaviours which are regarded as falling within its ambit. If transparency provides a model for good governance, obscurity provides a model for efficient government.

We have argued (for example) that housing need was an invention of the late 1920s and early 1930s, some time after municipal housebuilding had begun, in order to cope with an emerging 'crisis' caused by re-housing former slum-dwellers and the need for their management (as opposed to the administration of the housing stock). The term 'housing need' has been able to be manipulated precisely because it is obscure, required the creation of expertise to divine its ambit (which shifted over time), and objectified its subject.

Similarly, although a 'decent home for all at a price they can afford' has long been a slogan of government housing policies (regardless of political complexion), we have shown how affordability is essentially a problematic concept. It is a term that economists attempt to quantify and govern through, but is intimately connected to judgements about lifestyle and household need, decisions that are ultimately highly personal. The process of defining what is affordable requires judgements to be made, about *who* is to be housed, *how much* they can/will/should spend on housing, the *standard* of housing to be provided. How much households can afford for their housing costs depends not just on income, but also on the priority of housing consumption as against other costs. Victorian social reformers such as Seebohm Rowntree attempted to 'discover' affordability through social research methods; and the National Federation of Housing Associations attempted to govern the actions of its member associations through collecting data on rents and household incomes (in a largely failed attempt to control rent rises).

Similarly, another technique of regulation that has become a fundamental aspect of affordability – housing *subsidy* – is obscured through technical jargon. State intervention through subsidy has been a fundamental characteristic of social housing to make housing affordable for those in 'need'. Understandings of affordability are intimately linked with how we view need and the quality of housing to be provided. In the immediate aftermath of the two World Wars in the twentieth century, homes were built 'fit for heroes' which implied high cost accommodation pricing out the poor. Such governing of affordability has also been inextricably linked to housing tenure – governments have sought to control rent levels, but have not intervened to control the price of owner-occupied housing.

5. Shifting boundaries Obscurity also provides a link to our last theme – the continually shifting boundaries around social housing and its regulation. There are two aspects to this – the different conceptualizations of social housing, and the way in which this has changed over time. In our exploration of the meaning of social housing in Chapter 1, we asserted our conception of social housing as extending beyond the boundaries of housing provided by municipal councils and housing associations, to encompass the private rented sector (without which the social housing system would fall apart) and also the owner-occupied sector. We recognize that this is a controversial exposition, but its utility is (at least) twofold – first, private sectors have clearly been conceptualized as being part of the social at different times and for different reasons; second, council and housing association occupiers are often juxtaposed against private sector occupiers in a broadbrush, inadequate contrast.

We have also linked the concept of social housing into the rationalities of a system of 'social' provision – is it a system aiming to discipline and responsibilize housing occupiers, or to redistribute resources between classes, or to encourage social integration through work? This does not mean we are 'agnostic' about tenure, as Hilary Armstrong declared when she became housing minister in 1997, for it is through tenure that housing can be governed. Through controlling ownership we can control who has access to housing resources. And conversely, the loss of (public) control of tenure through the right to buy and stock transfer has fundamentally altered the connection between social housing provision and meeting housing need. The relationship between the tenures is important – when we talk about social housing as being the tenure of last resort, it tells us much about the way council and RSL tenure is perceived; but it also tells us much about the way the private sector is perceived.

However, even the concept of 'housing need' has been the subject of shifting boundaries, so that now governments justify state intervention to support key workers as a matter of meeting the needs of the economy – to afford teachers, social workers and low-paid service workers in areas of economic expansion requires state intervention. And as owner-occupation is now imaged as the tenure of responsible citizens, it is that tenure which must be supported. Indeed, some now are predicting that the accepted lines drawn between renting and owner-occupation will be blurred further, as policy-makers look for further mechanisms to allow tenants to gain an equity share in their home, and owner-occupiers to give up a portion of their ownership to meet changing household finances.

But it is not only the boundaries between tenures that are becoming more blurred. As government allegedly lost patience with social housing landlords' abilities to meet demand for affordable housing, it legislated to allow private developers access to public subsidy. Such a move then requires a rethinking of the modes of regulating providers of affordable housing, as the government regulator looks to the private sector for the skills to accredit developers as the new 'social' landlords. As in other areas of governmental intervention, the boundary between public and private too is becoming more blurred.

Notes |

Introduction

1. We use the terms 'housing association' and 'RSL' rather interchangeably. Historically, the term housing association referred to voluntary not-for-profit housing providers. The difficulty came with the Housing Act 1996 which replaced the term housing association with 'registered social landlord' when referring to all those social landlords that appeared on its register. Therefore, when discussing housing associations historically, it seems inappropriate to use RSL, and so you will find both terms used.

1 On Social Housing, Decline, Regulation and Government

1. All references commening 'PRO' refer to files held at the National Archive (formerly the Public Records Office).

2 Constructing the Domain

1. PRO references indicate reference to documents held at the National Archive (formerly the Public Records office).
2. Evidence of Stephen Brockway, Legal Adviser to the Housing Corporation, para 1.
3. Evidence of Stephen Brockway, para 7.

3 Needing Need

1. See p 129; see also Burnett (1986: 238), who refers to social surveys of London County Council tenants which categorized tenants across their employment status and standing; Holmans, 1987, pp 175 *et seq* contain evidence about family incomes of these council tenants. This 'disastrous and inequitable consequence' was doubly so because 'they got them ... with the assistance of a subvention from the other members of the community': Bowley, p 130.
2. In fact, few local authorities had conducted surveys of their tenants' incomes by 1933 – those who had found that 'a very small number of tenants were in a position to pay a higher rent': Ministry of Health, 1933.
3. In what follows, we are drawing on Cowan and Marsh (2004).

4 On Money

1. http://www.cih.org/news/view.php?id = 223#content

5 Regulatory Truths

1. References with the prefix 'LCC' or 'GLC' refer to records of the London County Council and Greater London Council accessed at the London Metropolitan Archives.

6 The 'Social' Contract

1. The method was to undertake 'a snapshot count of reports that were made to agencies in England and Wales on one day' (10 September 2003); 'over 1500 organisations took part and information was received from every Crime and Disorder Reduction Partnership area in England and Wales'.
2. One is also reminded of the rejection by the 1938 CHAC sub-committee of the 'Dutch method of dealing with difficult tenants ... based upon complete segregation' (CHAC, 1938: para 26).
3. Further detail on this can be found in Pawson *et al*, 2005, from which this paragraph is largely drawn.

7 Private Renting

1. This part was developed in conjunction with Alex Marsh as part of an ongoing project, 'Regulating/governing the private rented sector'.
2. This section would not have been possible without the assistance, discussion, and advance copy of Helen Carr's important work on tenancy deposits.
3. We are here referring, for example, to the subsequent deregulation contained in the Housing Act 1996.

8 Owner-Occupation

1. The Starr-Bowkett societies were 'speculative societies' (evidence of Thomas Fatkin to the 1885a Royal Commission: para 10,813), somewhat similar to pyramid selling of the 1980s. They took the names of their founders – further detail can be found in Cleary, 1965: ch 6.

Bibliography

Alder, J. and Handy, C. (2001) 'Donoghue and Poplar HARCA: Housing Associations and the Human rights Act 1998', *Journal of Housing Law*: 69–72.

Ambrosi, M. (2004) 'Hill rips up decency pledge', *Inside Housing*, 30 January.

Ashby, J. (1997) 'The inquiry into housing association governance', in P. Malpass (ed) *Ownership, Control and Accountability: The New Governance of Social Housing*, Coventry: Chartered Institute of Housing.

Audit Commission (1989) *Housing the Homeless: The Local Authority Role*, London: HMSO.

——(2004) *Housing Benefit Administration*, London: Audit Commission.

Ayres, I. and Braithwaite, J. (1992) *Responsive Regulation: Transcending the Deregulation Debate*, Oxford: Oxford University Press.

Baker, T. (2000) 'Insuring morality', 29(4), *Economy and Society*: 559–77.

Baldwin, R. (1997) 'Regulation after "command and control" ', in K. Hawkins (ed), *The Human Face of Law: Essays in Honour of Donald Harris*, Oxford: Oxford University Press.

Baldwin, R. and Cave, M. (1999) *Understanding Regulation: Theory, Strategy and Practice*, Oxford: Oxford University Press.

Baldwin, R., Scott, C. and Hood, C. (1998) 'Introduction', in R. Baldwin, C. Scott and C. Hood (eds) *A Reader on Regulation*, Oxford: Oxford University Press.

Baldwin, T. and Sherman, J. (2004) 'New plan for one million to buy homes splits Labour', *The Times*, 14 December.

Ball, M. (1983) *Housing Policy and Economic Power: The Political Economy of Owner Occupation*, London: Methuen.

—— (2004) *The Future of Private Renting in the UK*, London: Social Market Foundation.

Ball, M., Harloe, M. and Mertens, M. (1988) *Housing and Social Change in Europe and the USA*, London: Routledge.

Barker, K. (2004) *Delivering Stability: Securing Our Future Housing Needs*, www.barkerreview.org.uk

Barnes, P. (1984) *Building Societies: The Myth of Mutuality*, London: Pluto.

Baron, N. (1996) 'The role of rating agencies in the securitisation process', in L. Kendall and M. Fisherman (eds), *A Primer on Securitization*, Cambridge, MA: MIT Press.

Bauman, Z. (1998) *Work, Consumerism and the New Poor*, Buckingham: Open University Press.

—— (2001) *The Individualized Society*, Cambridge: Polity.

Beck, U. (1992) *Risk Society: Towards a New Modernity*, New York: Sage.

Bedale, C. (1980) 'Property relations and housing policy: Oldham in the late nineteenth and early twentieth centuries', in J. Melling (ed), *Housing, Social Policy and the State*, London: Croom Helm.

Bellman, H. (1927) *The Building Society Movement*, London: Methuen.

Berry, F. (1974) *Housing: The Great British Failure*, London: Croom Helm.

Beveridge, W. (1944) *Social Insurance and Allied Services*, London: HMSO.

Birch, J. (2004) 'Affordable to whom?', May/June, London: Roof: 18–19.

Black, J. (2000) 'Proceduralising regulation', Pt I, 20(4), *Oxford Journal of Legal Studies*, 579–614; Pt II, 21(1): 33–58.

——(2001) 'Decentring regulation: understanding the role of regulation and "self-regulation" in a "post-regulatory" world', 54, *Current Legal Problems*: 103–46.

——(2002a) 'Mapping the contours of contemporary financial services regulation', 2(3), *Journal of Corporate Law Studies*: 253–87.

——(2002b) 'Regulatory conversations', 29(1), *Journal of Law and Society*: 163–96.

——(2002c), 'Critical reflections on regulation', 27(1), *Australian Journal of Legal Philosophy*: 1–37.

Blandy, S. (2001) 'Housing standards in the private rented sector and the three Rs: regulation, responsibility and rights', in D. Cowan and A. Marsh (eds), *Two Steps Forward: Housing Policy in the New Millennium*, Bristol: Policy Press.

Blandy, S. and Robinson, D. (2001) 'Reforming leasehold: Discursive events and outcomes, 1984–2000', 28(3), *Journal of Law and Society*: 384–408.

Blitz, R. (2005) 'Affordable housing plans criticised', *Financial Times*, 7 April, 4.

Boddy, M. (1980) *The Building Societies*, Basingstoke: Macmillan.

——(1989) 'Financial deregulation and UK housing finance: government-building society relations and the Building Societies Act, 1986', 4(1), *Housing Studies*: 92–104.

Boddy, M. and Lambert, C. (1988) *The Government-Building Society Connection: From Mortgage Regulation to the Big Bang*, SAUS Working Paper 75, Bristol: School for Advanced Urban Studies, University of Bristol.

Bottoms, A. and Wiles, P. (1986) 'Housing tenure and residential community crime careers in Britain', in A. Reiss, and M. Tonry (eds), *Crime and*

Justice: A review of Research – Communities and Crime, Chicago: University of Chicago Press.

——(1997) 'Environmental criminology', in R. Morgan, and R. Reiner (eds), *The Oxford Handbook of Criminology*, Oxford: Oxford University Press.

Bowley, M. (1945) *Housing and the State: 1919–1945*, London: Allen & Unwin.

Braithwaite, J. (2000) 'The new regulatory state and the transformation of criminology', 40(2), *British Journal of Criminology*: 222–38.

Brion, M. and Tinker, A. (1980) *Women in Housing: Access and Influence*, London: Housing Centre Trust.

Brown, A. (2004) 'Anti-social behaviour, crime control and social control', 43(2), *The Howard Journal*: 203–11.

Burnett, J. (1986) *A Social History of Housing 1915–1985*, London: Methuen.

Cadbury Report (1992) *Committee on the Financial Aspects of Corporate Governance*, London: Financial Reporting Council.

Cairncross, L., Clapham, D. and Goodlad, R. (1997) *Housing Management, Consumers and Citizens*, London: Routledge.

Callon, M. and Latour, B. (1981) 'Unscrewing the big leviathan: how actors macro-structure reality and how sociologists help them to do so', in K. Knorr-Cetina and A. Cicourel (eds), *Advances in Social Theory*, Boston: Routledge & Kegan Paul.

Campbell, S. (2002) *A Review of Anti-Social Behaviour Orders*, Home Office Research Study 236, London: Home Office.

Carlen, P. (1994) 'The governance of homelessness: legality, lore and lexicon in the agency-maintenance of youth homelessness', 41, *Critical Social Policy*: 18–35.

Carr, H. (2005a) ' "Someone to watch over me": making supported housing work', 13(3), *Social and Legal Studies*: 387–408.

——(2005b) ' "People will say we're in love" Talking dirty about tenancy deposits', paper presented at the Socio-Legal studies Association Conference, University of Liverpool, 29–31 March.

Carr, H., Cottle, S., Baldwin, T. and King, M. (2005) *The Housing Act 2004: A Practical Guide*, Bristol: Jordans.

Carr, H. and Cowan, D. (forthcoming) 'The good, the bad, and the downright risky', in J. Flint (ed), *Anti-Social Behaviour*, Bristol: Policy Press.

Carr, H., Sefton-Green, D. and Tissier, D. (2001) 'Two steps forward for tenants?', in D. Cowan and A. Marsh (eds), *Two Steps Forward: Housing Policy into the New Millennium*, Bristol: Policy Press.

Carter, M. and Ginsburg, N. (1994) 'New government housing policies', 41, *Critical Social Policy*: 100–10.

Casey, R. and Allen, C. (2004) 'Public housing managers and the performance ethos: towards a "professional project of the self" ', 18(2), *Work, Employment and Society*: 395–412.

Castel, R. (1991) 'From dangerousness to risk', in G. Burchell, C. Gordon and P. Miller (eds), *The Foucault Effect: Studies in Governmentality*, Chicago: University of Chicago Press.

Central Housing Advisory Committee (CHAC) (1938) *The Management of Municipal Housing Estates*, Report of the House Management and Housing Associations Sub-Committee of the Central Housing Advisory Committee, London: HMSO.

——(1949) *Selection of Tenants and Transfers and Exchanges*, Third Report of the Housing Management Sub-Committee of the Central Housing Advisory Committee, London: HMSO.

——(1959) *Councils and their Houses: Management of Estates*, Eighth Report of the Housing Management Sub-Committee of the Central Housing Advisory Committee, London: HMSO.

——(1969) *Council Housing: Purposes, Procedures, Priorities*, London: HMSO.

Centre for Housing Research (1989) *The Nature and Effectiveness of Housing Management*, London: HMSO.

Chaplin, R., Jones, M., Martin, S., Pryke, M., Royce, C., Saw, P., Whitehead, C. and Hong Yang, J. (1995) *Rents and Risks: Investing in Housing Associations*, York: Joseph Rowntree Foundation.

Chilton, B. (1998) 'Speak now to shape the housing inspectorate', *Housing*, November: 28–9.

Clapham, D. (1997) 'A woman of her time', in J. Goodwin and C. Grant (eds), *Built to Last? Reflections on British Housing Policy*, London: Roof.

Clapham, D. and Kintrea, K. (1986) 'Rationing, choice and constraint: the allocation of public housing in Glasgow', 15(1), *Journal of Social Policy*: 51–66.

Clarke, J. and Newman, J. (1997) *The Managerial State*, London: Sage.

Cleary, E. (1965) *The Building Society Movement*, London: Elek.

Cloke, P., Millbourne, P. and Widdowfield, R. (2000) 'Change but no change: Dealing with homelessness under the 1996 Housing Act', 15(5), *Housing Studies*: 739–56.

Cohen Committee (1971) *Housing Associations: A Working Paper of the Central Housing Advisory Committee*, London: HMSO.

Cole, I. and Furbey, R. (1994) *The Eclipse of Council Housing*, London: Routledge.

Cole, I. and Goodchild, B. (1995) 'Local housing strategies in England: An assessment of their changing role and content', 23(1), *Policy and Politics*: 49–62.

Cole, I., Gidley, G., Ritchie, C., Simpson, D. and Wishart, B. (1996) *Creating Communities or Welfare Housing? A Study of New Housing Association*

Developments in Yorkshire and Humberside, Coventry: Chartered Institute of Housing.

Coleman, A. (1986) *Utopia on Trial*, London: Hilary Shipman.

Coleman, R., Sim, J. and Whyte, D. (2002) 'Power, politics and partnerships: the state of crime prevention on Merseyside', in G. Hughes and A. Edwards (eds), *Crime Control and Community: The New Politics of Public Safety*, Cullompton: Willan.

Collins, H. (1999), *Regulating Contracts*, Oxford: Oxford University Press.

Committee on Local Expenditure (1932) *Report of the Committee on Local Expenditure (England and Wales)*, Cmd 4200, London: HMSO.

Cooper, D. (1998) *Governing Out of Order: Space, Law and the Politics of Belonging*, London: Rivers Oram Press.

Cowan, D. (1997) *Homelessness: The (In-)Appropriate Applicant*, Aldershot: Dartmouth.

Cowan, D. (1999) *Housing Law and Policy*, Basingstoke: Macmillan.

——(ed.) (1996) *The Housing Act 1996: A Practical Guide*, Bristol: Jordans.

Cowan, D. Gilroy, R. and Pantazis, C. (1999) 'Risking housing need', 26(4), *Journal of Law and Society*: 403–26.

Cowan, D. and Lomax, D. (2001) 'Policing unauthorised camping', 30(3), *Journal of Law and Society*: 283–308.

Cowan, D. and Marsh, A. (2001a) 'New Labour, same old Tory housing policy', 64(2), *Modern Law Review*: 260–80.

——(2001b) 'There's regulatory crime and then there's landlord crime: from "Rachmanites" to "partners" ', 64(6), *Modern Law Review*: 831–54.

——(2005a) 'From need to choice, welfarism to advanced liberalism? Problematics of social housing allocation', 25(2), *Legal Studies*: 22–48.

——(2005b) 'Regulating/governing the private rented sector', Unpublished paper on file with the authors.

Cowan, D. and Pantazis, C. (2001) 'Social housing as crime control: reflections on the role of social housing in the rehousing of sex offenders', 10(3), *Social and Legal Studies*: 435–57.

Cowan, D. Halliday, S. with Hunter, C. Maginn, P. and Naylor, L. (2003) *The Appeal of Internal Review*, Oxford: Hart.

Craig, Peter (1986) 'The house that Jerry built? Building societies, the state and the politics of owner-occupation', 1(2), *Housing Studies*: 87–108.

Craig, P. (2001) 'The Courts, the Human Rights Act and judicial review', *Law Quarterly Review*: 589–609.

Crawford, A. (2003) ' "Contractual governance" of deviant behaviour', 30(4), *Journal of Law and Society*: 479–505.

Crook, A. and Moroney, M. (1995) 'Housing associations, private finance and risk avoidance: the impact on urban renewal and inner cities', 27(11), *Environment & Planning A*: 1695–712.

Cullingworth, J. (1973) *Problems of an Urban Society, Vol 2: The Content of Planning*, London: Allen & Unwin.

Damer, S. (1974) 'Wine Alley: the sociology of a dreadful enclosure', 22(2), *Sociological Review*: 221–48.

Damer, S. (1976) 'A note on housing allocation', in M. Edwards, F. Gray, S. Merrett and J. Swann (eds), *Housing and Class in Britain*, London: Russell Press.

Damer, S. (1980) 'State, class and housing: Glasgow 1885–1919', in J. Melling (ed), *Housing Social Policy and the State*, London: Croom Helm.

Damer, S. (2000) ' "Engineers of the human machine": The social practice of council housing management in Glasgow, 1895–1939', 37(11), *Urban Studies*: 2007–26.

Damer, S. and Madigan, R. (1974) 'The housing investigator', 25 July, *New Society*: 226.

Darke, J. (1994) 'Women and the meaning of home', in R. Gilroy and R. Woods (eds), *Housing Women*, London: Routledge.

Daunton, M. (1983) *House and Home in the Victorian City*, London: Edward Arnold.

——(1987) *A Property Owning Democracy?* London: Faber & Faber.

Day, P., Henderson, D. and Klein, R. (1993) *Home Rules: Regulation and Accountability in Social Housing*, York: Joseph Rowntree Foundation.

Deacon, A. (2004) 'Justifying conditionality: the case of anti-social tenants', 19(6), *Housing Studies*: 911–26.

Dean, M. (1992) 'A genealogy of the government of poverty', 21(3), *Economy and Society*: 215–51.

——(1999) *Governmentality: Power and Rule in Modern Society*, London: Sage.

Department of the Environment (DoE) (1977) *Housing Policy – A Consultative Document*, London: HMSO.

——(1987) *Housing: The Government's Proposals*, Cm 214, London: HMSO.

——(1994) *Access to Local Authority and Housing Association Tenancies*, London: DoE.

——(1995) *Our Future Homes: Opportunity, Choice and Responsibility*, Cm 2901, London: DoE.

Department of the Environment, Transport and the Regions (DETR) (1998), *Modern Local Government: In Touch with the People*, Cm 4014, London: The Stationary Office.

——(1999a) *Tenant Participation Compacts: A Consultation Paper*, London: DETR.

——(1999b) *National Framework for Tenant Participation Compacts*, London: DETR.

——(1999c) *Developing Good Practice in Tenant Participation*, London: DETR.

——(1999d) *Licensing of Housing in Multiple Occupation – England*, A Consultation Paper, London: DETR.

——(2000a) *Views on the Large Scale Voluntary Transfer Process*, London: DETR.

——(2000b) *Guide to Social Rent Reforms*, London: DETR.

——Department of Social Security (DSS) (2000) *Quality and Choice: A Decent Home for All – The Housing Green Paper*, London: DETR/DSS.

——Department of Social Security (DSS) (2001) *Quality and Choice: A Decent Home for All – The Way Forward*, London: DETR/DSS.

Department of Transport, Local Government and the Regions (DTLR) (2001) *Selective Licensing of Private Landlords*, A Consultation Paper, London: DTLR.

Department for Work and Pensions (DWP) (2002) *Building Choice and Responsibility: A Radical Agenda for Housing Benefit*, London: DWP.

——(2003) *Housing Benefit Sanctions and Anti-Social Behaviour*, London: DWP.

——(2004) *Standard Local Housing Allowances: Explanatory Memorandum and Commentary on Draft Regulations*, London: DWP.

Donzelot, J. (1979) *The Policing of Families*, London: Hutchison.

Dunleavy, P. (1980) *Urban Political Analysis: The Politics of Collective Consumption*, London: Macmillan.

Eaglesham, J. (2001) ' "Homes for Votes" led to dramatic fall', *Financial Times*, 14 December.

Elliott, C., Dawe, T. and Wood, N. (1994) ' "Vote-rigging" scandal stuns Tory flagship', *The Times*, 14 January.

Ericson, R. and Haggerty, K. (1997) *Policing the Risk Society*, Oxford: Oxford University Press.

Evans, R. (2004a) 'Regulator aims to sharpen skills to match developers', *Inside Housing*, 26 November: 26.

——(2004b) 'Regulator set to give power to private accreditation firm', *Inside Housing*, 3 December: 3.

——(2004c) 'The ultimate taboo: are tenants given too much say over homes?', *Inside Housing*, 30 January: 30.

——(2004d) 'Peabody at risk of stalling on new traffic light rating', *Inside Housing*, 16 January: 4.

Ewald, F. (1990) 'Norms, discipline and the law', 30, *Representations*: 138–161.

Fairclough, N. (1995) *Critical Discourse Analysis: The Critical Study of Language*, London: Longman.

Feintuck, M. (2004) *'The Public Interest' in Regulation*, Oxford: Oxford University Press.

Finlayson, G. (1990) 'A moving frontier: voluntarism and the state in British Social Welfare 1911–1949', 1(2), *Twentieth Century British History*: 183–206.

Fitzpatrick, P. (2000) 'Governmentality and the force of law', *European Yearbook of the Sociology of Law*: 3–24.

Flinn, M. (1965) *Report on the Sanitary Condition of the Labouring Population of Gt. Britain /by Edwin Chadwick, 1842*, Edinburgh: Edinburgh University Press.

Flint, J. (2002) 'Social housing agencies and the Governance of anti-social behaviour', 17(4), *Housing Studies*: 619–37.

Flint, J. (2003) 'Housing and ethopolitics: constructing identities of active consumption and responsible community', 32(4), *Economy and Society*: 611–29.

——(2004a) 'The responsible tenant: Housing governance and the politics of behaviour', 19(6), *Housing Studies*: 893–910.

——(2004b) 'Reconfiguring agency and responsibility in the governance of social housing in Scotland', 41(1), *Urban Studies*: 151–72.

Forrest, R., and Murie, A. (1991) *Selling the Welfare State: The Privatization of Public Housing*, London: Routledge.

Forrest, R., Lansley, S. and Murie, A. (1984) *A Foot on the Ladder? An Evaluation of Low Cost Home Ownership Initiatives*, Working Paper 41, Bristol: School for Advanced Urban Studies, University of Bristol.

Forrest, R., Murie, A. and Williams, P. (1990) *Home Ownership: Differentiation and Fragmentation*, London: Unwin Hyman.

Foster, C. (1992) *Privatization, Public Ownership and the Regulation of Natural Monopoly*, Oxford: Blackwell.

Foucault, M. (1977a) *Discipline and Punish: The Birth of the Prison*, London: Penguin.

——(1977b) 'Neitzsche, genealogy, history' in D.F. Bouchard (ed. and trans.) *Language, Counter-memory, Practice: Selected Essays and Interviews by Michael Foucault*, Oxford: Basil Blackwell.

——(1980) *Power/Knowledge: Selected Interviews and Other Writings 1972–1977*, C. Gordon (ed. and trans.), Brighton: Harvester Press.

——(1981) *The History of Sexuality, Volume 1: An Introduction*, London: Penguin.

——(1983) 'Afterword: The subject and power', in H. Dreyfus and P. Rabinow (eds), *Michel Foucault: Beyond Structuralism and Hermeneutics*, Chicago: University of Chicago Press.

——(1991) 'Governmentality', in G. Burchell, C. Gordon and P. Miller (eds), *The Foucault Effect: Studies in Governmentality*, Chicago: University of Chicago Press.

——(2003) *Society Must be Defended*, London: Penguin.

Francis, H. (1971) *Report of the Committee on the Rent Acts*, Cmnd 4609, London: HMSO.

Furbey, R., Wishart, B. and Grayson, J. (1996) 'Training for tenants: "Citizens" and the enterprise culture', 11(2), *Housing Studies*: 251–70.

Garland, D. (1996) 'The limits of the sovereign state: strategies of crime control in contemporary society', 36(3), *British Journal of Criminology*: 445–71.

——(2001) *The Culture of Control*, Oxford: Oxford University Press.

Garnett, D. (2000) *Housing Finance*, Coventry: Chartered Institute of Housing.

Garside, P. (1995) 'Central government, local authorities and the voluntary housing sector', in A. O'Day (ed) *Government and Institutions in the Post 1832 UK*, Lampeter: Mellon Press.

Gauldie, E. (1974) *Cruel Habitations: A History of Working-Class Housing 1780–1918*, London: Unwin.

Genn, H. and Genn, Y (1989) *The Effectiveness of Representation at Tribunals*, London: Lord Chancellor's Department.

Gibb, F. (2001) ' "Corrupt" Dame Shirley ordered to pay £26.4m', *The Times*, 14 December.

Gibb, K. (2001) 'Helping with housing costs? Unravelling the political economy of personal subsidy', in D. Cowan and A. Marsh (eds) *Two Steps Forward: Housing Policy for the New Millennium*, Bristol: The Policy Press.

Gibb K., Munro M., and Satsangi M. (1999) *Housing Finance in the UK: An Introduction*. London: Macmillann.

Gilroy, R. (1998) 'Bringing tenants into decision-making', in D. Cowan (ed.), *Housing: Participation and Exclusion*, Aldershot: Dartmouth.

Golding, P. and Middleton, S. (1982) *Images of Welfare*, Oxford: Blackwell.

Goodlad, R. (1993) *The Housing Authority as Enabler*, Coventry: Institute of Housing.

Goodlad, R. (2001) 'Developments in tenant participation: accounting for growth', in D. Cowan and A. Marsh (eds), *Two Steps Forward: Housing Policy into the New Millennium*, Bristol: Policy Press.

Goodlad, R. and Atkinson, R. (2004) 'Sacred cows, rational debates and the politics of the right to buy after devolution', 19(3), *Housing Studies*: 447–63.

Gordon, C. (1991) 'Governmental rationality: an introduction', in G. Burchell, C. Gordon and P. Miller (eds), *The Foucault Effect: Studies in Governmentality*, Chicago: University of Chicago Press.

Gray, F. (1976) 'The management of local authority housing', in M. Edwards, F. Gray, S. Merrett and J. Swann (eds), *Housing and Class in Britain*, London: Russell Press.

——(1979) 'Consumption: council house management', in S. Merrett, *State Housing in Britain*, London: Routledge and Kegan Paul.

——(1982) 'Owner-occupation and social relations', in S. Merrett, *Owner Occupation in Britain*, London: Routledge and Kegan Paul.

Greater London Council (GLC) (1979) *GLC response to the National Federation of Housing Associations' report of September 1979 on Project Control* [held on file at the London Metropolitan Archives: GLC/DG/SCR/1/3].

Griffiths, M., Parker, J., Smith, R., Stirling, T. and Trott, T. (1996) *Community Lettings: Local Allocations Policies in Practice*, York: Joseph Rowntree Foundation.

Guardian (2002), Interview with Mary Keegan, chairman of the Accountancy Standards Board, 16 February.

Gurney, C. (1999a) 'Pride and prejudice: discourses of normalisation in public and private accounts of home ownership', 14(2), *Housing Studies*: 163–85.

——(1999b) 'Lowering the drawbridge: A case study of analogy and metaphor in the social construction of home-ownership', 36(7), *Urban Studies*: 1705–22.

Hacking, I. (1991) 'How should we do the history of statistics?', in G. Burchell, C. Gordon, and P. Miller (eds), *The Foucault Effect: Studies in Governmentality*, Chicago: University of Chicago Press.

Haffner, M. and Oxley, M. (1999) 'Housing subsidies: definitions and comparisons', 14(2), *Housing Studies*: 145–62.

Halliday, S. (1998) 'Researching the Impact of judicial review on routine administrative decision-making', in D. Cowan (ed), *Housing: Participation and Exclusion*, Aldershot: Dartmouth.

——(2004) *Judicial Review and Compliance with Administrative Law*, Oxford: Hart.

Hancher, L. and Moran, M. (1989) 'Organising regulatory space', in L. Hancher, and M. Moran (eds), *Capitalism, Culture and Economic Regulation*, (reproduced in R. Baldwin, C. Scott and R. Hood (eds), *A Reader on Regulation*, Oxford: Oxford University Press).

Harloe, M. (1993) *The Social Construction of Social Housing* (Urban Research Program working paper; no.34), Canberra: Australian National University.

——(1995) *The People's Home? Social Rented Housing in Europe and America*, Oxford: Blackwell.

Harlow, C. and Rawlings, R. (1997) *Law and Administration*, 2nd edition, London: Butterworths.

Harvey, D. (1978) 'Labor, capital and class struggle around the built environment in advanced capitalist societies', in K. Cox (ed), *Urbanization and Conflict in Market Societies*, London: Methuen.

Hawkins, K. (2002) *Law as Last Resort: Prosecution Decision-Making in a Regulatory Agency*, Oxford: Oxford University Press.

Haworth, A. and Manzi, T. (1999) 'Managing the "underclass": Interpreting the moral discourse of housing management', 36(1), *Urban Studies*: 153–65.

Hencke, D. (1995) 'Homeless "put at risk" in asbestos-ridden tower blocks', *The Guardian*, 30 November.

——(1996) 'Westminster Tories who put families in asbestos flats may be prosecuted', *The Guardian*, 26 March.

Henderson, J. and Karn, V. (1987) *Race, Class and State Housing: Inequality and the Allocation of Public Housing in Britain*, Aldershot: Gower.

Hetherington, P. (2003), 'Driven to the limits', *The Guardian [Society]*, 12 March.

Higgins, P., James, P. and Roper, I. (2004) 'Best value: is it delivering?', August, *Public Money and Management*: 251–8.

Hill, O. (1875) *Homes of the London Poor*, London: MacMillan.

Hills, J. (1990) *Unravelling Housing Finance*, Oxford: Oxford University Press.

Hills, J. and Mullings, B. (1990), 'Housing: A decent home for all at a price within their means?', in Hills, J. (ed), *The State of Welfare: The Welfare State in Britain Since 1974*, Oxford: Clarendon.

H.M. Treasury (2000) *Public Private Partnerships: the Government's Approach*, London: The Stationary Office.

Hobsbawm, E. (1971) *Industry and Empire*, Harmondsworth: Penguin.

Hoggett, P. (1996) 'New modes of control in the public service', 74(1), *Public Administration*: 9–32.

Hole, J. (1866) *The Homes of the Working Classes*, London: Longmans.

Holmans, A. (1987) *Housing Policy in Britain*, London: Croom Helm.

Home Office (2003a) *TOGETHER: Tackling Anti-Social Behaviour, The One Day Count of Anti-Social Behaviour*, London: Home Office.

——(2003b) *Respect and Responsibility: Tackling Anti-Social Behaviour*, London: Home Office.

Home Ownership Task Force (2003) *A Home of My Own*, London: Housing Corporation.

Hood, C. (1991) 'A public management for all seasons', 69(1), *Public Administration*: 3–19.

Housing Corporation (1997) *Performance Standards*, London: Housing Corporation.

——(2000) Year 2000 Review of the Housing Corporation: Response of the Housing Corporation, London: Housing Corporation.

Housing Corporation (2002) *The Way Forward: Our Approach to Regulation*, London, Housing Corporation.

Hughes, D. and Lowe, S. (eds) (1991) *A New Century of Social Housing*, Leicester: University of Leicester Press.

Hugill, B. (1998) 'Clear threat', *The Guardian*, 4 March.

Hunt, A. (1992) 'Foucault's expulsion of law: Towards a retrieval', 17(1), *Law and Social Inquiry*: 1–38.

——(1999) *Governing Morals: A Social History of Moral Regulation*, Cambridge: Cambridge University Press.

Hunt, A. and Wickham, G. (1994) *Foucault and Law: Towards a Sociology of Law as Governance*, London: Pluto.

Hunter, C. (2001) 'Anti-social behaviour: can law be the answer?', in D. Cowan and A. Marsh (eds), *Two Steps Forward – Housing Policy into the new Millennium*, Bristol: Policy Press.

Hunter, C. and Nixon, J. (2001) 'Taking the blame and losing the home: women and anti-social behaviour', 23(4), *Journal of Social Welfare and Family Law*: 395–411.

Hunter, C. Nixon, J. and Shayer, S. (2000) *Neighbour Nuisance, Social Landlords and the Law*, Coventry: Chartered Institute of Housing.

Hunter, C. Blandy, S. Cowan, D. Nixon, J. Hitchings, E. Pantazis, C. and Parr, S. (2005) *The Exercise of Discretion in Rent Arrears Cases*, London: Department for Constitutional Affairs.

Jacobs, K. and Manzi, T. (2000) 'Performance indicators and social constructivism: conflict and control in housing management', 20(1), *Critical Social Policy*: 85–103.

Jeffers, S. and Hoggett, P. (1995) 'Like counting deckchairs on the Titanic: a study of institutional racism and housing allocations in Haringey and Lambeth', 10(3), *Housing Studies*: 325–44.

Johnston, L. and Shearing, C. (2003) *Governing Security: Explorations in Policing and Justice*, London: Routledge.

Jones, M. (1988) 'Utopia and reality: the utopia of public housing and its reality at Broadwater Farm', in N. Teymur, T. Markus and T. Woolley (eds), *Rehumanizing Housing*, London: Butterworths.

Karn, V., Kemeny, J. and Williams, P. (1985) *Home Ownership in the Inner City: Salvation or Despair?*, Aldershot: Gower.

Kay, A., Legg, C. and Foot, J. (undated) *The 1980 Tenants' Rights in Practice: A Study of the Implementation of the 1980 Housing Act Rights by Local Authorities 1980–1983*, London: Blackrose.

Kearns, A. (1997) 'Housing association committees' in P. Malpass (ed), *Ownership, Control and Accountability: The New Governance of Social Housing*, Coventry: Chartered Institute of Housing.

Kemp, P. (1993) 'Rebuilding the private rented sector', in P. Malpass and R. Means (eds), *Implementing Housing Policy*, Buckingham: Open University Press.

——(1997) 'Ideology, public policy and private rental housing since the war', in P. Williams (ed.), *Directions in Housing Policy: Towards Sustainable Housing Policies for the UK*, London: Paul Chapman.

——(2000) 'Housing benefit and welfare retrenchment in Britain', 29(2), *Journal of Social Policy*: 263–79.

Kemp, P. and Williams, P. (1991) 'Housing management: an historical perspective', in D. Hughes and S. Lowe (eds), *A New Century for Municipal Housing*, Leicester: University of Leicester Press.

Kempson, E. (1993) *Household Budgets and Housing Costs*, London: Policy Studies Institute.

Kerwer, D. (2002) 'Ratings agencies: setting a standard for global financial markets', *Economic Sociology – European Electronic Newsletter* Vol 3(3) http://www.siswo.uva.nl/ES/esjun02art4.html

Kleinman, M. (1993) 'Large-scale transfers of council housing to new landlords: is British social housing becoming more European?', 8(1), *Housing Studies*: 163–85.

Labour Housing Group (1985) *Manifesto for Housing*, London: Labour Housing Group.

Laffin, M. (1986) *Professionalism and Policy: The Role of the Professions in the Central-Local Government Relationship*, Aldershot: Gower.

Lambert, J., Paris, C. and Blackaby, C. (1978) *Housing Policy and the State: Allocation, Access and Control*, London: MacMillan.

Langstaff, M. (1992) 'Housing associations: a move to centre stage', in J. Birchall (ed), *Housing Policy in the 1990s*, Coventry: Chartered Institute of Housing.

Latour, B. (1986) 'The powers of association' in J. Law (ed.), *Power, Action and Belief* London: Routledge and Kegan Paul.

——(1987a) 'Visualisation and cognition: Thinking with eyes and hands', 6(1), *Knowledge and Society: Studies in the Sociology of Culture, Past and Present*: 1–40.

—— (1987b) *Science in Action*, Milton Keynes: Open University Press.

Laurie, E. (2002) *The Enduring Appeal of Reasonable Preference*, Unpublished PhD thesis, Southampton: University of Southampton.

Law, J. (1986) (ed), *Power, Action and Belief*, London, Routledge, Kegan and Paul.

Law Commission (2002) *Renting Homes 1: Status and Security*, Consultation Paper No 162, London: Law Commission.

LCC/MIN/7550 Minutes of Housing and Public Health Committee, London County Council [held at the Metropolitan Archives].

Leather, P. and Murie, A. (1986) 'The decline in public expenditure', in P. Malpass (ed) *The Housing Crisis*, Beckenham: Croom Helm.

Leigh, I. (2004) 'The new local government' in J. Jowell and D. Oliver (eds), *The Changing Constitution*, 5th edn, Oxford: Oxford University Press.

Levison, D. and Robertson, I. (1989) *Partners in Meeting Housing Need: Local Authority Nominations to Housing Associations in London: Good Practice Guide*, London: NFHA.

Levitas, R. (1998) *The Inclusive Society? Social Exclusion and New Labour*, Basingstoke: Palgrave.

Lewis, N.D. (2001) *Law and Governance*, London: Cavendish.

Lewis, N. and Harden, I. (1982) 'The Housing Corporation and "voluntary housing" ', in A. Barker (ed), *Quangos in Britain*, Basingstoke: Macmillan.

Lipsky, M. (1980) *Street-level Bureaucracy: Dilemmas of the Individual in Public Service*, New York: Russell Sage Foundation.

London Housing Associations Committee (LHAC) (1970) *Report on Housing Associations in London: 1970* (London Housing Associations Committee, London) [held at London Metropolitan Archives ref: P28–81 LON].

Loughlin, M. (1996) *Legality and Locality: The Role of Law in Central-Local Government Relations*, Oxford: Clarendon Press.

——(2000) 'Restructuring of central-local relations', in J. Jowell, and D. Oliver (eds), *The Changing Constitution*, Oxford: Oxford University Press.

Loveland, I. (1992) 'Square pegs, round holes: the "right" to council housing in the post-war era', 19(2), *Journal of Law and Society*: 339–61.

——(1995) *Housing Homeless Persons*, Oxford: Oxford University Press.

Luhmann, N. (1985) *A Sociological Theory of Law*, London, Routledge and Kegan Paul.

Lupton, M. (1998), 'Inspection or Inquisition?', November, *Housing*: 30–1.

Lupton, M., Hale, J., Sprigings, N., and Chartered Institute of Housing (2003) *Incentives and Beyond? The Transferability of the Irwell Valley Gold Service to other Social Landlords*, London: ODPM.

Luxton, P. (2001) *The Law of Charities*, Oxford: Oxford University Press.

Macadam, E. (1934) *The New Philanthropy: A Study of the Relations between the Statutory and Voluntary Social Services*, London: George Allen & Unwin.

Macey, J. and Baker, C. (1965) *Housing Management*, London: Estates Gazette.

Maclennan, D. and Williams, R. (1990) *Affordable Housing in Britain and America*, York: Joseph Rowntree Foundation.

Macneil, I. (2001) *The Relational Theory of Contract: Selected Works of Ian Macneil*, D. Campbell (ed), London: Sweet & Maxwell.

Magill, J. (1996a) *Westminster City Council Audit of Accounts 1987/88 to 1994/95: Designated Sales*, Vol 2: Introduction, Decisions and Statement of Reasons on the Section 19 Objection (Excluding Questions of Personal Liability), London: Deloitte and Touche.

——(1996b) *Westminster City Council Audit of Accounts 1987/88 to 1994/95: Designated Sales*, Vol 4: History of Events and Other Appendices, London: Deloitte and Touche.

Malpass, P. (1975) 'Professionalism and the role of architects in local authority housing', 82, *Royal Institute of British Architects Journal*: 6–29.

——(1990) *Reshaping Housing Policy: Subsidies, Rents and Residualisation*, London: Routledge.

——(1994) 'Policy Making and Local Governance: How Bristol failed to secure City Challenge funding (twice)', 22(4), *Policy and Politics*: 301–12.

——(1998) *Housing Philanthropy and the State: A History of the Guinness Trust*, Bristol: Faculty of the Built Environment, University of the West of England.

——(1999a) 'Housing policy: does it have a future?', 27(2), *Policy and Politics*: 217–32.

——(1999b) *The Work of the Century: The Origins and Growth of the Octavia Hill Housing Trust in Notting Hill*, London: Octavia Hill Housing Trust.

——(2000) *Housing Associations and Housing Policy*, Basingstoke: MacMillan.

——(2001) 'The uneven development of 'social rented housing': explaining the historically marginal position of Housing Associations in Britain', 16(2), *Housing Studies*: 225–42.

——(2003) 'The wobbly pillar? Housing and the British postwar welfare state', 32(4), *Journal of Social Policy*: 589–606.

——(2004) 'Fifty years of British housing policy: Leaving or leading the welfare state?', 4(2), *European Journal of Housing Policy*: 209–27.

Malpass, P. and Aughton, H. (1999) *Housing Finance: A Basic guide*, London: Shelter.

Malpass, P. and Murie, A. (1999) *Housing Policy and Practice*, 5th edn, London: Macmillan.

Marsh, A. (2001) 'Restructuring social housing rents', in D. Cowan and A. Marsh (eds), *Two Steps Forward: Housing Policy for the New Millennium*, Bristol: The Policy Press.

——(2004) 'The inexorable rise of the rational consumer? The Blair government and the reshaping of social housing', 4(2), *European Journal of Housing Policy*: 185–207.

Marsh, A. and Walker, B. (2006) 'Getting a policy to 'stick': centralising control of social rent setting in England', 33(1), *Policy and Politics*, forthcoming.

Marsh, A., Niner, P., Cowan, D., Forrest, R. and Kennett, P. (2000) *Harassment and Unlawful Eviction of Private Rented Sector Tenants and Park Home Residents*, London: DETR.

Marsh, A., Cowan, D., Cameron, A., Jones, M., Kiddle, C. and Whitehead, C. (2004) *Piloting Choice Based Lettings: An Evaluation*, London: ODPM.

Marston, G. (2004) 'Managerialism and public housing reform', 19(1), *Housing Studies*: 5–20.

Martin, S. (2000) 'Implementing "best value": local public services in transition', 78(1), *Public Administration*: 209–27.

McAdam, R. and Walker, T. (2003), 'Evaluating the best value framework in UK local government services', 24, *Public Administration and Development*: 183–96.

McCulloch, A. (1997) ' "You've fucked up the estate and now you're carrying a briefcase!" ', in Hoggett, P. (ed), *Contested Communities: Experiences, Struggles, Policies*, Bristol: Policy Press.

McDermont, M. (2003) 'The elusive nature of the "public function": *Poplar Housing and Regeneration Community Association Ltd v Donoghue*', 66(1), *Modern Law Review*: 113–23.

——(2005) *Managing the Tensions in 'Voluntary' Housing: A Study of the Role of the National Housing Federation in the Governance of Social Housing since 1935*, unpublished PhD thesis, Bristol: University of the West of England.

Mearns, A. (1883) *The Bitter Cry of Outcast London: An Inquiry into the Condition of the Abject Poor*, London: Review of Reviews.

Mele, C. (2005) 'The civil threat of eviction and the regulation and control of US Public Housing communities', in C. Mele and T. Miller (eds), *Civil Penalties, Social Consequences*, New York: Routledge.

Melling, J. (1980) 'Clydeside housing and the evolution of state rent control', in J. Melling (ed), *Housing, Social Policy and the State*, London: Croom Helm.

Merrett, S. (1979) *State Housing in Britain*, London: Routledge and Kegan Paul.

Miller, P. (2001) 'Governing by numbers: why calculative practices matter', 68(2), *Social Research*: 379–96.

Miller, P. and Rose, N. (1990) 'Governing economic life', 19 (1), *Economy and Society*: 1–31.

Milner Holland, Sir (1965) *Report of the Committee on Housing in Greater London*, Cmd 2605, London: HMSO.

Ministry of Health (1920) *Report of the Committee on the Increase of Rent and Mortgage Interest (War Restrictions) Acts*, The Salisbury Committee, Cmd 658, London: HMSO.

——(1923) *Final Report of the Inter-Departmental Committee on the Rent Restrictions Acts*, The Onslow Committee, Cmd 1803, London: HMSO.

——(1930) 11th *Annual Report 1929–1930*, Cmd 3667, London: HMSO.

——(1931a) 12th *Annual report 1930–31*, Cmd 3937, London: HMSO.

——(1931b) *Report of the Inter-Departmental Committee on the Rent Restrictions Acts*, The Marley Committee, Cmd 3911, London: HMSO.

——(1933) 14th *Annual report 1932–1933*, Cmd 4372, London: HMSO.

——(1934) 15th *Annual Report 1933–1934*, Cmd 4664, London: HMSO.

——(1937) *Reports of the Inter-Departmental Committee on theRent Restrictions Acts*, The Ridley Committee, Cmd 5621, London: HMSO.

——(1938) *The Management of Municipal Housing Estates*, Report of the House Management and Housing Associations Sub-Committee of the Central Housing Advisory Committee, London: HMSO.

Ministry of Housing and Local Government (MHLG) (1953) *Houses: The Next Step* Cmd 8996, London: HMSO.

Ministry of Reconstruction (1918) *Report of the Committee of the Ministry of Reconstruction on the Increase of Rent and Mortgage Interests (War Restrictions) Act 1915*, the Hunter Committee, London: HMSO.

Moody, S. (2000) 'Self giving in "charity": The role of law', in C. Mitchell and S. Moody (eds), *Foundations of Charity*, Oxford: Hart.

Morgan, B. (2003) 'The economization of politics: Meta-regulation as a form of nonjudicial legality', 12(4), *Social and Legal Studies*: 489–524.

Morgan, J. (2003) 'The alchemists search for the philosophers' stone: The status of registered social landlords under the Human Rights Act', 66(5), *Modern Law Review*: 700–25.

Morgan, P. (2005) 'Tenant futures – the future of tenants in social housing', Paper to the Housing Studies Association Conference, York, 6–8 April.

Morris, S. (1998) *Private Profit and Public Interest: Model Dwelling Companies and the Housing of the Working Classes in London 1840–1914*, unpublished PhD thesis, Oxford: University of Oxford.

Moyne (1933) *Report of the Departmental Committee on Housing*, Cmd 4397, London: HMSO.

Mullins, D. (1997) 'From regulatory capture to regulated competition: an interest group analysis of the regulation of housing associations in England', 12(3), *Housing Studies*: 301–19.

——(2002) 'Redefining "competition" as "competitiveness" – Best value activities of registered social landlords', April/June, *Public Money and Management*: 25–30.

Mullins, D., Niner, P. and Riseborough, M. (1995) *Evaluating Large Scale Voluntary Transfers of Local Authority Housing*, London: HMSO.

Murie, A. (1997a) 'The social rented sector, housing and the welfare state in the UK', 12(4), *Housing Studies*: 437–61.

——(1997b) 'Linking housing changes to crime', 31(5), *Social Policy and Administration*: 22–36.

Murie, A. (1998) 'Secure and contented citizens? Home ownership in Britain', in A. Marsh and D. Mullins (eds), *Housing and Public Policy: Citizenship, Choice and Control*, Buckingham: Open University Press.

——(2005) 'Building on the past', paper presented at the Housing Studies Association Conference, Spring 2005.

Murie, A., Niner, P. and Watson, C. (1976) *Housing Policy and the Housing System*, London: Allen & Unwin.

Murray, C. (1990) *The Underclass*, London: Institute of Economic Affairs.

Murray, K. (2002) 'Street smart', *Inside Housing*, 20 September.

National Association of Citizens Advice Bureaux (NACAB) (1998) *Unsafe Deposit*, London: NACAB.

National Federation of Housing Association (NFHA) (1993/94) *Facing the Future: Annual Report 1993/94*, London: NFHA.

——(NFHA) (1995a) *Competence and Accountability: Report of the Inquiry into Housing Association Governance*, London: NFHA.

——(1995b) *Much in Evidence: Selected Submissions to the Governance Inquiry*, London: NFHA.

——(1995/96) *A Step Ahead: National Federation of Housing Associations' Annual Report 1995/96*, London: NFHA.

——(1945) *The Official Bulletin, 36*, London: NFHS.

——(1946a) *The Official Bulletin, 37*, London: NFHS.

——(1946b) *The Official Bulletin, 38*, London: NFHS.

——(1946c) *National Federation of Housing Societies*, London, NFHS.

——(1946d) *The Official Bulletin, 39*, London: NFHS.

——(1959) *Quarterly Bulletin, 89*.

National Housing Federation (NHF) (1999) *Statement of Recommended Practice (SORP): Accounting for Registered Social Landlords*, London, NHF.

Nelken, D. (1983) *The Limits of the Legal Process: A Study of Landlords, Law and Crime*, London: Academic Press.

Nevin, B. and Leather, P. (2005) 'Understanding the drivers of housing market change in Britain's post industrial cities', Paper delivered to the Housing Studies Association Conference, York, 6–8 April.

Newman, O. (1974) *Defensible Space: Crime Prevention through Urban Design*, London: MacMillan.

Nixon, J., Blandy, S., Hunter, C., and Reeves, K. (2003) *Tackling Anti-Social Behaviour in Mixed Tenure Areas*, London: ODPM.

Noble, D. (1979) SSRC Workshop paper, Cambridge.

——(1981) 'From rules to discretion: the Housing Corporation', in M. Adler and S. Asquith (eds), *Discretion and Welfare*, London: Heinemann.

Nolan (1996) *Standards in Public Life: Local Public Spending Bodies*, Vol 1 (second report of the Committee on Standards in Public Life), Cm: 3270–I, London: HMSO.

O'Malley, P. (2004) *Risk, Uncertainty and Government*, London: Glasshouse.

O'Malley, P. and Palmer, D. (1996) 'Post-Keynesian policing', 25(2), *Economy and Society*, 137–55.

Office of the Deputy Prime Minister (ODPM) (2002) *Allocation of Accommodation: Code of Guidance for Local Housing Authorities*, London: ODPM.

——(2003a) *The Beacon Councils Scheme: How to Apply* (London: ODPM) http://www.odpm.gov.uk/stellent/groups/odpm_localgov/documents/downloadable/odpm_locgov_022465.pdf [site visited 11 March 2005].

——(2003b) *Sustainable Communities: Building for the Future*, London: ODPM.

——(2003c) *Housing Transfer Manual 2003 Programme*, London: ODPM.

——(2004) *The Right to Buy Scheme: Information to Help Tenants Decide Whether to Exercise the Right to Buy*, A Consultation Paper, London: ODPM.

——(2005) *Homebuy – Expanding the Opportunity to Own*, London: ODPM.

——/HM Treasury (2005) *Securing Better Outcomes: Developing a New Performance Framework*, London: ODPM.

Ogus, A. (1994) 'Rethinking self-regulation', 15(1) *Oxford Journal of Legal Studies*: 97–108 (reproduced in R. Baldwin, C. Scott and C. Hood (eds), *A Reader on Regulation*, Oxford: Oxford University Press).

Osborne, D. and Gaebler, T. (1993) *Reinventing Government: How the Entrepreneurial Spirit is Transforming the Public Sector*, New York: Plume.

Osborne, T. (1996) 'Security and vitality: drains liberalism and power in the nineteenth century', in A. Barry, N. Rose and T. Osborne (eds), *Foucault and Political Reason: Liberalism, Neo-Liberalism and Rationalities of Government*, London: UCL.

Osborne, T. and Rose, N. (1999) 'Governing cities: notes on the spatialisation of virtue', 17(5), *Environment and Planning D: Society and Space*: 737–60.

Owen, D. (1965) *English Philanthropy 1660–1960*, Oxford: Oxford University Press.

Page, D (1993) *Building for Communities*, York: Joseph Rowntree Foundation.

Papps, P. (1998) 'Anti-social behaviour strategies – individualistic or holistic?', 13(5), *Housing Studies*: 639–56.

Parker, C. (1999) 'Compliance professionalism and regulatory community: the Australian Trade Practices regime', 26(2), *Journal of Law and Society*: 215–39.

Parker, C., Braithwaite, J., Lacey, N., and Scott, C. (2004) *Regulation*, Oxford: Oxford University Press.

Partington, M. (1980) *Landlord and Tenant*, London: Weidenfeld & Nicolson.

Pawson, H. and Kintrea, K. (2002) 'Part of the problem or part of the solution? Social housing allocation policies and social exclusion in Britain', 31(4), *Journal of Social Policy*: 643–67.

Pawson, H., Flint, J., Scott, S., Atkinson, R., Bannister, J., McKenzie, C. and Mills C. (2005) *The Use of Possession Actions and Evictions by Social Landlords*, London: ODPM.

Policy Action Team (PAT) 5 (1999) *Housing Management*, London: Social Exclusion Unit.

—— (PAT) 7 (1999) *Unpopular Housing*, London: Social Exclusion Unit.

—— (PAT) 8 (2000) *Anti-Social Behaviour*, London: Social Exclusion Unit.

Pollock, A. (2004) *NHS plc: The Privatisation of Our Health Care*, London: Verso.

Power, A (1987) *Property Before People: The Management of Twentieth Century Council Housing*, London: Allen & Unwin.

Power, M. (1994) *The Audit Explosion*, London: Demos.

——(1997) *The Audit Society: Rituals of Verification*, Oxford: Oxford University Press.

——(2004) *The Risk Management of Everything*, London: Demos.

Price, S. (1958) *Building Societies: Their Origin and History*, London: Franey PRO HLG 29/213 – Ministry of Health paper 1933 [held at The National Archive].

——29/1097 – 'Consultations with the Charity Commission' [Ministry of Housing and Construction file held at The National Archive].

Procacci, G. (1991) 'Social economy and the government of poverty', in G. Burchell, C. Gordon and P. Miller (eds), *The Foucault Effect: Studies in Governmentality*, Chicago: University of Chicago Press.

Prosser, T. (1997) *Law and the Regulators*, Oxford: Clarendon Press.

——(2005) *The Limits of Competition Law: Markets and Public Services*, Oxford: Oxford University Press.

Randall, B. (2002) 'HA plc?', February, *Housing*: 20–1.

Randolph, B. (1993) 'The re-privatisation of housing associations' in P. Malpass and R. Means (eds), *Implementing Housing Policy*, Buckingham: Open University Press.

Reynolds, J. (1974) 'Statutory covenants of fitness and repair: social legislation and the judges', 37(3), *Modern Law Review*: 377–98.

Rex, J. and Moore, R. (1967) *Race, Community and Conflict: A Study of Sparkbrook*, Oxford: Oxford University Press.

Riseborough, M. (1998) 'More control and choice for users? Involving tenants in social housing management', in A. Marsh and D. Mullins (eds), *Housing and Public Policy*, Buckingham: Open University Press.

Robson, P. (2001) 'Housing Benefit', in D. Cowan, and A. Marsh (eds), *Two Steps Forward: Housing Policy for the new Millennium*, Bristol: Policy Press.

Rose, N. (1993) 'Government, authority and expertise in advanced liberalism', 22(3), *Economy and Society*: 283–99.

——(1996) 'The death of the social? Re-figuring the territory of government', 25(3), *Economy and Society*: 327–56.

——(1999) *Powers of Freedom: Reframing Political Thought*, Cambridge: Cambridge University Press.

——(2000) 'Government and control', 40(3), *British Journal of Criminology*: 321–39.

Rose, N. and Miller, P. (1992) 'Political power beyond the state: problematics of government', 43(2), *British Journal of Sociology*: 173–205.

Rose, N. and Valverde, M. (1998) 'Governed by law?', 7(4), *Social and Legal Studies*: 541–51.

Royal Commission (1871) *Royal Commission on Friendly and Benefit Building Societies*, First Report with Minutes of Evidence, London: HMSO.

——(1885a) *Royal Commission on the Housing of the Working Classes*, vol I, London: HMSO.

——(1885b) *Royal Commission on the Housing of the Working Classes*, vol II: Minutes of Evidence, London: HMSO.

Rowntree, S. (1901) *Poverty: A Study in Town Life*, London: MacMillan.

Rozenburg, J (2001) 'Porter told to pay £26m over "Homes for Votes" ', *Daily Telegraph*, 14 December.

Rugg, J. and Bevan, M. (2002) *An Evaluation of the Pilot Tenancy Deposit Scheme*, London: ODPM.

Rugg, J. and Rhodes, D. (2003) ' "Between a rock and a hard place": The failure to agree on regulation for the private rented sector in England', 18(6), *Housing Studies*. 937–46.

Sainsbury, R. (1989) 'Administrative justice: discretion and procedure in social security decision-making', in K. Hawkins (ed), *The Uses of Discretion*, Oxford: Oxford University Press.

Saugeres, L. (2000) 'Of tidy gardens and clean houses: housing officers as agents of social control', 31, *Geoforum*: 587–99.

Saunders, P. (1990) *A Nation of Home Owners*, London: Allen & Unwin.

Schifferes, S. (1976) 'Council tenants and housing policy in the 1930s: the contradictions of state intervention', in M. Edwards, F. Gray, S. Merrett and J. Swann (eds), *Housing and Class in Britain*, London: Russell Press.

Scott, C. (2001) 'Analysing regulatory space: fragmented resources and institutional design', *Public Law*: 329–53.

——(2002) 'Private regulation of the public sector: A neglected facet of contemporary governance', 29(1), *Journal of Law and Society*: 56–76.

Scott, S. and Parkey, H. (1998) 'Myths and reality: anti-social behaviour in Scotland', 13(3), *Housing Studies*: 325–45.

Select Committee (2004) *Select Committee on Office of the Deputy Prime Minister: Housing, Planning, Local Government and the Regions Decent homes fifth report [of session 2003–04]* Vol. 1 Report, together with formal minutes: House of Commons papers 2003–04 46–I.

Seyd, P. (1975) 'Shelter: the National Campaign for the Homeless', 46(3), *Political Quarterly*: 418–31.

Shearing, C. and Stenning, P. (1985) 'From the panopticon to Disneyworld: the development of discipline', in A. Doob and E. Greenspan (eds), *Perspectives in Criminal Law*, Ontario: Canada Law Book Inc.

Simmonds, A. (2002) 'Raising Rachman: the origins of the Rent Act, 1957', 45(4), *The Historical Journal*: 843–68.

Skinner, D. and Langdon, J. (1972) *The Story of Clay Cross*, Nottingham: Spokesman.

Smiles, S. (1859/2002) *Self-Help*, Oxford: Oxford University Press.

——(1989) *The Politics of 'Race' and Residence*, Cambridge: Polity.

Smith, S. and Mallinson, S. (1996) 'The problem with social housing: discretion, accountability and the welfare ideal', 24(3), *Policy and Politics*: 339–57.

Social Housing (2000) 'William Sutton plunges into the red as new SORP regime takes effect', July 15.

Somerville, P. (2001) 'Allocating housing – or "letting" people choose?', in D. Cowan and A. Marsh (eds), *Two Steps Forward: Housing Policy into the New Millennium*, Bristol: Policy Press.

Stenson, K. (1999) 'Crime control, governmentality and sovereignty', in R. Smandych (ed), *Governable Places: Readings on Governmentality and Crime Control*, Aldershot: Dartmouth.

——(2000) 'Crime control, social policy and liberalism' in G. Lewis, S. Gewirtz and J. Clarke (eds) *Rethinking Social Policy*, Milton Keynes: Open University Press.

Stevens, M., Whitehead, C. and Munro, M. (2005) 'Lessons from the past, challenges for the future: An evaluation of English Housing Policy since 1975', paper to the Housing Studies Association Conference, York.

Stewart, A. (1996) *Rethinking Housing Law*, London: Sweet & Maxwell.

Swenarton, M. (1981) *Homes fit for Heroes: The Politics and Architecture of Early State Housing in Britain*, London: Heinemann.

Teubner, G (1987) 'Juridification: concepts, aspects, limits, solutions', 21(1), *Law and Society Review*: 3–48 (reproduced in R. Baldwin, C. Hood and C. Scott (eds), *A Reader on Regulation*, Oxford: Oxford University Press).

Thane, P. (1996) *Foundations of the Welfare State*, London and New York: Longman.

Tickell, J. (2002) 'Independent spirit', 13 September, *Inside Housing*: 22–3.

Titmuss, R. (1970) *The Gift Relationship: from human blood to social policy*, London: Allen & Unwin.

Tombs, S. (2002) 'Understanding regulation?', 11(1), *Social and Legal Studies*: 113–33.

Tudor Walters (1918) *Report of the Committee Appointed to Consider Questions of Building Construction in Connection with the Provision of Dwellings for the Working Classes*, Cd 9191, London: HMSO.

Tunstall, R. (2003) ' "Mixed tenure" policy in the UK: privatisation, pluralism or euphemism?', 20(3), *Housing, Theory and Society*: 153–59.

University of Birmingham (1998) *How Local Authorities Used the Private Rented Sector Prior to the Housing Act 1996*, DETR Research Summary 86, London: DETR.

Valverde, M. (1996) ' "Despotism" and ethical liberal governance', 25(3), *Economy and Society*: 357–72.

——(2003a) *Law's Dream of a Common Knowledge*, Princeton: Princeton University Press.

——(2003b) 'Police science, British style: pub licensing and knowledges of urban disorder', 32(2), *Economy and Society*: 234–52.

Vincent-Jones, P. (2000) 'Central-local relations under the Local Government Act 1999: a new consensus?', 63(1), *Modern Law Review*: 84–103.

——(2001) 'From housing management to the management of housing: the challenge of Best Value', in D. Cowan and A. Marsh (eds), *Two Steps Forward*, Bristol, Policy Press.

Waddilove, L. (1970) *Housing To Let by Non-Profit Organisations* [document can be found at The National Archive PRO HLG 118/1390].

Walker, B. and Marsh, A. (2003) 'Setting the rents of social housing: the impact and implications of rent restructuring in England', 40(10), *Urban Studies*: 2023–47.

Walker, R. (1998) 'New public management and housing associations: From comfort to competition', 26(1), *Policy and Politics*: 71–87.

Walters, W. (2000) *Unemployment and Government: Genealogies of the Social*, Cambridge: Cambridge University Press.

Warburton, M. (1998) 'Inspecting the inspectorate', *Roof*, September/October.

Watchman, P. (1980), 'The origin of the 1915 Rent Act', 5(1), *Law and State*: 20–50.

Watson, S. (1999) 'A home is where the heart is: engendering notions of homelessness', in P. Kennett and A. Marsh (eds), *Homelessness: Exploring the New Terrain*, Bristol: Policy Press.

Weaver, M. (2004) 'Landlord forced to sell off homes to meet target' *The Guardian*, 4 October.

White, F. and Hollingsworth, K. (1999) *Audit, Accountability, and Government*, Oxford, Clarendon.

Whitehead, C. (2003) 'The economics of social housing' in T. O'Sullivan and K. Gibb (eds), *Housing Economics and Public Policy*, Oxford: Blackwell.

Whitehead, C., Stockdale, J. and Razzu, G. (2003) *The Economic and Social Costs of Anti-Social Behaviour: A Review*, London: London School of Economics.

Wilcox, S. (2005) 'Tangled up in rules', March/April, *Roof*: 14–15.

Wilson, D. (1997) 'Backdoor', 22(1), *Roof*: 44.

Winn, N. (2001), *Choice-based Lettings, the bIGPicture*, London: Housing Corporation.

Wolmar, C. (1982) 'Corporation critics', Sept/Oct, *Roof*: 12–14.

Index

Lightning Source UK Ltd.
Milton Keynes UK
UKOW040401150213

206313UK00003B/62/A